I AM NOT A GRASSHOPPER

DAVE HATFIELD

I Am Not A Grasshopper:
A True Story of Love Overcoming Hate
by Dave Hatfield

Published by Dave Hatfield
www.dave-hatfield.com
Cover by Kristen Ingebretson
Editing by Carly Catt
ISBN: 978-1-7377436-0-6
Printed in the United States of America
First Edition

To my wife, who has taught me what love and forgiveness look like.
And her friend Kay, whose courage is only equaled by her compassion.

FOREWORD

This book is an invitation to a life of impact and influence of truly eternal proportions of Dave Hatfield, a missionary in Kenya. His mission work in Kenya has been to the street children and the poor in the slums across different cities in Kenya. I met Dave Hatfield and his wife Kim nearly a decade ago in January 2013, when they visited Mully Children's Family in Ndalani. Out of this visit, insight and inspiration were born, translating to impacting children and families in the informal settlements in Nakuru, Kenya.

This book is full of priceless lessons of victory and the manifestation of the power of God in the most obscure and remote places. No one deserves to be born poor, helpless, without a home, and into a world of wickedness, gruesome evil and gross darkness. Yet, my friend Dave Hatfield is called and anointed to minister in such places. He has faced lack, shame, danger, harm and even death threats in his mission work to save a hurting generation of children scavenging in the streets, dumpsites, and slums. His story is that of Love overcoming hate, peace overcoming gang life, and hope overcoming despair and despondency.

The ministry to the street children and the marginalized

people in the society is one that I know of, and was called and commissioned by God to do. This journey is punctuated with persecution, days of sorrow, hurt and trouble, yet filled with joy, fulfillment, and satisfaction when the triumphant and victorious stories are told. The world can only know when these messages are recorded and passed on. Not only for posterity, but for also reviving a hopeless heart, renewing a frail spirit to strength, and demonstrating the working of God's power of Love to a people forgotten and despised by society.

Numbers 13:33 (KJV) says, "And there we saw the giants, the sons of Anak, which come of the giants: and we were in our own sight as grasshoppers, and so we were in their sight." The children of Israel beheld themselves as grasshoppers in their sight compared to the people of Canaan, who were said to be giants as sons of Anak. This report that the spies gave is described as "evil" in Numbers 13:32. It was out of order for the spies to express themselves (the children of Israel) as grasshoppers. They were in the place where they had the Almighty God on their side. In return, they wandered for forty years in the wilderness. God had to raise another generation that would take over the land of Canaan without fear or inferiority complex and with complete confidence in God. The evil report had tainted the perspective and the mindset of the Israelites. God desires that we see ourselves as He sees us in Christ Jesus. Christ, our image to behold and not that of lowly *insects*.

The ardent wisdom of the scriptures is that "as a man thinketh in his heart so is he . . ." Dave Hatfield has beautifully written this manuscript, *I Am Not A Grasshopper*, to paint an image for us that we are not mere 'grasshoppers' even in the face of 'giants', including calamity or the mountains of life.

The dumpsites and slums of Kenya are full of potential. There is an untold wealth of young persons that desire to be believed in and nurtured. The minds of many ask the same question that Nathaniel asked, "Nazareth!" exclaimed Nathanael. "Can anything good come from there?" "Just come and see for yourself," Philip declared (John 1:46 TLB). Nevertheless, the answer remains the same, "come and see for yourself!"

Reading stories that inspire the world with first-hand experience of these difficult places is nostalgic for me. They awaken a passion and drive that can only be satisfied when such scavenging children and families are delivered and given dignified livelihoods to stand on their own. These children become agents of hope and change to the world, an embodiment of admiration because they conquered. This is the place where fear is swallowed up in Love; failure is swallowed up in success; weakness in strength. However, it takes a man of courage and vision to become a refuge and a pillar to the scores of people who have been helped out of the dumpsite through Living Stone Global.

Love is an experience and a force. A force that compels the heart of Dave Hatfield and his wife to the countless children in his care. His words are, "when I see these kids at Maisha Mapya and know where they come from and what life is like for them, I just have to be here. There is no other place. I want to be the Love for them I never got." These are words that show what the true Love of God does to the heart of a man yielded to him.

On the premise of this Love, I invite you to the life in the streets and slums of Kenya as stunningly narrated by Dave Hatfield—a heart given to the transformation of children's lives.

Dr. Ev. Charles M. Mulli PhD, HSC
Founder and Chief Executive Officer
Mully Children's Family Kenya
Father to the Fatherless: The Charles Mulli Story

CONTENTS

WHY I AM TELLING YOU THIS STORY

I'm telling you this story so you won't be scared—scared of people who may look scary.

I'm telling you this so you can cast your fear of unfamiliar places aside and explore them. If you look closely, you will find beauty everywhere, even if you at first want to run away.

I'm telling you this because, given the current culture, you may feel small, helpless, and silenced. But you have infinite value and a voice to be heard.

I'm telling you this because you may be on the verge of something new—something great—that God has planned for you, but when you look at it with your human eyes, you only see the giants standing in your way.

I'm telling you this so you won't be afraid to humble yourself and ask for forgiveness. And so, if placed in a position to grant forgiveness, you will do it. You may find unspeakable joy.

I'm telling you this so you won't be scared of an all-powerful God who loves you but can take your last breath any second. I don't want you to miss out on the wonder and power of His love.

I'm also telling you this because if, like me, you feel alone and that you don't belong, there is a place for you. Quite possibly, it's with those scary people, in an unfamiliar place, with that scary God where you find safety, peace, love, forgiveness, and healing.

So walk a few steps with me on my journey as you prepare to take flight on your own. It will all be worth it.

THE TEXT

THERE'S nothing worse than a small casket. And I've seen way too many.

The tears. The pain. The mother's sorrow. The symbol of a life lost way too soon. The laughter that was never heard, and the joy that never radiated. It's agony. It's a dream cut short, leaving only the nightmare.

It is a failure.

The trembling in Dan's voice telling me about the mud wall that smothered Neema while she slept will never leave my ears. *Why didn't I fix her house before the storm?*

The look in Mama Emmanuel's eyes grieving the loss of her five-year-old boy from measles is always there, even when I close mine. I should have insisted she vaccinate her son.

Then there was baby Matthew. He fought bravely for every breath. After five months, he couldn't fight any longer. No one could have done anything about that.

We buried a preschool student each of the first three years we were open, even though only forty children were in class. While many other schools determine success by measuring test scores or observing if the kids were making friends, I just wanted our kids to survive the year.

Now COVID-19 is everywhere on the news. It's the silent killer ringing in everyone's ears. It's getting so much attention, you'd think nothing else was happening in the world. I wish people knew what our children faced in order to survive.

Over the last decade, poverty has been my pandemic. It steals life. It screams, but the sound never makes it past our slum residents' ears. It doesn't get into the headlines. No one enters the black hole called Gioto by choice. Poverty pulls the desperate in and lets nothing escape. Not a scream. Not a cry. Not even a five-month-old like Matthew. Even more sinister, poverty robs identity. It's faceless. No one knows the names of little kids living in a dumpsite in Africa.

But I do.

––––––

August 29, 2020

My phone danced on the nightstand from the vibration. "Sorry, honey. I should have silenced that stupid thing," I grumbled to my wife as I grasped for the annoying device. *Seriously? Two a.m.* My heart was already racing, but then I saw an unknown number with a Kenyan +254 prefix. It skipped a beat when I read the text.

THERE WAS A GANG ATTACK AT A SHOSHO'S [GRANDMA'S] HOUSE. 27 GUYS WITH PANGAS [MACHETES] AND KNIVES ATTACKED AND STABBED HER SON. ONE OF YOUR GIRLS AND HER SISTER SAW THE ATTACK. SOME MEN HAVE COME BACK TO THE HOUSE TWICE AND THREATENED TO BURN IT DOWN. THEY ARE LIVING IN FEAR. ~ ANONYMOUS

Sitting up, I reread the message. I could feel my community screaming.

Two hundred faces of children, four to ten years old, flashed faster and faster in my head. Each one beautiful—even though many have scars. Some were dressed in the rags they were wearing when I first met them. Others proudly sported their cheerful Maisha Mapya Learning Center uniforms. I know every name. I saw their smiles and heard each of their unique laughs. And I know what it's like to have wiped each of their tears.

My hands were shaking so much I could hardly press the right keys to reply. But I had to know which one of our seventy-eight girls was in danger. I was not losing another one.

Which one of our girls? Is she ok? ~ *me*

ANGEL ~ ANONYMOUS

All I could see were her big, round eyes and the cute gap in her front teeth prominently displayed in her beaming smile. Angel had overcome so much since her mom abandoned her at the dumpsite at only five months old to live with her grandma and two stepsisters. Her uncle lived with them too. She was lucky to have a man providing some protection from humans and other lurking predators.

Rumors flew around that Angel's mom came and watched her from afar. Sometimes, the father of her two stepsisters turned up. Angel thought he might be her dad too, but apparently he's not. Like so many things in the slums, it's nearly impossible to get the true story.

THEY GRABBED HER PUT A PANGA TO HER NECK AND THREATENED HER HEAD SCREAMING SOMEONE MUST PAY! SHE'S NEXT! ~ ANONYMOUS

I shut my eyes and wished it would all go away. But no matter how tight I squeezed, the vision of a wild-eyed, crazy man grabbing her hair with one hand and pressing a two-foot-long machete against the throat of our little Angel wouldn't fade. I could feel the beat of her racing heart and see the fear in her eyes.

And if they could attack Angel, what's stopping them from mangling more of our kids? Were any of them safe? I had to do something.

Why in the world would anyone want to attack Angel and her grandma?

Was it Kenya's most notorious gang, the bloodthirsty Mungiki? I'd read about them taking over slums by force. I had heard guys talk about them over the years, how they beheaded over one hundred *matatu* drivers in Nairobi. Were they here now, taking over Nakuru? Would they actually kill little girls?

Ten minutes later. Another text.

HER UNCLE IS IN REMAND [POLICE CUSTODY] ALONG WITH 3 FROM THE GANG AND THEY ARE THREATENING TO TAKE MORE HEADS IN HIS PLACE. ~ ANONYMOUS

Oh, no! Without her son around, Shosh couldn't possibly stand up to a horde of gangsters, especially the Mungiki. When those guys get arrested, the rest of the mob comes and makes a statement: Mess with us, and you get dead.

And why did the police detain Angel's uncle? He was the victim. What did he do other than get knifed?

And that was it. No more texts. Just me lying in bed next to Kim, my wife of thirty years, with my left index finger alternating between my upper lip and joining my middle finger to rub my forehead. Wide awake, I stared at the ceiling, wondering if God had forgotten these children again.

———

July 14, 2006

Kim hung up the phone, a curious look on her face as she turned to me.

"Guess what my brother said."

I shrugged. "I have no idea."

"He said, 'Hey, sis, guess what God wants me to do!'"

"What?"

"'He wants me to go to Africa. On a mission trip for two weeks. To Africa! Me! To Africa!' So I said, 'That sounds great. You should take Dave.'"

In her excitement, she volunteered me. Her response didn't seem out of the ordinary. My wife knew I'd love the adventure. When I worked on Wall Street, I traveled nearly every week to Las Vegas, New York, Honolulu, or wherever. If there was business to be done, I'd hop on a plane at a moment's notice.

Even our family was used to taking off on wild-hair escapades. We'd just gotten back from Portillo, Chile, shushing champagne powder on the slopes of the Andes in the middle of summer. Going on safari in Africa wouldn't be a big deal. It sounded fun.

But that innocent phone call set into motion the thing that changed my life.

Kim's brother and I attended the first training session for the trip and learned it wasn't a safari after all. Instead, it was God sending His people across the world to love those in need. I discovered I didn't know a thing about mission trips, Africa, poverty, or dumps. The poorest place I'd ever lived was where I was residing now—a small mountain town three hours east of San Francisco where I played golf in the summer and skied in the winter. And the only dump I knew was the cement refuse center where you tossed your bagged garbage into a trash compactor.

My phone rang the day before the second group gathering. It was Kim's brother.

"Dave, I'm sorry, I can't go."

"That's okay. You can catch the next meeting."

"No, Dave. I can't go. I can't go to Kenya." Life events happened that prevented him from making the trip. With all of the naïveté and enthusiasm newbie Christians are known for, I didn't even think twice about it.

"That's okay. I'm still going!" I replied.

He laughed. "You can't go without me!"

"Watch me. I've seen *The Lion King*, you know. *Hakuna matata* and all that."

In his place, our thirteen-year-old son, Andrew, joined the team. It seemed like a great father-son bonding adventure. Maybe we'd discover a few things about God too.

Overseas mission work was completely outside the scope of anything my little church in the mountains did on a regular basis. Although I think they sent a few dollars a month to a guy in South Africa and to one in South America.

The pastor emphasized if I accepted Jesus as Savior, I'd get into heaven. Of course, not everyone would get in. But if I believed with all my heart, mind, and soul, I was in. The main message focused on receiving God's grace. Tending to the spiritual and physical needs of the flock within the walls of the church got all the attention and resources. There wasn't much about doing outreach. When reading the scriptures, the pastor would sometimes say "the least of these," but I never really knew what it meant. I thought it referred to people who were worse off than me. Maybe it was the guy in greasy jeans seated next to me. It might have even meant they were lesser than me. I wasn't sure. But no matter what, he said I should be nice to them.

I wasn't sure about a lot of things. But one thing was certain: the last place I belonged was on a mission trip in the middle of Africa. I hadn't even read half the Bible. I was a retired stockbroker with a big ego, for Pete's sake, who was still wet from his baptism seven months earlier. I was completely unprepared for what was to come. But I obeyed God's call on my heart, and with my teenage son at my side, I boarded the plane with our team.

The Hilton slum in Nakuru, Kenya was like a black-and-white movie. Everything was some dismal shade of gray. Urban legend has it that Hilton got its name, along with London (the larger area that encompasses Hilton and Gioto), from some old-timers who used to escape there for afternoons of drinking, daydreaming, and storytelling. The location is Nakuru's highest vantage point and offers a panoramic view of the city and shimmering Lake Nakuru.

After a few too many brews, they would sarcastically joke that they were going to London and stay at the Hilton. Soon, London got its name, and Hilton followed suit. The only thing connecting the famous hotel brand with the slum in Nakuru is this cheeky story. If it were part of the Hilton hotel chain, it would get some seriously awful reviews.

There were no trees or bushes anywhere, just concrete and rock and dirt and dust. No birds sing. A few skinny goats and the occasional cow roam about. Wild dogs wander with their tongues hanging out, searching for shade.

As we traversed the volcanic rock streets looking for a place to park, the van tossed me about like the Indiana Jones ride at Disneyland. I put my hand on the roof to protect myself from hitting my head on the windows. It was too late for Andrew. He'd already smoked his dome twice against the glass while peering out trying to process what he was seeing. I wanted to ask if he was okay but didn't want him to feel like he needed *Daddy* hovering over him. He was on an adventure too.

Seven-foot stone walls surrounded rectangular courtyards like fortresses. Definitely there to keep things out. I wondered if they were also there to keep who knows what in. Hidden behind the rusted iron gates of each compound lay eight to ten single rooms with cinderblock walls and crude cement floors. Each six-foot by nine-foot room houses a family, usually a mom and three to six kids. There was no electricity, no water, no sanitation, and no hope. No matter where you looked, it was gray, dark, and ominous. The only splashes of color were random rainbows of shirts, pants, underwear, and towels strung up between each apartment to dry. Rent was $15 a month and a future full of despair.

But people were everywhere. Women were bent over open fires in the streets, boiling their meals of rice and beans. Drunk men stood with one hand on their hip and the other clutching a cup of their poison, watching the women. Others had already lost the day's battle and were passed out face down in the dirt. Half-clothed babies, sometimes wearing less than that, squat in the filth, playing. Flies covered everything, including the food and the kids. Seedy bars and hook-up places outnumbered the small businesses trying to make an honest living. Open sewage ran through the streets.

I'd seen images on TV like this but never stopped to notice they were actual people. I'd always clicked to the next channel before allowing any of it to sink in. I looked around at the others in the van hoping to connect with a sympathetic eye so we could stop and help. Instead, we kept driving.

I didn't know it, but compared to where we were headed, Hilton was upscale.

The smell of garbage hit me even before I saw a single piece of trash, the odor intensifying as we drove on. We parked and walked in the direction of the foulest stench. The environment abruptly changed from Hilton's tin-roofed shacks with stone walls and children running around to a bleak landscape with rubbish as far as I could see. Structures made of sticks, mud, rocks, paper, plastic—anything that provided a semblance of shelter—cluttered the horizon. Random plumes of smoke from self-combusting methane dotted the area and burned my eyes. I struggled not to gag from the putrid air. That first day we dared to set foot on the Gioto dumpsite in Nakuru, I learned a new definition of poor.

Before, being poor meant I didn't have what I wanted. On rare occasions, it meant I didn't have what I needed. In Gioto, your very existence is poor. There's no escaping it. The things that the million other humans in your city find useless and discard as trash become your essentials. They are your treasure. And garbage is your grocery store. I wasn't sure how I was going to fix this.

Emaciated feral dogs weren't looking for shade here. Like desperate hyenas, they were scrounging for their next meal. Their exposed teeth made me keep my distance. Squawking marabou storks, some five feet tall, with their hunched shoulders and long pointy beaks, gathered like evil judges deliberating a decision. In reality, they were combining forces to fend off the wild pigs for a bounty of rotten mangos. Survival was impossible here if you went at it alone. Even the animals knew that.

I tried not to let the shock own my face, but I'm pretty sure I displayed a gaping scowl. It was an overload to all my senses except one: I was afraid to touch anything.

Pastor Bill, an American missionary serving in Kenya, led us up a mountain of trash to have a better vantage point. He pointed in the distance. Another column of smoke drifted through the air.

"We can't go over there. They're in the caves brewing *chang'aa*. It's not safe for you."

Chang'aa, also known as *kumi kumi*, literally means "kill me quickly" and has a staggeringly high alcohol content. The cooks illegally brew chang'aa in fifty-five-gallon metal drums, using anything that ferments and gets you high. Usually, it starts as a simple mix of grains and fruit found in the dumpsite. Then toss in some yeast, add heat, and boil. They will sometimes add oil, gasoline, battery acid, bug repellant, glue, jet fuel, or even soiled underwear for an extra kick. Chang'aa fries your brain to a place without pain, beyond the reaches of this hell hole. One mistake in the recipe, and it's toxic methanol. Every year, people go blind or even die from a lethal batch of this homemade concoction. So why would anyone drink it? I've had some dark days in my past that I've drowned with beer, but there's nothing that would make me raise one of those cups to my lips. I'd rather die. Is it symptomatic of the despair that seeps out of this place?

I got the sense it was okay for Pastor Bill to go over there, just not us. He'd spent five years visiting the brewers and building relationships. They knew he wouldn't rat them out. Bringing visiting American foreigners to poke their noses into the illegal business wasn't wise. I did not question his decision in the slightest.

We slipped down the slope and continued toward the active area of the dump. The team huddled around the mission group leader. I stuck close to Pastor Bill. I could always sniff out the actual leaders versus those who were looking to be seen in authority. A large *lorry* (truck) filled to the brim with rubbish and with men hanging from the sides like railway conductors sped past us and kicked up even more debris. I would say dust, but when I think of dust, I think of soil. This was anything but that. This was rotten, decaying whatever from wherever that stunk to high heaven.

I don't know if it was the burning in my eyes or the density of the smoke that made it nearly impossible to see. But from what I could make out, a couple hundred yards ahead, more things were moving. Something was always moving. This garbage was alive.

Part of me wanted to run, go back and sit in the van, wash my hands and face, and wait to get some tea. Another part was curious. I wanted to explore because it was like being in the middle of a sci-fi movie. But the strongest force moving me forward was peer pressure, and after a penetrating glare from the missionary leader, I hurried to catch up. I didn't want to be like that guy they mentioned during our trip preparation who went with the Apostle Paul on a mission trip, couldn't hack it, quit, and returned home.

Stick-thin figures, barely recognizable as humans with filthy, torn rags hanging from their bodies moved in unison, like an army of ants. Had their arms been empty and outstretched, it would have been a scene right out of the *Night of the Living Dead*, but their hands gripped sacks of stuff three times their body size, slinging them over their shoulders.

Parked on top of a field of rubbish was the lorry that had raced past us earlier. The men who had been dangling from it were shoveling out the cargo of rotten bananas, mangos, and whatever else was in there. Girls as young as maybe fifteen and grandmas as old as seventy-five frantically combed through the garbage with their bare hands, searching for treasure.

Pastor Bill turned his head to me. In a quiet voice, he said, "If they're lucky, they might find a piece of metal or the leftovers from a meal at a restaurant. Mostly they pick out plastic bottles to recycle. If they work all day, they make twenty shillings, maybe fifty at most." That's about twenty to fifty cents.

Each person greeted Bill. "Pastor. Pastor. Mambo. Karibu," all while continuing their scavenging work. Most offered a friendly tone. I wondered how it would feel to have friends like these. Would they actually be like friends? Or would they always be hounding you for things? A few took a brief opportunity to stand and stretch their backs using it as an excuse to check out the strange-looking pale visitors from the West. The only one to stop was a woman who emerged from the middle of the pack. Pastor Bill shook her hand, and they smiled like they were long-lost best friends.

"This is Mama Amon. They call her the Mayor. Everyone loves her," Bill said with a laugh.

The Mayor didn't have a business suit or an office. She wore the same small-checked burgundy and beige apron as many of the surrounding women. It covered her from knees to shoulders and was filthy. I didn't know if it was to keep her clothes clean somehow or to protect her from the job's hazards.

She eyeballed us more than any of the others. Her laser-like focus made me consider if she was taking mental notes to give to a sketch artist later. One thing was for sure, the trappings of the ladies on the team, their nice dress and jewelry, caught her attention.

The pastor explained Mama Amon had positioned herself as the go-between for well-wishers from the West, with their goods and cash, and the other residents at the dump. She had a natural talent. She could convince visitors to reach deep into their pockets and give whatever they had brought with them. She was the mouthpiece for the community to get stuff. That's why they loved her. But the way she studied us made me wonder if, in some way, seeing people with all this wealth made her aware of all she didn't have.

I couldn't tell the Mayor from anyone else except by the gaping hole in her front teeth. You could have run a swizzle stick through it. As we left, making eye contact with each *mzungu* (white foreigner), she said, "Come back again. You are most welcome. Bring friends." I was thinking, how long would anyone stay my friend if I brought them to a place like this? But I felt the desire to reach for my wallet and give her a hundred bucks.

We walked on. There was so much to comprehend in this strange land, my head was spinning. The sound of broken glass at my feet made me stop and look down to see several shards poking out of one shoe and a discarded hypodermic needle stuck in the other.

When I looked up, I saw something that's still seared into my memory. My knees buckled. In the ocean of garbage, four shoeless toddlers, barely up to my knee, stood motionless. I had to squint to distinguish them from the sea of trash. Another child sat ten feet away, alone, crying. I walked over, took my hands out of my pockets, and wiped the tears—mine and hers. No adults were anywhere.

I know what it's like not to be wanted. My life has driven that point home. But I have no idea what this level of being unwanted is like. How abandoned do you have to be to end up belonging in a dumpsite, having the same value as a thrown-out piece of garbage? I couldn't unsee it. Nothing should live in this garbage dump—not even the flies.

I realized I had spent my entire life pretending kids like this didn't exist. They were always there, of course. I just didn't acknowledge them. I'd always avoided these places, the uncomfortable ones that made me look beyond my own wants. The logic was simple. If I didn't recognize these situations, I didn't have to do anything about them.

Now that I knew, it meant things would be different. Like every issue I've faced in my life, I had to fix this.

On the way back to the hotel, I asked Pastor Bill if it was possible to meet with the Kenyan family who started the ministry and school we were visiting. He arranged for us to have tea that afternoon.

I looked around the table. Everyone was well dressed and attentive. I hadn't changed clothes or showered. I only washed my hands. I never wanted to let go of what I had just experienced. I gathered myself and leaned forward. I tried to speak, but my eyes welled up and my throat tightened. The corners of my mouth only formed spasms, not words. All that came out was "the kids."

My face fell further, and my sounds got softer. "The kids." I looked across the room at Andrew laughing with the team drinking an ice-cold orange Fanta at another table.

I couldn't say much more. Pastor Bill rescued me by leaning over to the Kenyans, telling them, "We visited the dump today."

"The kids, what can we do?" I asked.

The eldest brother sat tall, adjusted his jacket and tie, and spoke for them. "When those children turn seven years, you can sponsor them. You can pay for them to come to our school. We will take them in."

I glanced over at Andrew again and thought of him and his younger brother spending the first seven years of their life in an unimaginable place like Gioto. I felt as helpless as the three-year-olds I saw earlier at the dump. I wished I could reach out to Kim for her tender encouragement. It was impossible to call her, however. And getting an international connection at the internet cafe in Nakurutown to send an email wasn't even worth the attempt.

God intervened and spoke through my lips. "No. Isn't there something we can do today? What can we do now?"

"Dave, children here don't start school until they reach age seven. Then they come to grade one. Thank you for the tea," the brother said with a strict sense of finality.

I wrestled all night and into the dawn with God. How could a loving God abandon children to this hellhole? How could He treat them like they were a mistake? I didn't want them to feel like I did growing up—that they didn't belong anywhere. I didn't want them to feel like the world would be better off without them, that they were nothing but a burden. I remember what that felt like, but I had the opportunity to prove to everyone that I wasn't a mistake. My outward success provided the cover I needed to keep those feelings buried deep within me. So deep that no one was ever going to find out why I had felt this way.

Over and over, I asked God, "How could You let this happen? Don't You care about those kids?" My plea continued. "Why haven't You done anything about this?"

"I have," He said. "I sent you." And He gave me an idea. It was clear as a bell. God had given me a dream—a purpose. It seemed so obvious. *But if it was going to be so easy, why hadn't anyone tried it before?*

I couldn't wait to share God's vision with the group the next day. "I know what we will do. God said, 'open a preschool.'" Even though I had no idea where to start, I knew it would become a reality. I'd never been so certain of anything in my life. "What do we have to do to open a school for kids four to seven years old?"

The locals looked around the table at each other as if to say, "This foreigner is crazy, but we like it." Pastor Bill said, "Just remember, if you start something, you can't quit. Everyone abandons that community."

And on September 13, 2010, we opened a humble preschool with eighteen four-year-olds. And God took over my life.

———

August 29, 2020

The image of those three-year-old kids cast aside at the dumpsite and Pastor Bill's plea not to desert the community had stuck with me since that day. When I closed my eyes, I saw those kids. When I plugged my ears, I heard Bill's words. In the deepest part of my soul, I felt God's love, faithfulness, and grace as He walked with me on this quest to win back this community for His Kingdom.

It wasn't a distant place anymore. I'd been going there for thirteen years. They weren't nameless toddlers with dirty faces and distended bellies to me anymore. Each one has a name and a story. Each one, their own pain. I've spent so much time in the dump that I often take on their desperation. We have become family.

And now I have a four-year-old scared out of her mind.

There's nothing worse than a small casket.

I just want to grab Angel, her sisters, Shosh, and run.

THE RESCUE

August 29, 2020

ALL I COULD DO WAS LAY motionless, running scenarios in my head of the gang's next vicious step with Angel. Kim stretched out next to me, ghostly white, and didn't make a peep. What could she say? "It'll be all right?" Neither one of us could utter the words of a worst case, but we knew the stains on their pangas proved this gang was out for blood.

I had to find out what my team in Kenya knew about the attack at Angel's. Typically, it doesn't take long for the rumor mill, or for cries for help, to reach their ears because they serve so many people in the community every day. But sometimes, in these darkest moments, when there's no one else to turn to, people like Anonymous reach out to me directly, even if I'm in America.

Over and over I typed out a message to the team.

They're gonna kill Angel.

Delete.

They're gonna burn down Gioto.

Delete.

They're gonna kill everybody.

Delete.

Make it stop!

Delete.

Delete! Delete! Delete! I pounded that key like a madman as my rage built toward these thugs. I didn't know what to say to the team or how to say it. I'd rather not say anything and pretend it would all go away. And I didn't want to throw people I loved into danger. So I waited and prayed, and typed and deleted, and looked at Kim like I could throw up, and prayed some more.

Bothering the team on a Sunday was the last thing I wanted to do. It was their day to go to church, decompress, and catch up on household chores they didn't have time to do during the week. But the gang had already savaged the uncle, and we had to act *now* to save Angel and her shosho before they made good on their threats to kill them.

On the other hand, Sunday might be the perfect day to rescue them since most of the one million residents in Nakuru go to church. Businesses and restaurants close for the day, like they used to in the US during the fifties. The normally traffic-jammed streets were empty. Maybe this would make it safe for my team to go out in broad daylight.

I typed the message one last time and looked at Kim. "I can't send it."

"Oh, honey, why not?"

"I can't break this news to them like this."

She glanced at me with tenderness.

"They have to hear my voice. They have to know it will be okay."

The brief, direct call stunned the team. I was afraid they'd be paralyzed. Without hesitating, four of our leaders, Dan, Maggie, Nafula, and Nia, dropped everything and volunteered. They arrived at Shosh's at 10:00 a.m. Nine gang members were already there, spewing more venom. They had surrounded the house, with their knives and machetes drawn, threatening grandma again. Angel cowered in the corner, huddling with her sisters.

It was outrageous this would happen on a Sunday. It was even worse that the attackers were disrespecting an elder. Even gangs once had standards. These guys didn't care about anything except spreading terror and spilling blood.

Dan told me that right after they arrived, the neighborhood crowd grew. No one dared to rescue Shosh, fearing the gang might turn their rage on them. Most stood motionless, trying to disappear. A few terrified moms, frantic that their kids might be next, sprinted to the dumpsite to get some guys who worked there to stop the fight before someone got slashed. Nobody messes with those dumpsite guys. They fight—and live—with no regard for consequences.

Often, they are the villains.

Six guys from the dump arrived to engage the gang, armed with nothing more than reputations and bravado. Tempers flared. Threats filled the air. And then it happened. Again.

One of the gang members grabbed Angel's hair and snapped her head back. He put a machete to her throat, screaming he'd slit it along with those of her sisters. Two of the dumpsite guys lunged at him and pulled Angel free. Ten more men were running from the dump toward the chaos to enter the fight. The gang leader saw them, shouted a single command, and his entire group fled before real trouble broke out.

Today, the dumpsite guys were the heroes.

For two and a half hours, our team pleaded with Shosh to leave while she and the kids were still able. Everyone knew those bloodletters would come back. But there was no convincing her. She refused to abandon her house because the gang threatened to burn it down. And if her place went up in flames, it would set off a chain reaction. The inferno would reduce her neighbors' homes to ashes too. Everyone would blame Shosh for bringing trouble, and they'd boot her out of the place she called home all her life.

If she got kicked out of a dumpsite, where in the world would she live?

Strangely, I felt the same. This place was my home now too. The people I love lived here. It's where I belonged. I'm not sure

I'd have the courage of the Shosh to stick it out, but I'd like to think I might.

Shosh wouldn't budge. The more my team pressed her to flee, the more she dug in. She exhibited the same tenacity that allowed her to survive the trials of life in this violent place and protect her girls.

As the team begged her to leave, a scout from the gang returned with taunting shouts of "When your son gets out of the cell, we'll kill him!" and "Today, we get your girls!"

Shosh anxiously rubbed her thumbs against her fingertips, lifting her hands until they reached her face. Then she wiped a tear. She'd always kept her granddaughters safe. Always. In her mind, no one could ever protect them like her. She could never trust their safety to someone else. Especially now.

The gangster pounded on the iron sheet gate and screeched, "Your girls get cut! *Kufa!* Dead!"

Both of Shosh's hands now cradled her own face. She tipped her head to the sky as if it was her last breath. "Take my Angel! Take my girls! Take them!" She collapsed into her lap, sobbing.

Shosh agreed to let us help the girls escape if we could get them to a relative's place forty-five minutes away. The team promised, trusting God to come through, without knowing how in the world it would happen—especially since we didn't have a vehicle. All we had was hope.

———

August 30, 2020

Who would be brave enough to transport the girls? I wished I could summon the Avengers and have Iron Man scoop them up. But all I had was my phone, my knees, and my faith. Who could I ask to come between a vengeful gang and the little girl they wanted to kill? The only person I thought of was the one who was already in it: Anonymous. *Lord, help us get the girls to safety.*

I pulled up Anonymous's text stream on my phone. Seeing the horror-filled messages still on my screen steeled my resolve.

> *Hi. Our team visited Angel today. Can you talk?* ~ *me*

YES, IF YOU EXCUSE ME EATING ~ ANONYMOUS

> *Do you have access to a car?* ~ *me*

NO ~ ANONYMOUS

No? I was surprised at the answer because Anonymous seemed to always be connected to some resource. I thought for sure he would have a car, a Blackhawk helicopter, and Tony Stark's phone number.

> *Ok. Thank you. We are trying to find transportation so the girls can escape. I thought I'd ask.* ~ *me*

SORRY ~ ANONYMOUS

"Sorry"? Why not "Sorry, but I know someone"? Why not "Sorry, but I have a friend"? Why not "Sorry, but I've got some guys who can get them out"? Just "Sorry"? That's not what I wanted to hear!

I scrambled to think of who might have anything more secure than a *piki* (motorbike) to get Angel and her sisters. I only knew one person with a car in Kenya. But did God really want me to reach out to him and hurl him into the middle of this? I didn't care. I'd already lost too many kids to stupid diseases and poverty. I couldn't bear another small casket. Out of desperation, I reached out to my longtime friend, Vic. For over a decade, he had seen our organization, Living Stone Global Foundation, change the lives of the people living in the slum. He'd always been willing to help us out in the past. Maybe he'd risk it this time too?

Because he owned a travel company, Vic had lots of vehicles. Some were classic safari vans that could go anywhere, like the hazardous terrain of a dumpsite.

I prayed, "Lord, help save these girls, please," and sent the text.

Hi Vic. We need to make arrangements for an emergency ride to rescue some kids. Are you up for it? ~ me

Thank you for contacting Elohim Tours and Travel. We're unavailable right now but will respond as soon as possible. Please let us know how we can help you. ~ Vic

Seriously, an automated reply?

Vic, we're in a jam and have to help 3 young girls escape the dumpsite. It MUST happen TOMORROW! Will you help? ~ me

After forty long minutes, three little letters brought hope.

yes ~ Vic

All it took was a simple text to the right person and $20 to get Angel and her sisters out of danger before the gang came back to claim their heads.

I was still grappling with what had gone on in the last forty-eight hours. Who were these gang guys, anyway? Were they the Mungiki or someone else? What's going to happen if I get into the middle of this? Will they turn on all our kids?

I messaged Dan to see if he thought I knew any of the gang guys. Dan ran our entire operation in Kenya and knew everybody in the neighborhood. They all called him Uncle Dan. Certainly, he knew these guys.

All he replied was "I don't think you do. I also don't know the guys."

The frustration of figuring out who this gang was, what they wanted, and why they were causing mayhem made my head spin. The idea of Angel losing her head made me sick to my stomach. What was God asking me to do, reach out to them? How would I even find guys like these?

————

August 31, 2020

Purposefully, I didn't silence my phone. This time, at 2:00 a.m., I got better news.

Daudi [Dave in Swahili] *the girls are moved safely ~ Vic*

Thank you, Jesus!

God bless you, Vic. You may have saved their lives. ~ me

I immediately texted the news of victory to my friend, Anonymous.

Angel and the girls are safely moved. Shosh is remaining. ~ me

THANK YOU SO MUCH FOR WHAT YOU HAVE DONE. ~ ANONYMOUS

All in God's strength. Thanks for the chance to help. ~ me

I thought that might be the end of it. Angel was out of harm's way. Shosh seemed to be okay. And God was glorified. Then Anonymous asked a leading question.

WILL YOU SPEAK TO THE CHIEF? ~ ANONYMOUS

THE CHIEF

August 31, 2020

MAYBE ANONYMOUS WAS on to something. If one man could get to the bottom of this mess, it would be the Chief. I didn't even know his real name. I only knew him as the Chief. But I knew the importance of his position.

It is the sworn duty of every chief to maintain law and order. Like a first-century Roman governor, a chief wants to maintain order, please the boss, and keep his high-status job. Ours had nearly unlimited authority over the seventy thousand people in our ward. And what wasn't under his authority was under his influence. Unlike an elected official, he didn't give a hoot about politics, pleasing people, or getting votes. He cared about keeping the peace and pleasing the president. He had the impossible task of peacemaker, mediator, negotiator, and law enforcer all rolled into one. Area chiefs were thrown in the middle of every kind of problem, whether it concerned land, marriage, inheritance, burial, school fees, or even troubles with witch doctors. I thought of him like Moses sitting before the Israelites, making judgments and maintaining harmony among the people.

Many Kenyans argue some chiefs are a heavy-handed burden

to their people. I hoped ours wasn't one of them. They accused them of being corrupt, autocratic, and dictatorial. Area chiefs had tremendous clout and could make things impossible for you if they wanted. It's a lot of power for one man. The Chief is an important person to have on your side, or at a minimum, to not have against you.

I wasn't introduced to the Chief as an honored guest or celebrated non-profit leader. I met the Chief as nearly everyone else does. I had caused a problem.

October 1, 2018

Nothing much about life had changed for the people in Gioto since I first stepped foot there in 2007, except that the state of decay was accelerating. The condition of the homes around the dumpsite ranged from atrocious to uninhabitable. The worst structures were indistinguishable from the pig stalls surrounding them. Most dwellings were constructed from some combination of salvaged paper, plastic, and scraps of wood. Cardboard seemed to be the roofing material of choice. I have no idea why. It makes a lousy roof because it is no match for East Africa's blazing sun and torrential rains.

Often, like discarded trash, our people felt thrown away too. They were no longer of any use, unwanted, and cast off to the outskirts of town. Living in these conditions humiliates them and crushes their spirits. We found one way to help them restore their dignity was to improve their shelters. A man's home is his castle and all that.

Our first remodel was for a man in his early thirties named Roberto. He was tenderhearted, but the demon of alcoholism possessed him. From the moment he woke until he passed out sometime later, he would drown himself in chang'aa, tormented by that dreadful brew. Then he'd wake up and begin the cycle all over again regardless of the time of day. Whenever Roberto saw us, he would stop us and beg us to pray for God to show mercy and remove the evil spirit of alcohol from him. Even though he hallucinated and heard voices frequently, his manner was always gentle, something unique among the drunkards in our town.

His house lay right on the border of Hilton and Gioto, an area that looked like the entrance to a gated community, only in reverse. Gone are the stone-walled compounds, tin roofs, and cement floors of the Hilton slum. Enter the burning desert of garbage called Gioto.

Roberto's place was in shambles. You wouldn't know the inside from the outside, as rotting trash was equally littered everywhere. His shack was among the worst around, being just random strips of cloth, paper, and sisal bags wrapped around a frame of crooked sticks. And of course, a cardboard roof. A hole in the wall stood in place of a door. A few rags beneath his cardboard mattress covered a fifty-five-gallon drum of chang'aa he'd buried for safekeeping and easy access. It's a good thing Roberto didn't smoke; the fumes were so noxious, the place would have exploded.

Bright and early, Dan, Maggie, Kim, and I rounded the corner to Roberto's place to make his hut a home. A couple of local *fundis* (construction experts) we'd hired to rebuild the house joined us. Every chance we got, we provided jobs for those living around us. It put a little money into the economy and showed people they could make things better with resources from within the community. They have skills, talents, and worth. Plus, I don't really know which end of the hammer to use.

I was dreaming of the look on Roberto's face when he had a *mabati* (iron sheet) roof over his head. How much joy would it bring him to have it not rain inside anymore? I also wondered if he would be smashed out of his mind or massively hungover when we arrived. I would be thrilled with coherent.

He saw us before we entered his humble compound. With an enormous smile, he clapped his hands together. "HAHA, DAUDI!

TODAY IS THE DAY!" It was the loudest sound I had ever heard come out of his gentle mouth. He put one arm around me and the other around Dan and led us inside his plot. His clothes were clean, and I could smell the fresh soap from his bath. He was sporting his favorite Rasta beanie, a wooden bead peace necklace, and a magnetic smile.

"When we get done, I'm going to sweep out the inside, clean up the outside, and plant flowers. It is going to be beautiful!" He may have been whistling.

Could this be the same man? Did a drop of hope send his demons on the run?

Two days later, we finished the work. Roberto was so thrilled he ran around the dumpsite, waving his hands over his head, nearly hysterical. He was praising Jesus, telling his friends God hadn't forgotten him, and inviting everyone to visit his new home. I wanted to follow close behind and echo that God hadn't forsaken any of us, but I was having too much fun watching him dance like King David with all his might before the Lord as he disappeared in the distance. Seeing Roberto's reaction made me want to fix every home in Gioto. So that's what we set out to do.

And that's when our problem started.

The next shanty we targeted was for Peter, a man in his early forties who lived in the heart of the dumpsite. At the entrance to his place, stuck on top of the corner post, was a creepy, white mannequin's head. The pole next to it was bare. As we walked in, I looked at Dan, tilted my head, crossed my eyes, stuck out my tongue, and pointed at my chin and then the empty pole. I nervously joked that I hoped my likeness wouldn't be staring back at him from up there after we finished.

The house's cardboard and rock ceiling was collapsing. I couldn't even stand upright under it. In the center of the back wall, hanging upside down, was a 1998 calendar with a photo of a tender-skinned, blue-eyed, blond-haired Jesus.

I wanted to raise the roof, wrap the house in iron sheets, and restore Jesus to His full and upright position. Even more, I wanted

Peter to know how much we loved him and hoped that, in the end, he would gleefully fly around the dumpsite like Roberto.

The fundis demolished Peter's old structure in no time, securing new posts firmly in the ground. They kindly removed the mzungu mannequin's head. Early in the afternoon, Maggie went to oversee the progress. She called me the moment she arrived. I could barely hear because Mama Amon was screaming in the background, hysterical.

Mama Amon's influence had skyrocketed over the past ten years. No longer was she simply the unofficial mayor. Now she was the empress. Gone was the burgundy and beige apron of a peasant scavenger. In its place was a fashionable dress and fine shoes. She sported a flashy gold watch, which I had seen her sometimes remove before she addressed her subjects. Even the unmistakable gap in her teeth was gone. She had made so much money skimming from the well-wishers' good nature that she didn't live full time in Gioto anymore. Instead, she owned a comfortable home with a view in an upscale part of town. She maintained an enormous compound in Gioto, but it was only to show her dominance over her pawns and serve as the headquarters for her extortion ring.

I had always wondered what happened to her. How had she gone from someone who seemed to do good for the others in the community to becoming a tyrant with a reputation for brutality? Was it pure greed?

I learned the minute Maggie had arrived, all hell had broken loose.

"Hang in there, Maggie. We'll be right over." I grabbed Dan and Kim, and we walked to the dumpsite like we were an hour late for an important meeting. From a distance, I could see the ruckus. Mama Amon was in Maggie's face, and a crowd was forming.

Lord, do Your thing. Help us be Your love for this community. Bring Your peace, bring Your righteousness. Your will be done.

All eyes were on me as I climbed the knoll of decomposing

trash and approached the home. None were watching more closely than Dan and Maggie. With each step closer, Mama Amon yelled faster and louder. "No one does a thing without my approval! Who do you think you are! *Toka hapa!* (Get out of here!) These people are mine! This place is mine! Toka hapa!"

Her English tongue lashing morphed into a Swahili rant. She may have even been inventing Swenglish swear words. Her eyes yellowed as her rage built. But the angrier she got, the more God's peace flowed through my veins, though I despised what she had done to the people. Even my breathing slowed. I turned my head slowly to acknowledge the crowd gathering around us. People three rows deep now surrounded Peter's plot. With a soft smile and tenderness in my voice, I raised both hands palms out, shoulder high, and addressed them. "You know, we love you. We're here to do good. We are here in peace and want to create a safer home for this gentleman." Several in the crowd nodded in approval. Keeping their eyes fixed on me, a few motioned to their friends and tugged their ears, silently asking for translation. One said, "Asante."

Mama Amon's shrill tried to drown out my speech, but yapping like a toy poodle, she now had backed away forty yards. I didn't have to raise my voice above that of a dinner conversation.

"We intend to improve every single home in the dumpsite like we're doing here. We're here to love you and do good. But we won't force it on you. Some people aren't happy we're here." The crowd, now over a hundred people, knew exactly who I was talking about as I smirked in her direction.

"We are going to leave now. Don't worry, we are not abandoning you. We will be back the minute we are welcome," I said. Then Kim, Maggie, Dan, and I cautiously sidestepped down the slippery mound of slime. We'd repeated the same promise we've made for years: "We'll try if you'll try. We will not force anything on anybody—not even good."

How we do things and engage with the community is even more important than what we do. In order to influence, we first must establish relationship. The people need to feel valued and loved.

So often, I have witnessed well-intended groups come to the slum, do the project they want to do, take some pictures, then pack up and leave, having little community engagement. As a result, they may do more long-term harm than short-term good. For a community crushed by shame and hopelessness, foreigners doing a project while the locals sit and watch on the sidelines confirms the fear they have all along: *We can't do this for ourselves. We're not capable. We need someone else to do it. We're as useless as the trash we live in.* It can create a vicious cycle that makes people give up for good. And then they drown themselves in fifty-five-gallon drums of chang'aa—the devil declares another battle won.

Building into people, not merely constructing iron and wood structures, is what makes me tick. Working side by side with the residents to improve their dwellings is just the beginning of building their value. It's not the square footage of the house or the extravagance of the furnishings that matters—it's the reconstruction of their identity. It's instilling the feeling of worth. Eventually, it leads to understanding that we are all made in God's image and dearly loved by our Creator.

As we hiked the short distance back to the school we'd established, Maisha Mapya Learning Center, I turned to Maggie. "Hey, the next time I go to the store, remind me to get some Tic Tacs please."

She looked at me sideways, just as I had hoped. "Um, sure, Daudi. I will get them."

"I'm going to give them to you to offer to Mama Amon next time she gets in your face. Her breath had to be baaaad."

"Maybe get her a toothbrush too," Maggie added. We laughed and continued to school. It broke the tension of a tough afternoon. But Mama Amon's brash display of dominance over her people and their silence at being her pawns made me wonder even more about the power she had over them.

Then Dan's phone rang.

In a small voice, he answered, *"Habari yako"* (Hello). His head didn't move, but his eyes looked up at me with concern. *"Sawa sawa"* (Okay).

"Daudi, that was the MCA. He wants us to meet with him and the Chief immediately."

"What's an MCA?"

"It's the Municipal County Assemblyman. He's the top politician in our area. He heard about what we are doing, and he's not happy."

"How can he not be happy with us fixing houses?"

"We must go right now."

"Who's the Chief?"

Dan didn't answer my question. Instead he said, "Nothing good happens when you have to see the Chief."

We picked up our pace to get to Maisha Mapya before our guests arrived. Dan instructed James, our campus host, to get some sodas for them. *Nice touch, Dan.* Kim and Maggie joined us in the admin office. We sat for twenty minutes staring at each other in uncomfortable silence. Dan's eyes darted across the ground the entire time. I wanted to shake up the sodas to break the tension and make him laugh but decided against it.

Sam, the MCA, entered the room with a giant smile, hand already extended. Not really what I was expecting. I feared it would be some steaming-mad egomaniac in a power suit with shiny shoes, looking to rip someone a new one—that someone being me.

We stood to greet Sam, then sat and enjoyed our drinks, exchanging pleasantries. It's one thing I love about Kenyan culture and one I hope to incorporate more into the way I treat people everywhere: even if there is an issue between two parties, they always begin with "How are you?" and "How is your family?" They establish a human connection before dealing with the situation at hand.

Dan asked Sam if the Chief was coming. Sam scooted his chair closer to the table. "No, Dan, he wants me to handle this."

Mama Amon suddenly burst in through our office door—uninvited and unannounced. Immediately, she took a position at the head of the table and began screaming at me, pointing her long, bony finger at my face. She didn't even sit down. I was surprised Sam didn't utter a word. Her rant began with "THIS MZUNGU . . . bleep, bleep bleep, blah blah blah. . . ." The nerve of this woman was extraordinary, barging into my school and reading me the riot act. Fortunately, my lack of understanding of Swahili came in handy. I had no idea what she was saying. But I gathered it was not complimentary.

I looked at Sam again as he sat there, pretending not to see me. Why was this prominent man allowing her to continue unimpeded? Why wouldn't he shut her up?

Her face grew even more enraged, and hatred spewed from her, aimed to destroy and devour me. The darting glances from Maggie and Dan were telling, as they shrank in their seats. They knew exactly what she was saying. They looked at me like beaten puppies, their eyes saying, "Isn't this hurting you, Daddy?" Kim was looking at me too, feeling defensive for her husband, who was apparently being accused of all kinds of things.

After forty-five minutes, the lady ran out of insults. Her stamina had been impressive. As she sat down, I smiled, folded my hands on the table, and turned to Sam still wondering why he had allowed this display.

"Sam, since we don't know each other well, would you please share with me more about who you are?"

He leaned in and gathered his hands together on top of the table. "I am the duly elected municipal assemblyman for this area. I represent and serve seventy thousand people here in Nakuru West."

"Wow, Sam, that's awesome! That's a big job. I want you to know we fully recognize your authority. Not only that, but we want to be your best citizens in the area. We are here to love the community and make life better for everyone, especially those who are hurting."

He relaxed, sat back in his chair, and exhaled.

Motioning to Mama Amon, I asked politely, "Now, who is she?"

"The people at the dump elected her to represent them," Sam said.

Mama Amon jumped to her feet and interjected, "That's not right! Seventeen years ago, God appointed *me* to rule over these people!"

I blinked hard. Twice. It was the most incredible thing to hear this woman declare herself the supreme leader of the people in the presence of the people's elected leader.

"Is it true, Sam? She is self-appointed?"

His eyes widened. "I guess so." He shrugged. I couldn't tell if that was a concession or if he was tired of her antics, but I expected him to be more assertive.

I continued. "I've seen her behavior, even what she displayed here during this meeting." Everyone knew I was referring to the forty-five-minute hate-filled tirade still ringing in our ears. Now it was my turn for a power play.

"I don't know which god she is referring to, but it is not the same God who sent me here to love, heal, and transform this community. Since she holds no official elected position, I won't recognize the authority she claims to have. She has no position of leadership or influence. She has no rightful seat at this table. She is welcome to take part in any services or programs we offer the general community, but she has no special standing. Are you okay with that, Sam?"

After a brief pause, he nodded in agreement. I couldn't believe it. The devil just lost a tooth!

I'm not sure Mama Amon's English was fluent enough to understand fully what had transpired. With her glare still fixed on me, the corners of her mouth turned down and nostrils flared. In the deafening silence with arms crossed over her chest, she attempted to make eye contact with each person at the table, searching for some sign of agreement or support. I was the only one who engaged her squinting stare. I smiled, sort of like the Mona Lisa. God's gracious peace filled me completely.

"So, we can continue fixing the homes, Sam?"

"Yes."

The meeting adjourned, and by the time we got to the bottom of the stairs to head from the building, Dan's phone was ringing.

"Daudi, it's the Chief. We must meet him first thing in the morning. He is not happy."

Are we really going to go through this again? Mama Amon had doubled down and continued to assert her influence. She called the Chief from inside our admin office to complain about our presence in the community. He immediately summoned us to stand before him. Who was this woman to have that much juice?

———

It's only a fifteen-minute walk from Maisha Mapya to the Chief's headquarters. Along the way, I tried to get a sense from Dan about why he was so worried.

"Daudi, everyone is afraid of him. Politicians like Sam are very powerful in Kenya. It's true. But government officials are even more. I've only seen the Chief out and about in the neighborhood. He comes walking through the streets dressed in camo with his guards. Every time, someone is going to jail. Every time. I've been here my whole life, and I've never met him like this —called to his office. He can send me to prison just because he feels like it. He didn't sound happy on the phone. Oh, Daudi, what if . . ."

I gulped and interrupted before he could finish. "Let's see what God does, Dan." I was hoping the meeting would be as friendly as with Sam and that Dan's fears had the best of him.

When we arrived at the Chief's office, Dan sheepishly poked his head in and was told to "Get out!" and wait outside. Dan's eyes widened as his head went down and, with his tail between his legs, he sat next to me, trying to be invisible. After the beautiful progress with Sam and seemingly getting Mama Amon out of our affairs, I feared our victory might be short-lived.

A teenage boy with dreadlocks, ripped jeans, and a tie-dyed One Love T-shirt slipped out of the office without turning his back on the Chief. The Chief gave him a threatening goodbye. "Tell those thugs at K2 they are in my sights! I will chase them out like I did the others!"

A stern voice from behind the desk in the office said, "Come in." As we entered, a man in his forties sat focused on the stacks of papers that littered his desk. The collar of his forest green dress shirt peeked out over his olive-colored cable-knit sweater. The office was smaller than I imagined for a man of his position. Random notices were taped to the peeling, yellow-painted walls. Prominently displayed behind him were the Kenyan flag and a framed picture of President Uhuru Kenyatta, son of the nation's first president, Jomo Kenyatta.

Some people have a larger-than-life reputation. The Chief's cold eyes looked me up and down, sizing up who this mzungu was in his office causing him problems. He crossed his arms and inhaled. It was the exact opposite reception that Sam had given me.

"What do you think you are doing!"

I looked at Dan, being careful not to turn my face away from the Chief, and didn't say a word. I knew I would jump to defend our actions and sell the Chief on all the great work we do, which would precisely be the wrong thing to do. So I followed Dan's lead.

"Good afternoon, Chief. Thank you for calling us here. I am Danson from Maisha Mapya. We have a school for the kids at the dumpsite."

The Chief turned his gaze from Dan to me.

Dan's right hand was rubbing his pant leg as he rocked in his chair. "This is Dave Hatfield." Now Dan's right leg was bouncing. "He is the founder of our school and helps the kids in so many ways."

Arms still folded, the Chief's eyes widened. "What do you think you are doing!"

Dan's charming, submissive introduction had made no impact. I held my tongue.

Unfortunately, the Chief sat taller and broke the silence. "You can not go about doing whatever you want. Do you hear me?" His speech quickened and his volume increased too.

I looked at Dan still rocking in his chair. Now his complexion was blotchy.

"I get a call . . ." The Chief tapped two fingers on his cell phone and scowled. ". . . the lady at the dump says you are building houses. How can I be a good leader if I do not know what is going on in my backyard?" He looked up from the phone. "Answer that!"

I had no idea what to say. Dan fidgeted with his fingernails.

The Chief went on. "What do you think you are doing? I need to know!" He paused for what seemed like an hour before saying, "What am I going to do with you?"

Dan knew exactly what the Chief was going to say. He'd heard it clearly in his imagination: *"Dan, you're going to jail. Somebody's got to go to jail for this, and it's you. You are the local guy. There won't be any headlines in the paper sending a Kenyan kid to jail. I do it all the time. You will have twenty giant cellmates. That will be the end of Dan. You'll probably never be heard from again."*

At the same time, I knew exactly what the Chief was going to say: *"Mr. Mzungu, or whatever your name is, I'm going to close your school and kick you out of the country. You'll never be able to come to Kenya again. You'll never see the kids you love again. The place you feel you belong, the place God sent you to, will return to a wasteland. And along with it, you won't have fixed anything. You'll just be a failure. A mistake. A nobody. People will laugh at you and your god. I'll feed your kids to Mama Amon."*

The Chief's right hand rose to rub his perspiring forehead, then slid down his face and stopped at his chin while he pondered. He exhaled, "Both of you . . ." *Oh, we're* both *going to prison.* His gaze captured all four of our eyes, and it was only broken when he smoothed both hands under his eyes and across his face. Now *my* forehead was perspiring. "What am I going to do with both of you?" he said again, only this time he was genuinely perplexed.

I cleared my throat. "I'm sorry sir, Chief. Please accept my personal apologies and apologies on behalf of our entire organization." I wanted to continue and explain we were fixing broken-down homes, but I could tell it wouldn't get us very far. He was establishing his authority, and it was working. He went on and on and on about how he got a call from a lady screaming about us building new homes for her people. Somehow, she was making things difficult for him. I couldn't believe he was letting her upset him like this. Was she a relative? Was she bribing him?

I repeated, "Kindly accept our apologies. I was unaware we had to contact you first. But that is no excuse, sir. We should have known. I take full responsibility for it, and I am sorry to cause issues for you. It's my fault. Will you accept my apology, sir?"

He sat back in his chair, folded his hands in his lap, and nodded. "Yes. But seriously, next time you must include me first before you do anything in the community. Do you understand?"

"Sawa sawa. We will."

"Now, please tell me what you want to do."

We discussed our desire to improve the homes at the dumpsite that were falling apart. The Chief agreed it was a good idea, then laid some ground rules.

"First, we will meet with the MCA, and together we can pick exactly which homes to improve."

In the end, the Chief appeared to be a reasonable, sober, community-minded official. The combination of my fear and lack of understanding of local protocols had gotten the best of me. I thanked him for his concern and grace, apologized one last time, and Dan and I slid out. Plus, I had a plan to mend the relationship. Once outside the government compound, I said, "Dan, for the next few weeks, I want you to call the Chief every day with what we are doing. Every. Single. Day. I want you to call him until he says, 'You don't have to call me with these things anymore.'"

Dan chuckled. "I get it." Over the next few weeks, he befriended the Chief, calling him daily without missing a beat.

But Mama Amon was not surrendering without a fight. A month later, I saw her with Sam at the entrance to Gioto rubbing elbows and laughing.

In the end, working with the Chief and Sam's approval, we transformed every tattered shack into an iron sheet fortress and restored dignity. The community felt loved. And Roberto again danced for his friends.

———

August 31, 2020

While I guessed Anonymous had reached out to me to see if I could get the Chief to intimidate the gangs, in reality, he had contacted me for a more subtle reason. The request came on behalf of Angel's shosho. Anonymous was somehow aware I knew the Chief. It seems everyone around here knows everyone else's business.

Right after the attack on her family, Shosh lumbered as fast as possible to the local police precinct to get help. The cops didn't lift a finger. They wouldn't even write the incident down. She insisted: "I not leaving until you make report." They laughed. The more she pushed, the more they resisted. Finally, they barked at her, "Get out, old woman!" It seems the only thing they were interested in was arresting Shosh's son and three gang members.

All this made Shosh more worried about her safety. Why wouldn't the police want to hear from an eyewitness? If the police wouldn't protect her, who would? Everyone knows a female dumpsite dweller is vulnerable. And it solidified her resolve to keep Angel in hiding.

Anonymous reached out to me to see if I could get Shosh

some protection. But just because I knew the Chief didn't mean I had any influence on the police. My main concern had been scrambling to get Angel and her sisters beyond the reach of the gang's machetes. And now they were safe, hidden in the cleft of the Lord's protection at their auntie's. I wasn't interested in opening Pandora's box by battling the police right now. For the first time in a few days, my nerve endings were calming down.

For a few nights, there was peace.

THE NIGHTMARE

September 3, 2020

THERE WERE 2 MURDERS IN HILTON LAST NIGHT. BOTH KNIFE. ~
ANONYMOUS

MY CHEST TIGHTENED. "THEY GOT ANGEL!" I gasped. It was like
a car hit me. I leaned over to Kim, who was already asleep. I held
on to her as tight as I could and put my head on her shoulder as
tears flowed. All I could think of was Angel slashed to pieces lying
in a pool of blood.

"Kim," I said softly.

She sat up with a look like I'd already delivered the news
because I only call her Kim when something tragic happens.
"What's wrong?"

"They killed somebody last night, maybe it's Angel."

"What? Oh, no . . . Jesus have mercy!"

We both huddled around my phone as if somehow, we could
reverse the hands of time. I held her extra tight, feeling the life of
each breath in her lungs.

"What if they got Angel? Or Shosh? What if . . ."

I knew things had been too quiet over the past few days. I

couldn't believe it. I didn't want to believe it. I'd experienced a lot of catastrophes in the past dozen years, but murder? Was that even possible? All my trembling hands typed out in response was

OH NO! ~ me

Before I could ask if it was Angel, Anonymous replied.

AS OF YET, ONE WE DON'T KNOW WHO DID IT. THE OTHER I THINK IS KNOWN. A HARDWORKING GUY WHO WAS LIKED AND RAN A POOL CLUB. THE OTHER GUY, HIS BODY WAS FOUND THIS MORNING. THE VIOLENCE IS ON ANOTHER LEVEL THESE DAYS. ~ ANONYMOUS

"Oh, what if it's Dan!" I cradled my face with both hands. "What if I dragged him into this whole thing to just get him killed?"

Kim looked at me speechless.

"Oh, Lord, please don't let it be Dan."

"I know, honey, he's been like a son," Kim replied. My heart beat in my throat. One side of my brain was reading the text, the other trying to figure out what the heck was going on and how to keep it all together. I dropped my phone off the edge of the bed and scrambled to find it only to push it further away. I had to know if it was Dan.

Is Dan ok? ~ me

I DON'T THINK IT'S ANYONE AT MAISHA BUT IT HAS SHAKEN EVERYONE. IT HAS ROCKED THE COMMUNITY. ~ ANONYMOUS

You don't *think* so? I had to know! My mind was spinning. I could feel everything we'd worked for being ripped apart. I had to get Dan and all the rest of them out of Maisha and as far away as possible. All the kids. All the staff. Everyone! We need to go into hiding like Angel or at least I need to go and protect them.

I'm sorry. I wish I was there. ~ me

I don't know what we'd do, but we're pretty good at engaging with people. Be safe and be smart. ~ me

I fixed my eyes on Kim, not knowing if I really wished I was in the middle of the mayhem in Kenya or not. But I had to know for certain Dan and the others were alive. At the same time, I didn't want to scare my friend to death and blurt out that two guys got mutilated. He was still emotionally recovering from the attack at Angel's. The news of ruthless butchering a few hundred yards from our school's gates would rock him to his core. I had to text him. I had to know Dan wasn't in the morgue. But how could I soften the blow?

Hello Dan. Have you heard about the incidents of last night? ~ me

Nothing. No response. "What is taking him so long?" I asked Kim. "Oh, I hope he's alive."

For two excruciating minutes, there was no reply.

Hello Dave. Haven't heard of anything yet. What's the issue? ~ Dan

Oh, thank God. Thank You, Jesus. Thank You. Thank You. I read those words again, hearing each syllable in the sweet sound of Dan's voice.

Dan didn't have a clue. I was happy his little fingers were typing back to me, but I was about to shred his heart by telling him the news of killers roaming our streets.

He and I had been through a lot together. We'd fended off

greedy politicians who blatantly asked for bribes. We'd routinely handled violent men who were drunk out of their minds. We'd grieved the senseless loss of a five-month-old baby. We'd shared the outrage of tracking down abusers who defiled a five-year-old girl just outside our gates. We'd even helped a six-year-old boy whose dad whipped him so badly it split his shirt and skin wide open. Then the monster threw his son into a fifteen-foot-deep pit toilet to die. The scars on the boy's back are there forever to tell the story.

It takes a lot to shock Dan. Would fearing murderers be too much to handle for this twenty-nine-year-old?

Dan is resilient, but he's sensitive too. He has a gentle spirit, a mischievous grin, and a fun-loving nature. However, he always has an eye out for the other shoe that is waiting to drop. If I make a harsh comment without first giving a compliment, he cowers. It is not my intention to intimidate him, but there's something in his past that causes it. I can only imagine what.

I knew he had a tough time as a kid, and I've been like a father to him almost from the day he joined our organization as an intern four years ago. He came to us as a bright-eyed college student with big dreams of making his mark in technology and business, and instead, God moved in his heart and gave him a family. We've walked side by side for hours doing good in our community. I'm not sure he knows he's being mentored, but hopefully he knows he's being loved. He's learning how to pass that love on to the children around him. Dan's not quite a dad to the thousands of kids in our neighborhood yet, but he is, at a minimum, their Uncle Dan.

The six months of COVID-19 lockdowns had taken a toll on Dan. He had grown into serving the needs of two hundred children attending the school, but he now had fifteen thousand people depending on the center for food every day. Dan's responsibilities had skyrocketed in a measure that would crush most people. Not to mention the increased isolation and loneliness he was experiencing from government restrictions and curfews.

I desperately wanted to be there in person to cushion the blow. At times, my phone provided the connection we needed. But when all hell is breaking loose, there is no way to make up for the 9,500 miles separating us. I needed to sit down in the same room as Dan, look into his eyes, and reassure him it would be okay and God would do something amazing. At least I hoped He would.

Was pushing a few keys and having some electrons whooshed off to the other side of the world really the best I could do? I had no choice. I swallowed hard and typed out the words, knowing they would be a gut punch.

Oh, Dan, I hate to inform you there were 2 murders in Hilton last night. ~ me

Woo . . . now this is just too much to take in . . . Hilton has just changed drastically and it really hurts ~ Dan

I'm sorry. ~ me

What should we tell the staff ~ Dan

The truth. And under NO circumstances does anyone go out alone. What do you think? ~ me

Yea . . . lets stick around the school area for now coz we cant understand what exactly is happening ~ Dan

I completely agree. Do you think it's best to inform all the staff members? ~ me

Yea . . . we can just highlight this so everyone can be on the lookout. Things are getting out of hand day after another. God have mercy. ~ Dan

Ok Dan. Maybe it's best if you call everyone rather than text. It might be too abrupt otherwise. ~ me

I didn't want him to do to others what I had just done to him. His call would comfort the staff, something a cold, voiceless text could never do. I wished I could have seen the look in his eyes to know if he was as okay as the words he typed conveyed. I doubted it. Our fingers can press keys that cover up our fears.

Yea . . . I will pass on the info . . . Thanks for that. ~ Dan

Do you think it's safe for James to be on the property? ~ me

I was concerned about James Wafula who lived on the school grounds and worked hard in the kitchen too. He's a Luhya, a tribe known for being big and muscular. He's a good guy to have around if there is any trouble because he's strong and can look intimidating even though he's as gentle as a lamb. He likes to joke, calling *me* Wafula because I used to hit the gym when I was younger. The situation with the gangs was uncertain and potentially deadly, and I wanted to make sure he would be safe as could be. I wondered if he should stay or flee and visit his family in the village.

I'd strategically built a mini fortress to protect the property without making it look like a prison. The stone wall perimeter with razor wire on top is meant to deter intruders and create a safe environment inside the campus. We had also hired a twenty-four-hour security guard to keep watch. His uniform says he has authority and training, and his phone can call for backup, but truthfully, he's no match for a riotous bunch of slaughterers.

One last thing, Dan. Can you check on Angel? ~ me

sure ~ Dan

I collapsed into Kim's embrace, grateful that our friend was secure for the moment. Being held by my wife was the safest place this side of heaven.

I had to keep checking to make sure those closest to me were out of harm's way. Nia, my executive assistant, was next on the list to contact. She is well-educated and possesses excellent HR and admin skills. In the few months Nia had been working with us, she untangled the mess I'd unknowingly created over the past decade while building our nonprofit.

Since Nia grew up outside the slum community, she lacked the expert street smarts Dan possessed. But being new to the area didn't stop her from being overconfident, thinking she knew everything about what went on. I think it's something that flowed from her career success. I know I was guilty of the same when I first came to Gioto. I thought I understood the problems and had quick fixes. Since Nia was still getting used to the ways of the place, I didn't have a clue how she would react to blood being splattered on the streets near the school.

I was told about the events of last night. Are you ok? ~ me

Good morning, Dave. I'm ok, thank you for asking. I do not know what is causing the unrest in the community. Please join us in prayer for safety and peace. ~ Nia

Amen ~ me

I didn't receive any frantic texts back from Dan or Nia, so I assumed the rest of the staff was out of danger. Angel too. The relief I felt was short lived as my mind began spinning horror stories. Would there be more murders tonight? Was the slaying spree over or just beginning?

This was not only about rescuing Angel anymore. Now it was about Sarah, and Salome, and Sharlini. It was about all two hundred children. It was not only about Dan. It was about Mary and Maggie and Nia and all the staff too. It was about the parents and aunties and uncles and everyone. Not one was safe! And who was behind all this? Was it really the Mungiki? Was it some drugged-out psycho lunatic? Maybe it was someone I know? Would this get tribal like in 2008 after the elections where thousands of people died? Is Maisha Mapya about to become a blood-stained burial ground? My questions had me trembling.

———

September 4, 2020

Bzzzt. Bzzzt. Another message from Anonymous.

> THEY ARE SAYING THEY WILL TRANSFER ALL THE POLICE AT THAT POST AS THEY DON'T DO THEIR JOB. PARENTS OF THE GANG SHOULD ALSO BE ARRESTED. ~ ANONYMOUS

Darned right they didn't do their jobs. Why not fire them and toss them in jail too? There are too many corrupt cops already. No one would miss a single one of them. And why do they want to arrest the parents? If the authorities know the gangs so well, why not get the members? What do their parents have to do with any of this?

> *Have these arrests been made? ~ me*

> I DON'T THINK SO. IT WAS SPOKEN ABOUT JUST THIS MORNING. ~ ANONYMOUS

I thought about the Mungiki, then I wondered about Mama Amon and her boys. She had her fingers in most of the horrific stuff that happened around here since the beginning of time. Maybe she was at the center of this. My fear kept me from asking about faceless, organized butchers, so I asked about the devil I knew rather than the one I didn't.

> *Do you think it's Mama Amon? ~ me*

Probably ~ Anonymous

Probably! I couldn't tell if Anonymous was being sarcastic or not, but his response didn't rule out Mama Amon being the culprit. How could she ever go from being a feckless scavenger to a murderous gangster? Was she Mungiki? Was that what rotted her heart?

> *Ok. From talking with people who do ministry with gangs, they said sometimes the police are on the take and therefore do not respond to gang activity. ~ me*

True ~ Anonymous

> *Please let me know if the arrests take place. I know a nonprofit that tolerates Mama Amon and distributes services through her, even though I have pleaded with them not to. If she's arrested, I'd like to let them know about that. Be brave. Be smart. Our team is there to help you if you need us. ~ me*

I don't even know why I typed the last part since I don't know who Anonymous was. Was he a neighbor? A gang guy? A grandpa like me? Was he even a he? I looked at the little phone icon on the screen and thought about calling. I wanted to hear the voice. I wanted to know if I knew him. But I didn't want to risk having him be afraid of me knowing his true identity. If he got nervous, maybe he would break contact. I was getting good info from someone on the inside. That alone was going to have to satisfy me.

Even better, I knew the One who knew everything going on. *Lord, help me to see what's happening? Help me know Your heart. I'll do whatever You want.* I started thinking more seriously about going to Kenya and seeing if I could calm things down. But this stupid pandemic had me stuck in a four-hundred-square-foot apartment in California. COVID-19 had all travel locked down, and Kim was sick—not with COVID-19, but with some mysterious ailment that had plagued her for over five years. Even if we had a way to get there, she couldn't go. Given her disease, there's no way she could be exposed to more toxins and the stress of travel, let alone the unknown cause of the mayhem. I also knew I couldn't make the trip without her. I did that ten years ago, and it was unbearable. The combination of constant spiritual attacks and being unable to explain to her what happened during the trip when I got back made us agree that I would never go alone again. And the circumstances were nothing like these. There were no gang attacks, no murders. Staying home undoubtedly was the safest option. I wouldn't get sick. I wouldn't get stabbed. Kim wouldn't be a widow. Maybe God wanted me to direct our efforts from the secure distance of remaining in America?

Again, I reached out to our staff to find out what was going on. Even though they had grappled with thugs face to face earlier in the week at Angel's house, was it going to be too much to lean on them again? I checked in with Dan to see if I could get some more news.

How was the day, Dan? ~ me

Nothing much to say about it, Dave. I have talked to the Chief about the incident and the govt plans to take action. Only that we dont know when. ~ Dan

Ok. I'm here if you need to talk. Are all of the staff ok? How about our kids? ~ me

Everyone we know is fine. Just dealing with it. God have mercy. ~ Dan

I did my daily check-in with Nia too.

How was the day, Nia? ~ me

Hello, Dave. I'm thanking God for the gift of a new day and the renewed strength to serve Him more even when situations seem dark. ~ *Nia*

Ok, Kim and I are here for you. ~ *me*

"To every child—I dream of a world where you can laugh, dance, sing, learn, live in peace, and be happy." Malala Yousafzai . . . this is my prayer for our community. Mama Kim had suggested we need prayer intercessors to pray for our community. ~ *Nia*

I second this dream. ~ *me*

———

September 5, 2020

I tossed and turned most of the night and told God all my troubles. I'm not sure I gave Him much of an opportunity to respond. I had to know if He wanted me to stay with Kim and risk having everything fall apart at Maisha or fly into the vortex in Nakuru. And if I went, did He want me to break my promise to Kim and go alone?

I woke up to another text from Anonymous.

UNCONFIRMED REPORT THAT MAMA AMON IS ARRESTED. LET ME SEE IF I CAN CONFIRM. APPARENTLY THE GANG HAVE SAID THEY ARE COMING FOR 7 MORE HEADS. TODAY THE NEIGHBORHOOD CHILDREN WEREN'T OUT PLAYING LIKE NORMAL. IT'S TENSE. ~ ANONYMOUS

I didn't know which was more shocking. Mama Amon's arrest or the gang's never-ending thirst for blood. Are all our kids curled up quivering in the corner like Angel? And is Mama Amon part of the gang or is it her boys? Does this mean it's not the Mungiki? Why had I even thought it might have been them? I guess stuff you read in the newspapers and gossip you hear can create unnecessary fears. The devil loves to stir up lies.

Are you doing ok? ~ me

I'M OK. HOW'S YOUR TEAM? ~ ANONYMOUS

They are tired from last week and just dealing with it. I wish I was there to strengthen them. And maybe the community at large. Maybe I'm overstating my influence but I know the Lord could calm some fear thru me. ~ me

No. I THINK YOU WOULD BE USED IN AMAZING WAYS. ~ ANONYMOUS

That line scared me so much I ignored it.

I wonder if Pastor Edgar [the pastor of a local church] would come to school one day and pray with the team. They need a shepherd. It would be so helpful. Our team is young. It would be great for them to have a moment where they didnt feel like they have to hold the whole thing together on their shoulders. ~ me

IMAGINE IF ALL THOSE WORKING IN THE COMMUNITY WERE UNITED . . . ~ ANONYMOUS

Exactly ~ me

ANY PLANS TO COME? ~ ANONYMOUS

Is God using Anonymous to test my heart? Should I go? I offered up an excuse.

We're praying about it. We'd love to come but Kim faces some health issues. ~ me

OH, I'M SORRY TO HEAR THAT. WE LOVE YOU BOTH. ~
ANONYMOUS

It's not a quick fix thing. Please be praying for her. ~ me

Kim was reading the entire thread as we lay next to each other. Her tender eyes looked at me as her eyebrows drew together, wondering what God was placing in my heart. She knew if God was calling me, He'd make a way. She also knew I'd answer, which scared the wits out of her.

"Honey, should I go?" I asked.

"Maybe." She paused. "They need you. But I need you too. And the doctors . . ."

"I know. How could I ever go without you, especially with all that's going on? But I'm starting to feel God pulling me to go."

She's seen that look on my face before and knew I was serious.

"But if I go, I won't go by myself. I can't believe God would want me to break my promise."

With a deep look of love in her eyes, she responded, "I understand. If you can find somebody to go with you, I'd understand."

———

September 6, 2020

MAMA AMON IS ARRESTED. ~ ANONYMOUS

Was this a confirmation or another rumor? Could the beast who's been at the epicenter of everything bad that's happened for nearly two decades have met her demise, or was her arrest going to set off a firestorm of more killing?

I asked Dan to check and see if this report was accurate. He phoned the one person who would know for sure, the Chief.

"It's true, but people like her have connections to bribe their way out of anything, including jail," the Chief told Dan.

He was right. It was only a matter of hours before Mama Amon was back on the streets.

———

September 7, 2020

Nothing. No messages. I turned my phone up to full volume. All day long I checked it. I'd never felt so far away from my people. My heart longed to know what was happening. How could I not be there with them?

———

September 8, 2020

Finally, Nia reached out.

Hi Daudi. How are you today? Hope you and Kim had a restful night. I'm just leaving Maisha mapya. We had a session with pastor Edgar and his team. Oooooh Dave we really needed this session. So many tears. The team opened up about what they were feeling, individual prayer session. Todays word from mark 6 ministered by Joy broke my heart. I didn't know I had fear and I was angry at what is happening in our community. Pastor Edgar took time to listen to all of us and personally ministered to each and every one of us. Thank you. We needed this. ~ Nia

So glad there was some healing. God is good. We are in His hand. ~ me

I didn't hear anything for days from anyone. Nothing from Anonymous. Nothing from the team. I wondered if we were in the eye of the hurricane or if the storm had passed. God's voice was getting louder in my head, and He was flooding me with scripture from the Sermon on the Mount: "Blessed are the peacemakers: for they shall be called the children of God" (Matthew 5:9).

———

September 15, 2020

I HEARD THE GANG WENT TO HILTON LAST NIGHT. MANY OF THEM ON BIKES LIKE BEFORE. THE PEOPLE THEY ARE AFTER WERE IN HIDING. THERE WAS NO VIOLENCE. ~ ANONYMOUS

I finally spoke with our team today. Things are tense. Normal guys on the street have pangas. They stopped one of our staff. Made him lower his mask to show his face and gave him the okay to pass without incident. The spies are out and everyone is suspected. ~ me

BECAUSE OF WHAT HAPPENED WITH MAMA AMON'S SON. HE WENT TO THE MORTUARY TO SEE THE BODY OF ONE OF THE VICTIMS. CULTURALLY THE KILLER WILL GO AND SEE THE BODY AT THE MORTUARY. THE OTHER GUY HAD 53 STAB WOUNDS. IT STIRRED UP A LOT OF TENSION YESTERDAY. ~ ANONYMOUS

The thought of a gutted corpse ripped apart by some sick monster turned my stomach. Fifty-three hate-filled slashes. Is it even in one piece? How many times do you have to stab someone to kill them? What beast stands over their victim to put a signature saying, "I'm your killer"? I'd watched too many TV shows to think that this would be the end of it. Someone with this amount of hate would never stop.

Kim's wide eyes expressed, "You're not going to go, are you?"

THE CALL

MY FEAR BUILT at the thought of there not just being murders but mutilations. And what might come next?

September 18, 2020

DID YOU HEAR THEY BURNT MAMA AMON'S HOUSE IN THE DUMPSITE? ~ ANONYMOUS

Oh wow, no hadn't heard. ~ *me*

IT'S TRUE. I PASSED BY ON THE WAY BACK. ~ ANONYMOUS

Was this in retaliation for her son claiming his prize at the morgue? Are they coming for her next? Who would dare take on Mama Amon? The prisons can't hold her. Not even the Chief can stop her. Who would have the guts to take her on?

Twenty minutes later, waiting to join a Zoom call with the board of directors from Kapu Africa, my eyes were still fixed on the text message. My stare turned into a blank gaze as I replayed the events of the past two weeks in my mind. Gang attacks. Dead bodies. Cops being reassigned. A little girl in hiding. A stubborn shosho who won't budge. Killers going to the mortuary to claim their victims. Fifteen thousand people armed and on edge. Mama Amon arrested and released a few hours later. More threats. And now, her house incinerated. Her fingerprints had to be all over this mess somehow. I'd call her Jezebel, but I don't think it's wicked enough. How about Beelzebub? Maybe Jezebeelzebub would be closer.

Anonymous confirmed that Mama Amon's compound was in ashes. For an instant, I fantasized this would be the moment we would be rid of her. Finally, the sinister, ruthless woman who had brutally ruled over the dumpsite for a generation would be gone forever.

But who would be brave enough to challenge the Goliath of our neighborhood? Anyone who had tried had been chased out of town by her thugs or met an untimely end. The truly unlucky ones were still there—oppressed, victimized, and exploited as props for her to run her financial empire of terror. She paraded the most hurting scavengers, the ones with missing limbs or those holding on to their lives by a thread, in front of well-wishers to appeal to their good nature and extract the maximum amount of money from them. If someone burned down her place, did it mean they were gunning for her spot on the top of the heap? Or had they simply had enough of her tyranny?

And how hard would she strike back if she found herself backed into a corner? Mama Amon was scary, but for some reason, I was not afraid of her. She just gave me the willies. I think she might have actually been terrified of *me.* Not because I'd burned down her house but by persistently loving the people in the dumpsite and having the love of the Lord work through me. I'd won their hearts and led them to the source of all love, Jesus. She was afraid of losing her status as empress and savior and becoming another nobody in a land of castaways.

My daydream broke as familiar names with vaguely familiar faces appeared on my screen one by one. I had met these gentlemen a year earlier. Since then, their organization, Kapu

Africa, has been the source of nearly a million meals for our neighbors in their moment of deep need.

I was introduced to *Kapu* (basket) when the warm-hearted Director of the Nutrition Department at Egerton University, a lady named Dr. Liz, brought a team of graduate students to Maisha Mapya to assess the students' health. They weighed, measured, and calculated the BMI of each child. The results confirmed what her eyes and experience had already told her. The kids of our community were severely malnourished. The youngest children, the four- and five-year-olds, were half-starved.

Dr. Liz grew up in difficult circumstances and needed financial sponsorship to attend primary and high school. A generous couple from the UK, who she never met, gave this girl a chance by providing monthly finances. Liz excelled in academics and aced her national exams, earning a scholarship to the University of Australia. Later she obtained a PhD from the University of Prague. Dr. Liz knew the life our children experienced and their potential. So when she saw our children's living conditions and struggle to have life-sustaining food, she called her friends at Kapu, knowing that they had the heart to help.

Kapu Africa was born when the Midwest Food Bank's Christian founder wanted to feed hungry kids in East Africa. They hired a degreed nutritionist to adapt the original secret formula of the meals created by Archer Daniels Midland and the University of Illinois. She studied the list of readily available Kenyan ingredients and discovered a new recipe of rice, lentils, full-fat soy, fractured cowpeas, vitamins, and minerals. It turned out to be even healthier than the initial mix and has a whopping seventeen grams of protein per serving.

It's cheap, nutritious, and best of all, every ingredient is sourced in the region. Not one thing is imported, so it cuts costs and boosts the local economy. They heard the need and immediately donated 50,000 meals to us.

Since then, every time I reached out, the folks at Kapu answered the call. Whether it be rushed shipments or topping off orders with additional free meals, time and time again, they rose to the challenge.

And to think that it almost never happened.

September 11, 2019

I woke up with the usual sorrow that September 11 brings. Even though it had been eighteen years, I could still see the two planes exploding as they hit the World Trade Center towers. I saw the rubble crashing down onto 7 World Trade where I had worked for Salomon Brothers. I saw people with fire raging below them and no possibility of escape making the impossible choice to leap to their deaths. I lost friends that day. They were moms and dads and sons and daughters that would never see their families again. I loathe the hatred of the men who boarded the planes that killed 2,996 people on 9/11. There were lots of caskets that day. Some large. Some small. Some empty, serving only as a symbol because the charred remains of so many were never found. The war it created and the divide among people still rip at my heart.

When I arrived at school, the sound of children playing in the field and the hope of a new group visiting our school soothed my grief. The board of directors from Kapu Africa was coming to see first-hand the impact of the new project where they had donated all those meals.

The team had just visited Kibera, the largest informal settlement in Kenya. International organizations from all over the globe had established permanent offices there and invested billions of dollars in improving life for the two million people in the area. Yet, isolated slum communities such as ours, with only 15,000 people, litter cities throughout Kenya. They receive less attention and far less support than places like Kibera. For our small corner of the world, help comes from a few small nonprofits, local businesses, and some churches. But today, the Kapu board was coming to see *us*, this little school, in this little place, where only the abandoned live.

I was thrilled they were coming because it was rare any organization from the US came to see us, let alone one that distributes 250 million dollars of food per year to places all over the world. I wanted the board members to see our needs, feel our heart, and become long-term partners.

As they entered the gates, their heads were on a swivel, marveling at the beautiful, colorful buildings and hearing the joyful sound of children running around. When the bell rang, the students scurried to their classrooms, many giggling most of the way. The Kapu team was intrigued and wanted to explore every aspect of our facility.

"Would you like to greet the kids in their classrooms?" I asked. The leader exclaimed, "Can't wait!" We visited each grade in ascending order, beginning with our tiny four-year-olds. The preschoolers jumped to their feet. Some said, "Welcome." Others said, "Karibu." A few just blushed. We went from class to class. With each increasing grade, you could see the progress in their social and English skills. By the time we entered grade three, children with beaming smiles stood in unison with their arms at their sides. They recited, "Welcome to Maisha Mapya. Our school motto is 'Learn, Love, and Transform.' Thank you for visiting us. You are most welcome."

Then a few kids raised their hands and asked questions. "How do you like Kenya?" and "What does it feel like to ride in an airplane?" and "How did you get started feeding so many people?" Anastacia simply said, "Thank you for bringing us food."

The humble smiles of the team conveyed a whole-hearted "you're welcome." One of the members' eyes was glistening. I think he was saying his personal thanks to the Lord for His generosity in helping these priceless children.

The Kapu board was intrigued to see our kitchen setup. We'd recently finished an upgrade complete with two giant *jikos* (wood-fired cookers) and ample room for our three-person crew to prepare four hundred meals a day for our kids. Heads nodded at the well-designed layout.

Then, we led them on a tour through the neighborhood.

They were familiar with poverty. They know the conditions in poor rural villages and vast urban slums. They even knew the endless void of despair called Kibera, the Nubian word for "jungle," and it's millions of people. But for what our community lacked in numbers of desperate people, it made up for in intensity. No one from Kapu had ever set foot in a place like the Gioto dumpsite.

As we left the crowded dirt roads of the Hilton slum, the same thing happened to the Kapu team that happened to me back in 2007. Experiencing the complexities of the dumpsite, their hearts opened, and their minds expanded. The ferociousness of the conditions touched every sense and etched a permanent memory. It was hard to fathom how anyone, let alone a child, could survive in such an environment. However, while the realities of Gioto life were staggering, that wasn't what left the most lasting impression upon them.

With the tour completed, we returned to the safe surroundings of our campus. Over a cool drink, the lead Kapu director revealed a candid thought. He said the atmosphere at Maisha felt so lovely and the kids were doing so well that the group had wondered if they'd made a mistake. That was before they saw the students' living conditions. "I never imagined the beautiful children that were running and laughing in the playground would come from a place like that. Just looking at them in school, we thought your kids came from a more middle-class area. We weren't sure you needed our help. Then we saw their homes. I'm still trying to take it in." His well-trained eye caught something else. He said, "But you do have some issues. Some of the children's hair is turning reddish orange at the roots and their skin is losing its shine, turning dull and slightly gray. It's a telltale sign of malnutrition."

One of the directors, a guy from Connecticut named Joe, said,

"Wow. That was intense! How did you ever get the people to embrace you? When we walked through Kibera, we got some stares. It can be intimidating." He was referring to the familiar sounds of the people smiling and calling out to us as we walked around. "Maisha Mapya!" and *"Daudi. Rafiki. Karibu!"* which means, "Dave. My friend. Welcome!" Along with the greetings came an endless stream of high fives—the more drunk the resident, the louder the outburst and harder the slap. By the end of a typical forty-five-minute walkabout, the pad of my hand just below the thumb is often black and blue. The pain is worth it. Stephen Crane had his red badge of courage. I have my black and blue badge of love. I wouldn't trade it for anything.

Joe ended with, "I love what you're doing here. I'll be back."

I thought to myself, *"If I had a nickel for everyone who has made that promise . . ."*

September 18, 2020

Maybe Joe hadn't made it back to Maisha Mapya yet, but at least he and his friends were on this Zoom call ready to hear what had been happening in our community since COVID-19 hit.

"Dave, Dave, are you there?"

Part of me was there. Most of me was still contemplating who torched Mama Amon's place and fearing how viciously she would make the whole community suffer for whoever's bravado dared to challenge her. Plus, the gang threatened seven heads. Were they merely echoing her words? But there wasn't time for that now. I had to focus on connecting with the Kapu board.

"Hi, guys, thanks for meeting with me. Thanks for all the meals you've donated. Thanks for how quickly you respond to meeting the food needs of my community. It's amazing that deliveries arrive in less than twenty-four hours from the time I order it. Let me bring you up to speed on what's been happening."

I thought about what had transpired since March this year and COVID-19's shock to the planet. It was beyond comprehension that the entire world would shut down.

During normal economic times, things were hard enough for my people. The World Bank set the international poverty line at $1.90 a day. That's the threshold to purchase goods needed to support one adult. It's about half of what I spend on my cup of Starbucks. In the US, the federal poverty line is $35 a day per adult.

Most of the people in the Gioto dumpsite would love to earn $1.90 in a day. Unfortunately, many don't achieve that in a week. They earn twenty to fifty cents by scavenging ten hours a day through rotting garbage. If there are two working parents, which is rare, they will make forty cents to one dollar a day to support their family. In many cases, one or both of our students' parents have died from AIDS or other diseases or simply abandoned their kids, and their grandmother or aunt is raising them. The family structure in our community is often one adult female supporting three to six children. The hearts of the older women can be exceptionally tender as they take in any child in need. In some cases, there can be over ten children living with a lone seventy-year-old woman.

The dumpsite is on government-owned land. Many scavengers are mere squatters because they can't afford $15 a month to rent an eight-foot by nine-foot place in the Hilton slum.

When COVID-19 hit our community, the unimaginable happened.

All the restaurants and hotels closed in Nakuru. Instantly, no rubbish was taken to the dump. For those who picked through the trash for their food, there was no garbage to pick through—not one scrap. Within a week, the ten-foot-high mountains of refuse became a barren field. The pigs were gone. The birds were gone. Even the smoke had drifted away. Only the dirt and despondent humans remained. For people who don't have one morsel to spare, this was a fatal situation.

Facing 15,000 people on the verge of starvation and the mandatory closure of all schools in Kenya on March 15, 2020, we switched our efforts from educating our kids to keeping them alive. The economic effects of a global pandemic brought that kind of focus.

I began to tell the board, "The people in Gioto are on life support. There's no garbage. Nothing for them to scavenge through. With your help, we've been bringing 80,000 meals a month to them."

My thoughts sputtered with horror images of the previous few weeks.

Angel's neck got snapped back.

But I tried to continue the conversation. "We've brought meals."

Fifty-three slashes.

"We . . ."

I could feel myself losing it.

Panga's everywhere. Threats. Fear. Uncles. Grandmas. Mungiki. Blood. Mama Amon's boys. Fifty-three.

"Guys . . ."

She's gonna strike back ruthlessly.

As hard as I tried, I couldn't stay on topic for even a split second with my phone still flashing the text: *Did you hear they burnt Mama Amon's house in the dumpsite?* I feared she would burn down the whole place as retribution and out of pure hatred. She'd attack Maisha, our kids, everything.

Instantly, the agenda of the video call shifted to the current crisis in Hilton. People were living in fear, and the economy was in shambles. Alcoholism and drug abuse were on the rise, hopelessness and despair were at an all-time high, and people were now killing each other and burning down homes.

I had to share. "Guys, everything in my being says I need to go to Nakuru. There's been a lot of gang violence and even two murders." The faces on the screen were motionless. Most had their mouths open. "God said He will use me to bring peace."

I think I was saying that as much to convince myself as them.

"Kim is ill and can't travel, and I promised her I would not go alone. I have to go. But I can't go alone."

In the silence that followed my comment, I heard a voice say, "Maybe I'll go?"

It was Joe. A guy I hardly knew and wouldn't be able to pick out of a line-up. It threw me for a loop because I had been stuck in the place of self-pity, not having the option to go. It was easy for me to say I'd rush into a gang war when it wasn't possible to do so. But for the first time, it seemed like there was a chance.

"I told the guys on the board I always wanted to go back to Maisha Mapya. So maybe now's the time? Let me talk with Sandy, and I'll get back to you," he said.

I was excited to tell Kim but wasn't sure how she'd take it. Now for the first time, the reality of her husband venturing out in the pandemic-ridden world was possible. Not to mention I'd be pursuing killers, armed only with love and the Holy Spirit.

Joe's wife Sandy was all for it, and five days later, we had our plane tickets. Joe even made all the flight arrangements on our behalf. He would fly out of Boston, and I'd leave from San Francisco. Then, we'd meet in Frankfurt, Germany, for the final leg to Nairobi, Kenya's capital city. The eight-hour flight would give us some time to get to know each other. It also ensured we would not get separated en route and have to search for one another in a city of over four million people.

Joe was living up to his promise. He was coming back to Maisha Mapya. It looked like I owed someone a nickel.

September 25, 2020

HAVE YOU SEEN THE NATION? ~ ANONYMOUS

Along with that simple line was a link to an article in Kenya's leading newspaper, the *Daily Nation*: "Special security team was formed to tackle Nakuru criminal gangs." The incidents in our neighborhood had now reached the national news. *Could things be even bigger than I thought?*

I turned to Kim. "Listen to this . . ." I read the Nakuru County Commissioner's words.

> *We have kicked off a major operation to weed out all the criminals. We will not tolerate the resurgence of any criminal gang. Those involved will face the full force of law. We will deal with criminal elements ruthlessly. I urge residents to be candid and report any criminals to help police arrest them.*

Geez, I wonder if this is going to mess things up for us. I wanted to fly under the radar and connect with the lost in my community, no matter how brutal or criminal they are—even if it was Mama Amon. No dealing with the police. No reporting anything to anyone.

All I could do was shake my head at how out of touch these officials seemed. Doesn't the county commissioner know the cops are on the take? Doesn't he know the local police wouldn't even write down Shosh's complaint? How are they going to *ruthlessly* deal with the troublemakers if they don't acknowledge they exist? It took the courage of Dan, Maggie, Nia, Nafula, and Vic to get our Angel to safety. It took the dumpsite guys being heroes to save the day.

Kim said, "Keep reading."

> *We have already arrested over fifty members of outlawed groupings in Nakuru County in the past weeks. They have already been charged in court, and this will continue until we wipe them out of Nakuru.*

This sounded like things were under control. The problem was being handled. There's nothing to worry about, according to the local government. Well, what about all of our 15,000 residents walking around with weapons scared out of their minds?

The report continued with "facts" that were less than accurate.

The crackdown comes weeks after two criminal gangs clashed at Nakuru's London estate (Hilton), leading to the deaths of two gang members, one of whom was Ugandan.

Well, at least they got it right that one was Ugandan, but neither were gang members. Anonymous had told me one guy owned a bar where gangs hung out, but he wasn't one of them. He was a well-liked, easy-going businessman. So who were these two criminal gangs? How many criminal gangs were there?

The article went on.

Residents say the dreaded gang has mutated into a more dangerous outfit, enjoying the protection of some local politicians.

Is Sam on the take? The Chief? Is that how Mama Amon has such sway over them? Another part of the story brought fear.

The members are usually idle, unemployed youth from the slums who are armed with machetes, metal bars, swords, and sometimes guns. Despite regular swoops and arrests of members of the group, it has kept on resurfacing. Gang members are aged between thirteen and thirty.

Thirteen to thirty? Oh no! We've got a couple thirteen-year-olds in school. How many of my kids and their families are trapped in this?

Seeing the issue in actual print proved the whole thing wasn't just in my head. An entire new line of concerns presented themselves. What's going to happen to the oldest children in my school? Are they next? How can I prepare them to stand up to these thugs? The thought of them forced into gang life, leaving school—or worse, bringing that culture into our school—elevated my prayers and solidified my resolve to go to Nakuru.

Despite the uncertainty, my drive to fix this was extreme. But it paled in comparison to God's relentless pull on my heart to go. *"Go. Bring peace. GO!"* It wasn't an audible call. It wasn't a thought. It was an internal voice. It penetrated every cell, radiating for me to go straight into the heart of the conflict. *"Go and be a blessing."* God spoke those words to Abram centuries ago, and He was speaking them to me today.

I kept repeating to Kim, "I've got to go, honey. I can't stay here. I've got to go."

THE TEST

September 2020

To TRAVEL during a global pandemic turned out to be, in a word, complicated. I thought my biggest hurdle was going to be convincing someone to come along. But God took care of that with my willing acquaintance, Joe. Sure, I had a plane ticket, and fortunately, my five-year entry visa and passport were still valid. But that didn't mean I was going anywhere in the world of COVID-19. I knew the devil wanted to do whatever he could to thwart God's goodness and keep me as far from Nakuru as possible. Restrictions were changing continually, seemingly without notice. Every day, I searched the internet for anything that might throw a monkey wrench into our travel plans.

After getting a typhoid booster, I had everything I needed except for one thing: a negative COVID-19 test result. It sounded easy enough, and testing sites were popping up everywhere, but the fine print made it impossible. First of all, it had to be valid within ninety-six hours of arriving in Kenya. This would be tricky because it takes about forty hours to get from the place Kim and I were renting in California to Jomo Kenyatta International Airport in Nairobi. Second, it couldn't just be any test, like the rapid test the president of the United States gets, but a polymerase chain reaction, or PCR test. These tests were the gold standard for diagnosing COVID-19. With the pandemic spreading like wildfire, the authorities didn't want to take any chances of the virus tagging along with airline passengers from country to country. I didn't know where to get a PCR test or if it was possible to get a result the same day.

I took a few deep breaths to calm my racing heart. Living on a ranch in a small, rural community in northern California had its strengths, like being extremely peaceful and beautiful, but getting anything done swiftly was not one of them. I called my "big city" doctor in the San Francisco Bay Area. I assumed he would be my best bet for a sophisticated, quick test result. He said, "I'm sorry. I'll only test you if you're symptomatic." I thought about coughing up a lung like Ferris Bueller but thanked him instead. I phoned the Calaveras County Health Department where I lived. They had established a command center at the local county fairgrounds to battle COVID-19.

I dialed the phone to see if they could help. "Yes, you can get a PCR test."

"Awesome!" My excitement built. I knew God hadn't abandoned me. First, He provided Joe, and now this.

"You will receive the results in four to six days."

My heart fell off a cliff. No, no, NO! It wouldn't work. That certificate wouldn't be valid for the Kenyan authorities when I landed. It was another dead end.

I racked my brain. I couldn't be the only person attempting to trek from California to Kenya. I took a deep breath. *Lord, show me a way.*

God gave me a fresh glimmer. My heart spoke to my mind, "Reach out to the Kenyan consulate in Los Angeles."

For years, Kim and I purchased single entry travel visas for each visit to Kenya. Often, this meant completing the paperwork and paying fees three or four times a year. When

Kenya offered the opportunity to get a five-year visa, we jumped at the chance.

The website said it was hassle-free. It turned out to be anything but. It was a lot more involved than filling out the form correctly, sending along a couple of photos, and providing a credit card payment. We'd filled out everything perfectly online and still had to meet with an immigration officer. In Nakuru! Then we had to meet with the Kenyan consulate too. In Los Angeles! We didn't end up saving much time, but we did save a few precious dollars, and it allowed us to be assured entry into Kenya at the drop of a hat.

We'd spent so much time with the Los Angeles Kenyan consulate staff that we were on a first name basis. The more they learned about our work in the Hilton slums, the more help we received.

I reached out in a desperate, last-ditch effort for advice on how to get a timely COVID-19 test. My friend at the consulate, Marlene, informed me that most people traveling to Kenya were Kenyan citizens who had gotten stuck in the US because of the COVID-19 lockdowns. They wanted to return home.

"It is possible to receive quick PCR test results," Marlene said. "You can get one near the airport or through a hospital emergency room. Oh, and you need to complete an additional online form to get a QR code. No one knows about this, but you need to do it to get into the country. Have a blessed trip!" She hung up and emailed me the link to the secret form.

I phoned the local hospital to see if they could deliver PCR results within a few hours of taking the test.

"Absolutely," said the anonymous voice on the phone.

With a wry smile, I shook my head. Why do I try to use my intellect first, only to find it lacking and *then pray?* Why do I wait? Why don't I start with prayer more often? The yo-yo of my emotions calmed down. God had provided the path. All I needed now was to take the test and get the right paperwork.

Kim and I continued to pray, prepare, and pack. We touched

base with Joe and Sandy a few times. I wanted our wives to connect so they could support one another while Joe and I were abroad. You never know what's going to happen. I wanted the ones who loved us the most to know each other and be a source of comfort for one another if something tragic happened.

———

October 7, 2020

My bags were packed and ready to roll. All I needed was the coveted negative PCR test result. The fifteen-minute drive to the local emergency room gave me a few moments to "Pray without ceasing," as 1 Thessalonians 5:16 says. There's no rule you have to pray with your eyes closed. It's a good thing because I do it a lot while driving.

Lord, what am I stepping into? Do you want me to even do this? Have I lost my mind? Am I risking the safety of everyone at the school? Can I even get there? Amen.

For the first time, even though I felt healthy, I wondered if I had asymptomatic COVID-19, or if I would get a false positive test result and wouldn't be able to catch my flight the next day. Actually having COVID-19 was the last thing on my mind. My bigger concern was helping Angel keep her head and the consequences of asking to be thrust into a gang conflict.

The hospital parking lot was nearly full as I pulled in. Many of the cars had their engines off with people sitting in the driver's seats staring at their phones. Mask on and hands freshly sanitized, I headed to the emergency room entrance. It felt foolhardy to be perfectly healthy and freely walk into the one place the mysterious, odorless, silent killer would certainly exist—just to get permission to fly. I didn't have a choice, though. If I wanted the certificate to board the plane, I had to go in. *Lord, You are Jehovah Nissi—my banner, my protector. Please protect me now.*

They only permitted me to take one step inside the building. A nurse, who looked like she had just stepped off the lunar module, greeted me in a full-body suit, complete with oxygen tank and headgear. She may have been smiling, or maybe not. Who could tell through her protective spacesuit?

She pointed a temperature gun at my head before asking, "May I help you?"

I almost answered with, "Greetings, earthling," but instead went with, "I phoned earlier and am here to get a PCR test for travel."

She motioned to a stack of papers on the desk.

"Please complete this form and wait in your car. Do not get out of your car. Did you hear me? Do not get out of your vehicle."

I had the feeling she wasn't messing around.

She asked, "What is your phone number? We will text you. After we text you, pull around to where the ambulances drop off patients. Do not get out of your car!"

I followed her instructions to the letter. They sure were taking this COVID-19 thing seriously. It emphasized the reality of something I'd only heard about on the news and read on the internet. I didn't know anyone who had contracted the virus.

Almost immediately, I received the text and drove into the ambulance entrance. Fully masked, I rolled down the window and waited. The fresh air was pleasant. The hospital doors opened, and a nurse clad in standard green scrubs walked out. She glanced down at her chart. Her eyes softened and sparkled above her mask as she approached.

"Hi, Dave." It was said in such a warm, welcoming tone, as if she knew me. Without question, she was smiling.

I glanced at the nametag. Suzanna.

Suzanna is a friend I've known for over a dozen years but hadn't seen in a few. Her youngest son was in the same youth group as ours. She had received email updates about our ministry and how we loved the kids in Kenya. She has seen God grow our school from eighteen preschoolers to two hundred students through fourth grade in the last six years.

It was unexpected to have someone I knew help me out. I thought for a moment how hard being on the front lines of the pandemic must be. She'd probably seen people come in looking healthy, test positive, and die a week later, so I didn't want to pile my troubles on top of her.

"Hey, Suzanna. Good to see you. Well, good to see your eyes at least."

I thought she'd laugh, but instead she said, "Don't punch me." *What? Why would I hit her?*

"Seriously, Dave, keep your arms at your sides. Sit on your hands if you have to. Some people have smacked me when I take these swabs."

And before I knew it, a wire coat hanger looking thing appeared out of nowhere and was shoved in my nose way past anywhere anything should be and wiggled around. It was irritating but didn't hurt—much. Then without a breath, a quick switch to the other nostril and she did the same drill. *Okay, that one hurt!* Somehow, I was able to keep my hands at my sides, but now I understand how an up-and-coming Muhammed Ali might have decked her.

"Okay, all done. That wasn't so bad, was it? You can drive on. We should have the results in a couple of days. Say hi to Kim."

"No . . ." My eyes began welling up. "No. No. No. That won't work. What am I going to do?"

I'm not sure I was making any sense or even an audible sound, but she could read my tears. "Are you okay?"

I was on the cusp of being on that plane. God had cleared obstacle after obstacle. The promised land of Nakuru was just on the horizon. Why had He raised my hope just to flatten me now? My desperation began to bubble over.

"What am I going to do, Suzanna? I called my doctor. I called the county, the consulate. A couple of days? I need those results right now—*today*. Right now. Where can I get one? The gangs are going wild. Kids are killing each other. Little girls are selling themselves to get food and are getting pregnant. There were murders. There's going to be more if I don't stop them. My flight leaves tomorrow morning. I've got to be on it. I can't wait a couple of days!"

"Wait, slow down. What are you saying?"

I explained how the economic effects of the COVID-19 shutdowns had the desperation of my people at a peak and that the Hilton community was on fire. I didn't know what I would do, but I knew I was to show up and love the people. God would do the rest. I spelled out the ninety-six-hour restriction on test results and why I had to have the certificate today.

Now her eyes were tearing too. She pointed at a note on her clipboard. "I'm sorry. We have strict orders and are only doing immediate tests for symptomatic patients."

My heart sank further. Although it was embarrassing, there was no hiding my tears.

"The supplies of the reagent are so short. We just don't have enough," she said. "We're sending tests to a lab and getting results in a day or two. Maybe I can get it tomorrow."

The corners of my mouth quivered underneath my mask. "Please . . . please, Suzanna, is there *anything* you can do? I have to be on that plane."

"I don't think so. But I'll try." She turned and walked into the sterile hospital. I watched the back of her head disappear along with my chances of getting to Kenya.

My prayers intensified. *Please, Lord, make a way. Do it now! Or do you not want me to go? Are you protecting me?*

The emergency room doors opened and out raced a doctor, his head held high. The expression on his face and his eye contact honored me as a first responder. "I heard you have to go help some kids. We can do this. I will find enough reagent. I will. You need to catch that flight!"

Hallelujah! Only God could arrange something like this. If it had been any other nurse, just a random person administering the test, they might never have had the heart to bend the rules. God placed Suzanna in the exact right spot at the exact right time to be a compassionate heroine and plead for me. God lives everywhere, including emergency rooms in small towns in the middle of nowhere. And based on the love in that doc's eyes, I'd say it wasn't the first time he had experienced it.

With tears dripping and my smile fully restored, I pulled my car back into the parking lot. I joined the sea of other patients tapping away on phones, waiting for whatever was to come next. It gave me time to think.

The fear of an invisible, unknown killer was paralyzing the globe. We understood so little about it, but to stop the spread, we shut down the world. We closed businesses, schools, and churches. We locked ourselves in our dwellings. We were told by the authorities it was hopeless. No matter what we did, three to four million innocent men, women, and children in America would die from COVID-19 before the year was out. We had to close the country so that people would not be dying in the hallways of our hospitals while waiting to be hooked up to ventilators. So America does what she always does. We banded together in an effort to "flatten the curve" and battle this threat to our families, friends, and neighbors.

All the attention to COVID-19 thankfully was mobilizing the world in a way never seen before. As of August 2020, there's been about one hundred twenty-five million cases of COVID-19 in the world and 2.7 million deaths. The world looked at this virus, came together, and concluded, "We must act. We must get control of this. Even though we don't know much about it, we have to find out. Let's stop everything we are doing and deal with this plague that is causing so much suffering." Over and over I heard the phrase, "This threat is unprecedented."

I'm struggling with our response to another pandemic that we actually know a lot about. It is the pandemic of poverty. We may not have a cure, but we can certainly flatten the curve of hunger. We just have to try.

Three million children a year starve to death. That's one every ten seconds. Two million people die from malaria every year, most of them children under five years old in sub-Saharan Africa. Another five hundred million people get infected. What if we had a COVID-19-sized task force to save kids who eat garbage, suffer sexual abuse, and live in dumpsites?

I looked around at the people sitting in their cars waiting for their test results. Nearly every one of them had their smart phone in one hand and a cup of Starbucks or a snack in the other. Including me.

Stranded in my car, I scrolled through my old messages from Kenya. The stream from Anonymous sank deeper and deeper into my soul. I spent the next two hours praying for Angel, Shosh, the gang guys, and all our staff. My prayers for Kim were for her to not feel abandoned and a distant second to the ministry. I asked God to give me His eyes and heart every single day. Then I received a text from Suzanna. I didn't even know she had my number.

Dave, I've got your test results. Pick them up in medical records. ~ Suzanna

That was it. No hint as to the outcome. I bolted to the main entrance, got my temperature checked, hands sanitized, and went up the elevator to see my fate. *Lord, You're working miracles. Don't stop now.*

The volunteer at the medical records desk asked for my name. "Dave Hatfield," I answered.

"Oh, Suzanna dropped these off a few moments ago. Here you go."

The paper was crisp, although the ink was splotchy. None of that mattered because I had not one but five precious copies of my *negative* PCR test results in hand. *You did it, God. You did it. You did it. You did it! I'm coming, Angel. I'm coming, Shosh!*

I shot Suzanna a quick text.

Thank you and the staff for your kindness in helping me. Thanks for your compassion. You all were so great :) ~ me

You are very welcome. Have a great trip. Go love those kids! ~ Suzanna

I couldn't drive home fast enough to see Kim. My face beamed as I broke through the door waving the certificate. "Look what God did!"

THE AIRPORT

October 7, 2020

FOR THE FIRST TIME, I could relate to Shosh. She didn't know how to protect Angel. She just knew she had to try. It was the same for me. I had no clue how to safeguard Angel, the entire community, and keep the dream of Maisha Mapya alive. But I had to try. Instead of Shosh's cry of "Take my girls, take my Angel," mine was "Hang on, I'm coming!"

Our luggage was already stuffed into our little Prius for the three-hour trip to the Bay Area. Kim drove to the hotel as I watched familiar sights go by—the foothills of the California gold country, Altamont Pass, Bay Bridge, Alcatraz, and finally, the iconic San Francisco skyline.

All we wanted to do was check in, grab dinner, and get some rest. Sometimes I don't eat well when I'm in Kenya, so I craved something delicious and filling to remember my last taste of home. As we drove through Millbrae, window after window displayed signs reading, "Closed," "Out of Business," even "COVID Sucks." We found a little hole-in-the-wall called O' Sole Mio, which served takeout. Kim ordered lemon-garlic shrimp with sauteed veggies and risotto. I had penne with sausage and peppers, something I was certain wouldn't be on the menu for the next few weeks.

Back in our hotel room, sitting crisscross-applesauce on the bed, eating pasta out of aluminum takeout bowls with plastic utensils reminded me of the early days of our marriage. We tuned into the vice-presidential debate. It was more civilized than the embarrassing presidential brawl between President Trump and Vice President Biden a week earlier.

The intensity of the political division in the US breaks my heart. The inability to discuss differences of opinion while honoring those with whom we disagree is tearing our nation apart. We are two warring tribes called democrats and republicans. We are devouring one another, all in the name of being "right" while claiming the moral high ground. I hope, if given the chance, I can have better success at bringing two clashing groups together when I get to Kenya than is on display in my native country.

After the yummy meal, Kim and I looked at the clock, kissed each other good night, and tried to get some sleep. I didn't want the day to end. It meant I wouldn't hold her for a fortnight, and for the first time in ten years, we wouldn't be traveling to Kenya together. Snuggling Kim for the last time and facing all the threats ahead brought tears, which gently and quietly rolled down my cheeks. Some were tears of gratitude to an amazing God. Some were tears of sorrow for our suffering community. Some were for my wife's illness. Most were that I would miss her deeply. I tried not to sniffle, but I know I did. Finally, her relaxed breathing and occasional twitch signaled she was done for the day.

I held my wife tight and whispered, "Forgive me for leaving you. I hope to be back before you know it." I wanted to promise her I'd come back. But I couldn't. I'd read too much of the Bible to believe that those who follow God's will always come back, or if they do that their lives are the same as before.

October 8, 2020

My phone sounded the alarm dark and early at 4:30 a.m. As I turned it off, I was glad to see there were no texts, no new issues to handle. It had been a noisy night. When I booked our stay online, I didn't realize I didn't reserve a room at a hotel. I'd booked a cheap motel, you know, the ones with your door exposed to the outside. It turned out it wasn't in the safest part of town either, and I think they may have rented rooms by the hour. I could have used a do over because I rarely sleep much on plane flights. Now I was exhausted even before we arrived at the airport.

We spent little time gathering our things and left quickly to check in three hours before my 8:30 a.m. flight. I wondered if something would keep Joe from making the trip at the last second. The ten-minute drive to the San Francisco airport was too short. When we pulled to the curb to offload my luggage, the reality of what lay ahead hit me.

Kim gave me a look reminding me of the day we were married. I had pulled her veil up to reveal eyes radiating with love. I returned her love in similar fashion standing curbside, only my face was now much more spotted and wrinkled from our years in the hot African sun. I closed my eyes and tried to imprint her look on my brain so I could recall it at any moment over the next few weeks. My wife is even more beautiful than the day I met her at the Oakland Coliseum on a blind date at game three of the World Series in 1988. That was 11,678 days ago.

I don't know if I ever looked into my wife's hazel eyes thinking I may never see her again or that our lives might be altered forever. Then Kim drove off into the rising morning sun. I just stood there as the vehicle got smaller and smaller, wondering what I was going to do.

For the last decade, we've made up to three flights a year from California to Kenya together, often as a family. I'm pretty good at hanging out in airports when I have my loved ones around; the best times were with our kids. Being entertainers at heart, they almost always did stupid stuff to pass the hours, often mimicking antics learned from their dad, including holding ear wiggling competitions. Even at age ten, little Scotty was usually the champ. He could move his ears back and forth as I barked out instructions like a drill sergeant, "forward and back, hold and forward, hold, back, hold!" The kid was astonishing and could position his ears anyplace he wanted. I told him it was a recessive gene from monkeys and hippos, which cracked his big brother up. Andrew's laugh is contagious. He could make a living as a hype man in a comedy club.

There was a time we stopped at an Asian restaurant near the Amsterdam airport. It took ten hours to fly from California to the Netherlands only for the plane to sit on the tarmac for two hours. By the time we disembarked, the boys were starving, especially our growing teenager Andrew. The restaurant was ritzier than we expected with white linens, dim lighting, and the rest. Kim and I left the boys at the table to find the restroom. While we were gone, Andrew couldn't help himself from the tempting looking items placed in the middle of the table. When we came back, he said that the breadsticks tasted funny and were super crunchy. I looked at Kim, shrugged my shoulders, and said, "Oh, buddy, those aren't breadsticks." My Dutch was not good enough to apologize properly to the server for my thirteen-year-old son eating the centerpiece. Now it was Scotty's turn to provide the laugh track.

Those memories kept me company as I got through security and searched for an open coffee shop. Sure, I wanted a warm delicious cup of brew. But even more, knowing I had thirty-five hours of mandatorily face-masked travel ahead, I wanted an excuse to be able to remove the annoying COVID-19 cover for a while. God blessed me with my favorite brand—Peet's. Only a skeleton crew of airport employees were on hand. I overheard many of them had returned to work just this week. They were all friendlier than usual. I guess they missed the interaction with live, not virtual, human beings and were happy to have a job to put food on their tables.

I had my choice of seats at the usually crowded computer charging station outside my gate. Only one other gentleman was sitting there, outfitted in a sport coat, slacks, and shiny shoes, holding a paper coffee cup. Silently, we tipped our cups and acknowledged each other as travel warriors undeterred by COVID-19 fears and going about our battles. He was on his way to slay business dragons. I was following God into the unknown certainty of walking with Jesus.

———

It had been a long time since I'd sat in an airport alone. Many of those times, like the man sitting across from me, I was the guy in a Brooks Brothers power suit with the American dream in my heart and the next big deal fixed squarely in my sights. My business career took flight as soon as I left home for college at UCLA in the 1980s during Wall Street's glory days.

My dad was an orphan and grew up in the Midwest during the Depression. He served in WWII and became an insurance agent after the war. He talked about stockbrokers being the "wealthy guys," the elite. To have a fat wallet and the status to go with it sounded good to me. If I could become an investment hotshot, I'd win my dad's affection and be more successful than he was. Maybe my mom would like me too? To get started, I asked my economics professor which firm was the biggest and the best.

"Merrill Lynch."

"Awesome. Where can I find them?"

"Wherever there's money."

In my small world, the first place that popped into my mind was Hollywood.

So, I bought a pair of gray trousers, a white cotton dress shirt, a blue blazer, and a peach colored knit tie. All for about $80. I revved up my sweet 1978 gold Toyota Celica, shifted from first into second gear, and headed to 7070 Hollywood Boulevard, right across the street from Grauman's Chinese Theatre and home of the Hollywood Walk of Fame. I wondered which celebrities I'd see. I made a right turn on Wilshire, then left on La Brea until I hit Hollywood Boulevard. My heart was racing with excitement even though the area looked pretty sketchy. Certainly not what I was expecting after hanging out in Westwood. And it looked nothing like Bel Air. The streets were gray and dingy. Dudes were lying in the gutter, and there was litter everywhere.

Undeterred, I found the building where gold letters, slightly tarnished but still sparkling, spelled out the names Merrill, Lynch, Pierce, Fenner & Smith. From just outside the door, I noticed red LED letters and numbers streaming by. A few old codgers with folded newspapers sat on a bench eyeing the symbols as they went by. One was chomping on an unlit cigar.

Pointing at the board I said, "Hello, gentleman. What's that?"

"It's a ticker tape, son."

"What's it do?"

"Is all that college making you stupid, kid?"

"I want to work here. Can you tell me who I should see?"

Another guy in a raincoat motioned to an office inside. As I turned my back, he snickered under his breath with his posse. "Good luck, Tenderfoot."

Tenderfoot? I had an instant flashback to when I was eleven on my first camp-out with the Boy Scouts, and our Senior Patrol Officer offered me a sip of vodka out of a baby food jar.

Their heckling only solidified my resolve. *Remember what Mom always said: "You can do anything you set your mind to."* I opened the glass door and headed to the boss's office, wondering what his name was. There was an office outside his; it was empty, but the desk was full of papers and the phones were ringing. I questioned whether I should wait, and if that would make me appear weak or polite. *What the heck, I'm going in.*

My extended right hand led the way through the door.

A middle-aged man dressed in a navy pinstripe suit, who had

already lost the island of hair on the top of his head, sat behind the desk.

"Hi, I'm Dave Hatfield. I'd like to work here. Do you have any job openings?"

He never looked up, continuing to stare at the newspaper in his hands. He grunted a dismissive, "Nope."

Think quick. You can do anything you set your mind to.

"Are there things people around here don't like to do? I'll do those."

He remained fixed on the paper, not even a hint of motion to look up. "Nope. Everybody loves what they do, kid."

I didn't believe that for a minute. Looking around the wider office floor, the place was a mess. Some people looked wired, like they'd had fifty cups of coffee, others looked like they were lost wandering in a sandstorm.

"Do you mean if I come in and do the things that no one wants to do and you didn't have to pay me, I couldn't do that?"

Finally, I saw the man's face. A friendly smile said, "I'll see you Monday. I'm Bob."

That set off a tyrannosaurus-rex-sized appetite to devour everything about business and accumulating wealth. I had business plans, time management tools, Day-Timers, and "proven steps to success." I read every book Zig Ziglar, Brian Tracy, and Dale Carnegie wrote. I nearly memorized Stephen Covey's *The 7 Habits of Highly Successful People*. Covey's book preaches living in a state of constant improvement, and I was going to evolve at a pace that would astonish Darwin. Tony Robbins's message played on a continuous loop in the cassette deck in my car. Follow him and he promised to *"awaken the giant within."* I believed him. The next few years of my life proved it. He told me to mirror people's body language and they would trust me. Bill Clinton later shared his secret of the handshake. Match the pressure you're receiving, and people will like you. There were sure-fire can't-fail sales close techniques. I never felt good about any of them. But I loved what the result of success did for me. The giant was awake and stomping on the little inferior people. If I was more successful than everyone, then obviously I was better than them. I'd be important. I'd be superior. Instead of being the mistake my mom taunted me with, I'd be the center of the universe.

Eventually, I said goodbye to Bob, the mailroom, and the small fries at Merrill. They had served their purpose. And I became one of the youngest financial consultants ever hired into a Wall Street training program. At the fresh-faced age of twenty-three, I became a broker at Shearson American Express in Beverly Hills. Beverly. Hills. The same year, I represented the firm giving investment lectures on a transatlantic crossing on the luxurious *Queen Elizabeth 2*. Every three years, I moved to a more and more prestigious firm. I took pride in being independent and self-made; things my parents valued above all else. I was living the life I had put my mind to.

Covey's book also stresses combining different people's strengths and pairing with others to achieve goals that could not be done alone. So while at Kidder, Peabody & Company, I teamed up with a smart, handsome, charismatic stockbroker who became my best friend. Together, we accomplished more than either of us could do on our own. Every year, we did more and more business. Every year, we were better than ever before. Nothing could slow, let alone stop me. The desire for more drove me. The need for acceptance and recognition only added fuel to the fire.

I was on the speed dial of the salesmen at Nordstrom. Each season as new merchandise arrived, I'd get a few items custom fit by their tailors. I'd spend $500 on a suit, $100 on a shirt, $100 on a tie, $300 on shoes, and whatever it took to have a Montblanc pen snowcap peeking out of my jacket pocket.

My partner spent twice as much on his suits, and the stylish gear set him even further apart from me. Kim bought me a thousand-dollar watch once. I was afraid to wear it because I might scratch it. My partner had a few twenty-five-thousand-dollar watches in his collection.

When we opened the West Coast office for Salomon Brothers

Private Investment Department in 1992, the firm wouldn't permit us to have a client who was worth less than fifty million dollars. And I wasn't allowed to fly coach to see a client. I had to travel in first class. The firm had a posh private dining room to hold meetings in our office, complete with an executive chef, sous chef, pastry chef, and sommelier. There was floor to ceiling hardwood everywhere. They polished the table to the finest shine you'd ever see. When I looked at my reflection, I saw success and prestige wrapped in a designer pin-striped suit.

We had some of the world's most famous athletes as clients. A few entertainers too. But our careers exploded during the riverboat gambling boom in the early '90s. We flew to Las Vegas every week and did business with most of the casino owners. Many of these families were worth hundreds of millions of dollars. A few became billionaires. They'd invite us to stay in the high-roller suites and live large.

A few years went by, I walked into the office, and my best friend and business partner said, "Do you have a minute?" Nothing good ever follows that phrase, and this time was no different. He rocked back in his chair and coldly said he was terminating our partnership and taking the big clients . . . but I could have a few of the crumbs.

Like the walls of Jericho, in an instant, my life came crashing down.

My dream was gone. The paradigm my life was built upon collapsed and was proven to be false. I'd put my faith in believing I could do anything I set my mind to, and it turned out to be a lie. In a flash, it vanished. The access. The money. My ego. In their place was betrayal, embarrassment, and humiliation. Later, they would be replaced by anger. But it was too soon for that. Head held high, I strutted out the door and hit the down arrow on the elevator.

The only thing to greet me in the garage was the echo of slamming my car door. Once safely inside the tinted windows, the dam holding my tears burst. I was completely crushed.

Annihilated. Worthless. *What do I tell Kim?* She married a driven
guy who had the lifestyle to prove it. Now that my rocket ship of
success epically failed, would she kick me out too? Maybe my
mom was right. Maybe I was a mistake?

My wife's true nature revealed itself when I walked in the
door.

"Are you okay?" she said, reading my face. I broke the news to
her. "I'm so sorry. We'll be okay," was all she said. Then, her arms
wrapped around me like a warm blanket, returning feeling to my
decimated spirit.

I went to work each day for the next month, surrounded by
strangers who I once thought were my friends. Everyone's eyes
turned away just slightly, not enough to be rude, but enough to
send the message that in no way were they associated with me. My
diet consisted of depression and shame for every meal.

My vitriol escalated every day. Every time I saw my former
partner, I thought about saying, *"Seriously, dude, you were my best
friend, and after all we've been through, you humiliate me like this. Why
wouldn't you have talked to me about this?"* I never uttered a word and
simply swallowed my bitterness.

I'd go into my new office, the same little one without an ocean
view where he broke the news to me, and look at the clock,
counting the minutes until lunchtime. I'd wait to enter the elevator
alone, hit "G," and get in my car and drive—anywhere. I'd go
into residential neighborhoods and park my Mercedes 500SL. I
started to hate that car and everything it represented. I'd take out
my brown paper sack lunch that Kim had lovingly prepared, eat
my peanut butter and jelly sandwich, and choke down a few chips.
Day after day, it was the same thing.

A month into it, I'd had enough. I weighed my options over
and over. I could sue him, our boss, and the company. I could sue
them all. I could leave the firm and fight for our old clients.
Maybe Goldman would still be interested in hiring me? I knew
most of my partner's dirty little secrets and he knew mine. We
could just battle it out. Or I could come in every day and stare at

them, firing daggers of guilt their way. Revenge consumed my ugly heart. I knew implementing any of these strategies would make me a bitter old man at the young age of forty-one. Not what I wanted to be. I did not want to become a broken-beyond-repair parent ranting at my kids. I'd been on the receiving end of that. But what will I be if I walk away? How does the world treat a cast-out nobody?

Standing at the crossroads, I finally reached into my desk drawer and pulled out the crumpled piece of paper that had been my bible. The worn, twenty-three-year-old tattered scrap with my goals on it stared back at me. I looked at every item and put a check mark next to the ones I'd accomplished. There wasn't a single item left unchecked. Most had two or three. I'd achieved the dream the world had set out for me. The climb was remarkable. The descent, devastating. I looked at the list one last time and finally saw it for what it was worth. I scrunched it up and threw it in the trash and walked out of the office for the last time.

I just didn't have the strength to fight. It was time to move on. To what, I had no idea. But I couldn't take the pain caused by chasing what I had put my mind to anymore. My life wasn't simply broken—it was shattered. There weren't enough of the king's horses or king's men to put Humpty Dumpty back together this time.

The selfish act of my business partner led me to move my family to a small mountain town in Northern California where I heard the gospel message for the first time. Who would ever have imagined that loss would eventually lead to me finding my true place of belonging: serving a community of fellow outcasts living in a dumpsite in the middle of Africa? Circumstances could not be more polar opposite from the first-class flights, fine meals, and thousand-dollar bottles of wine from my Wall Street career. Neither could my thinking. The gradual understanding of Scripture replaced the decades of false truths indoctrinated into me by my parents, professors, culture, and business leaders. Slowly, these new teachings changed the way I looked at life.

"Do nothing out of selfish ambition" (Philippians 2:3 NIV) took the place of "You can do anything you set your mind to" (Ben Franklin). My mom thought it was her, but Ben coined it first. Everything I had done was out of selfish ambition to do whatever it was I set my mind to.

Philippians 2:3 (NIV) goes on: "Rather, in humility, value others above yourselves." In my arrogance, I had no place for humility. According to my warped view, there was no value to others who accomplished less than me. I only looked up at others who had more, never down to those who may be struggling. I never looked. Not once.

Verse four continues, "Not looking to your own interests but each of you to the interests of the others." I wouldn't have known the interests of others if they stared me in the face. I didn't even know others had interests, and if they did, none of them were any concern of mine.

Instead of pursuing more for myself, God wanted me to give everything I had to Him—the source from which everything comes.

I was still made of the same stuff that drove me to walk into the Merrill Lynch Hollywood office and ask to work in the mailroom for free. I had those same fingerprints. I had that same wiring. Only now I had a different playbook. I wasn't obsessed with building Dave's kingdom; I was honored to serve in God's.

Romans 12:2 (NLT) states, "Don't copy the behavior and customs of this world, but let God transform you into a new person by changing the way you think." By the power of the Holy Spirit, I thought in new ways and became a new person.

Stephen Covey taught that the first three habits of highly successful people lead you to move from dependence to independence. He called it "self-mastery." God was teaching me something altogether different—not to depend on myself, no matter how talented I was or how finely I honed my skills, but to put my confidence in Him. He was transforming me from a *One Minute Manager* into an eternal servant. I no longer had to be *In*

Search of Excellence. I had the One who is excellence Himself living inside me.

———

Stepping into the unknown of confronting gangs would take much more than the keen negotiation tactics of a Wall Street veteran. My old strategies would be useless. I wasn't competing against another human to win a piece of business. I was fighting the devil for a soul. I was battling to beat back deception, darkness, and evil with truth, light, and love. This was going to take a heart and mind like Christ with ears tuned to God's voice and a joyful obedience to do whatever He asked. I was not fighting flesh and blood, but the principalities of darkness in the unseen world.

The sole preparation I did for all the meetings scheduled in the coming two weeks with the staff was to prepare my soul. And for all the unscheduled ones, I simply had to surrender everything to God. I had to fill myself as full of His Spirit as possible and rely on Him to pour it out as needed. Sitting in the terminal alone, I realized that, much like a firefighter battles physical flames, I was about to battle a raging spiritual fire. Firefighters don't bring their spouses and children along as they rush into a burning building. They look into their eyes, kiss them goodbye, and say, "'I'll see you soon," not knowing if they will or not. But they don't bring them with them. It was the same for me. Kim and the boys weren't with me this time, and it was by God's design. They were tucked away safely until I could see them again—hopefully soon, and hopefully in one piece.

But even though my wife and kids weren't with me, I wasn't alone. I would never be alone. Never. I had my God. His Word served as some comfort: "Even though I walk through the valley of the shadow of death, I will fear no evil, for you are with me" (Psalm 23:4 ESV).

I boarded the plane bound for Chicago. Like the terminal in

San Francisco, the plane was half full. Joe texted to let me know he was on his way to Boston. I would see him in Frankfurt. I rode the shuttle to the international terminal for the flight to Germany. It was an echo chamber. Travelers, paralyzed by COVID-19 fears, were nowhere to be found.

I checked my two fifty-pound pieces of luggage through to the ultimate destination of Nairobi. All I had to do was wrestle with my overstuffed computer backpack and pull my wobbly one-wheeled carry-on down the aisle to my economy seat. Before the flight, I worried about having enough overhead bin space to place my bags. It proved to be an unfounded fear. Like the terminal, the plane to Frankfurt was nearly empty. There was only one person in each row of nine seats. While the vacant seats provided additional legroom, they served as a tangible reminder that my wife wasn't leaning on my shoulder, something that always comforts me more than having space to stretch my legs. I reached to the Lord for comfort instead.

The only thing with fewer people in it than the plane was the airport in Frankfurt. Not a single shop was open. I couldn't even get a cup of coffee.

But I did meet Joe, my companion from Kapu, whom God sent to be with me the next two weeks. He recognized me first, and his smile grew. The spring in his step quickened. We broke all protocols and hugged unsocially distanced at the gate. We spent the next four hours telling stories of our times in Kenya and getting to know each other.

Finally, I asked, "Joe, how'd you and Sandy meet?"

"Through church."

The muffled sound of the gate attendant called before he could answer further, "Now boarding Lufthansa flight 590 nonstop to Jomo Kenyatta International, Nairobi, Kenya."

Joe had made our seating arrangements. We sat on aisles across from one another. He took one look at the five empty seats to his right, grabbed some pillows, a soft blanket, and rolled over and slept much of the way.

I tried to read. I tried to watch a movie. I closed my eyes and tried to remember Kim's departing kiss. I tried to ignore the heartache of not being with her. I didn't succeed at any of them. Instead, my mind was filled with uncertainties. We'd only be on the ground in Nakuru for thirteen days. What good can I possibly do in only thirteen days? Would we incite more violence trying to make things better?

We landed in Nairobi without issues, although multiple temperature screenings and interrogations of our recent travel and health conditions made getting through customs take three times longer than usual. I was happy to see all the caution and protections around containing COVID-19.

I always feel a little like Jason Bourne when I land in Kenya and transfer my phone's SIM card from ATT to the local carrier, Safaricom. This time was no different, and once the switch was made, there was already a text waiting.

DID YOU HEAR MAMA AMON TURNED UP MONDAY WITH SIX POLICE OFFICERS WITH GUNS? ~ ANONYMOUS

Oh no, who are they hunting? So not only can she not be held in prison, now she has cops as her hit squad. How much worse is this going to get?

Just landed ~ me

ONE OF THE POLICE IS THE ONE WHO ARRESTED HER LAST WEEK ~ ANONYMOUS

This lady is relentless. Doesn't she ever rest? They burned her house to the ground. Her sons were suspected of being in a gang. She gets arrested, and now, only a few days later, she shows up at the dumpsite with six armed police as her escorts, including the one who arrested her! Now she had a literal police force to keep anyone away who dared interfere with her affairs. Mama Amon should be on the other end of those cops' machine guns and locked up in a dark hole in an undisclosed location. Her mobster boys should be down there too.

I kept this to myself. It was late, and I didn't want to worry Joe. We picked up our luggage and headed to the taxi. After thirty hours of travel, Joe's grin was still there.

THE ARRIVAL

October 9, 2020

COVID-19 RESTRICTIONS AFFECTED all aspects of travel, including, sadly, the cuisine. Hermetically sealed, food-like substances were the only things on my tray during the flights. They were every bit as tasty as this description sounds. When we got to Nakuru, fifty-seven hours after my delicious pasta plate with sausage and peppers in Millbrae, the rumble in my tummy said it was well past time to eat. The fog in my head said it was time to go to bed.

I introduced Joe to what would be our diner for most of the trip, the Nairobi Java House, or simply, Java. It's my favorite spot. The food is decent with a few tastes of home and doesn't make me spend several days within seven feet of a commode. And the service is top-notch.

Twenty years ago, it was nearly impossible to find a robust cup of coffee in Kenya, which is ironic since so much of what we drink in the US comes from the hills and valleys there. For the life of me, the best cup I could find was a watery serving of Nescafé, which never lived up to the claim on its packet of "ultimate coffee goodness." An American relief worker teamed up with two

Kenyans and started Java to attract tourists who had ample cash and started a profitable franchise that continues to grow today. To ensure it was a safe place for tourists to eat and give them a leg up on the locals, they filtered the water. Soon they gained a reputation a sure fire place for foreigners. You can get anything from a guacamole bacon cheeseburger to *chicken dhania* (coriander chicken curry) with *ugali* (stiff maize flour porridge) and *sukuma wiki* (collard greens, onions, and spices). Currently there are seventy full-blown diners across Africa with a menu able to satisfy a variety of palettes.

There are two Javas in Nakuru now. One in the middle of the commotion of Nakurutown and the other at the more relaxed, upscale, retail Westside Mall. It's the go-to spot for me and the rest of the mzungu herd. If you're looking for white foreigners in Nakuru, odds are you can find them passing through Java sometime during the day.

Just outside the shop, a masked greeter silently motioned to the handwashing station. She pointed a temperature gun at my head, showed me the readout, nodded, and waved me in. Java's burnt orange interior and prominent bright yellow sun logo on the wall was just as I remembered it. The most significant change from when I was there in February with Kim was fewer seats and far fewer customers.

The staff noticed me immediately, and their welcome made me feel like I was Norm entering the bar in *Cheers*.

Hempstone, a server who sends me an occasional overseas WhatsApp message, sauntered up, brushed the corner of my chair, and handed me a menu. There is no social distancing among friends. "Long time, Wafula, how's the States?"

"Okay, my friend, just glad to be back in Nakuru with you."

"Where's Mama?" he asked.

"She's okay. Just sitting out this quick business trip. We'll come together next time."

Joe wasted no time diving into the deep end of the menu. "I'll try the Java chicken curry, please."

"Chicken, chips, and a salad for me. *Asante*, Hempstone."
Asante is "thank you" in Swahili. Often, I try to sprinkle in what
little I know to connect with my local friends.

When the meal arrived, Joe looked at me, bowed his head,
and prayed, "Heavenly Father, we pray Thy nearness upon us
today as we strive to do Thy will. We pray for grace to make good
decisions, and we pray we could be thankful Thou hast put us in
this place this day to share the blessings with others Thou hast
given to us."

I looked up, anticipating the closing amen, but Joe continued.
"We realize, Lord, to whom much is given, much is expected, so
we pray we could use whatever skills or assets we've been given to
honor Thee and to share with others. We pray for those that have
not yet come to know Thee as their Savior and pray that Thou
would prick their hearts, that they would see there is a better way.
We are most thankful for the shed blood of Jesus Christ, which
offers all mankind the opportunity of life eternal with Thee in the
heavens above."

Still not a hint of an amen.

"We pray for Thy abiding nearness this day as we give all
honor and glory to Thee. We also pray a blessing on the food and
drink before us and ask it could nourish our bodies much as Thy
Word nourishes our soul. We pray that Thy, and not our, will be
done this day. And Lord, we want to remember the staff at
Maisha Mapya who give their time and talents to help the
children who attend there. Please, Lord, give them wisdom
beyond their years to continue to show love and respect to the
school children as well as their parents and all those in the
community near the school. We thank Thee in the name of our
risen Savior, Jesus Christ. Amen."

It was the most I'd heard Joe say at one time, and also the first
time I'd ever heard anyone pray in the King James Version of the
Bible with all the Thees and Thous. I was afraid he might be
super legalistic. I wondered if he would be okay with an informal,
conversational Christian like me. How would he handle me

having few rules except loving God and loving people? I'd probably find out soon.

"In our church, we want to remember God's holiness, so we use some King James language in our prayers." Joe was already reading me like a book. "Sandy and I were married by faith."

He had said that earlier at the airport. I should have asked what it meant, but I didn't. Did it mean it was an arranged marriage?

The meal arrived, and it was as tasty as the conversation was proving to be satisfying.

"What are you looking forward to this week, Joe?"

"I want to help you however I can. Just let me know. I'll do anything that can be helpful. Oh, if we have time, maybe we can go to Lake Nakuru to see the flamingos?" I didn't want to break it to poor Joe that the flamingos haven't been around for several years.

Now, with our tanks full, all we had to do was make it to the hotel to get a good night's sleep.

My primary method of transportation around town is either a tuk-tuk or Wasili. Occasionally, I'll take a matatu. Tuk-tuks are three-wheeled vehicles with *zero* horsepower. Okay, maybe one petting zoo pony power. Their motors start with a pull string like your lawnmower. Hills of any kind are an issue. They have shock absorbers made of, well, nothing because the tuk-tuks don't have any. Their principal use is for transporting cargo around town and, maybe, the occasional person.

Wasili has been around for a couple of years and is like Uber in the US. It is generally a nice compact car with four wheels and the ability to go over thirty miles per hour. There's a simple app on my phone to request a car that picks me up at my location. The ride costs the same as a tuk-tuk and is much easier on my backside. It's one of the most significant improvements to the Kenyan transportation system in years.

Matatus are the preferred local transportation method. They are six or eight passenger vans with an extra row of seats added.

So, with the social closeness of the Kenyan culture (pre-COVID-19), you can easily fit a dozen humans, a few chickens, and maybe a goat or two in a single matatu (I've actually experienced this). They are by far the cheapest mode of transportation, running at about 10 percent of the cost of a Wasili. Rides are even cheap for mzungus like me, even though we pay double the rate, maybe twenty Kenyan shillings (twenty US cents) to get most places around town. But at six feet tall, weighing two hundred pounds, there are only two seats where I comfortably fit. The one in the middle of the back row where I can stretch my legs into the aisle. And the one closest to the open sliding door, which is reserved for the *makanga* (similar to a railway ticket salesman) to convince potential passengers to hire them.

We opted for a Wasili for the ten-minute ride to the Rose Diamond Resort hotel. An engaging driver picked us up. Joe offered to sit in the back seat. I hopped in the front. "Hi. What's your name?" I asked.

"I'm Wallace." His voice sounded exactly like Chris Rock's Marty the Zebra in *Madagascar*.

"Hey, Wallace." I decided to strike first. "It's good to meet you. I'm Daudi Wafula Kamau."

He was laughing so hard his hands came off the wheel. One hand covered his masked mouth and the other pointed at me. "You're Wafula?"

"Yep."

It's my favorite icebreaker. The last thing a Wasili driver is thinking is that the white guy he just picked up from Java would have a Swahili name with surnames from not one but two of the most common tribes. I've been using this schtick for years to create relationships with strangers who've become fast friends.

Joe was laughing too. He might have been taking notes on standup.

I glanced at a text on my phone from Kim.

Hey, honey. How are you? Are you okay? ~ *Kim*

I'm okay. ~ me

"Hey Wallace, how's business? I bet it's been slow with no tourism and not many people around."

Wallace now knew I knew more than just one Swahili word and understood a bit more of his situation than he initially thought. I continued. "Who's your best customer?"

"Oh, it's the guys at Trinity Church. I'm the unofficial van for them!"

I knew the guys at Trinity, so I figured I'd string Wallace along a bit more just to blow his mind. "Do you mean Pastor Edgar?"

"You know Edgar?"

"Yep. I love Edgar."

"There is no way you know Edgar," Wallace said, thinking he would call my bluff.

"Do you have a phone, Wallace? Call him."

He whipped out his phone so fast and dialed. We merged into traffic. This guy was a multitasker.

As it was ringing, I said, "Ask him who his favorite white guy at the dumpsite is."

Wallace's smile poked out the side of his face mask. He couldn't wait to see if this was true or just another gag. Edgar, who was now on the phone, overheard and answered, "Hahaha, it's Dave Hatfield. Daddy Dave! How are you my friend?"

With a slight tilt of my head and one raised eyebrow, I said, "Told ya, Wally."

Stuff like that makes life come alive for me. Plus, it's fun and brings joy to people.

We pulled into the hotel. I knew business stunk for Wally with no tourists around, so I handed him four hundred shillings, about double the standard rate.

"Can you pick us here at the hotel tomorrow at 8:00 a.m. for a fifteen-minute ride?"

Wallace glanced down at the bills in his hand. He knew if he said yes, he would earn enough to meet his family's expenses for the day.

He looked up at me, shook his head, and said, "Wafula, I am sorry, Sunday is my day of worship. I just can not make it."

I loved that about Wallace. He put his God first. Carrying that thought with me was something that helped me all week.

"How about Monday then, Wallace, 7:30 a.m.? Right here at the hotel?"

"Will do. See you then."

Fast friends, me and Wally. All it took was a ten-minute ride.

He dropped us at the porte-cochère of the Rose Diamond Resort, the only four-star hotel in the city. It's about the price of a Travelodge in the US, but nearly double the cost of staying in the next best hotel in Nakuru. Kim and I have tried other establishments, but the last place we stayed had more locusts in the hotel than guests. Residing at the Rose Diamond means getting a good night's sleep, healthy food, and no surprises.

"Welcome back, Mr. Hatfield. We're delighted you're here," said the doorman. "Kindly allow us to sanitize your bags."

"It's good to be with you again. Thank you."

"My pleasure."

Whenever the polite, exceptionally well-trained staff ends a conversation with those words, I always feel like I'm at the Ritz-Carlton. Yet, incredibly, such a luxurious resort is only an eight-minute drive from the Gioto dumpsite.

Kim and I carry certain notoriety there. We're not their typical clientele of prominent businessmen, rock stars, and dignitaries. Because of Kim's illness and the need to be in the most sanitary places possible, we stayed there for seventy-one nights in 2018. Each day, we'd come to breakfast bright and early and freshly dressed. I would wear blue jeans, the school's Hilton's Heroes T-shirt, and my trusty Kenyan beaded bracelet while Kim sported a colorful African skirt and blouse. We could see the staff whispering when we returned late in the day. We looked tired, dirty, and had a distinct dumpsite odor about us. I'm sure they were curious about what we did all day. Often, they played American '80s and '90s tunes during meals, and whenever Michael Jackson's *Somebody's Watching Me* came on, Kim and I just laughed. It astonished the staff that a couple from America came to Nakuru to serve the people living in the dump on the other side of town.

It feels extravagant to stay in the city's best hotel and causes me cognitive dissonance being in such lovely surroundings while serving a community in utter despair. But since our stay was so short, Joe and I didn't have a minute to waste. The last thing we needed was lodging troubles.

The cozy, well-appointed room on the top floor had two twin beds and a splendid view of an open field with a beautiful African tulip tree in full display, showing off its bright orange blooms. An overflowing bowl of fresh fruit had been placed on the table to welcome us along with a note, "Karibu nymbani, Mr. Hatfield."

I set my phone down and noticed a WhatsApp message awaited me. It wasn't from Anonymous. It was from Bethany, a delightful young woman who had visited Maisha Mapya on a mission team last spring.

Dave! Today is the day! The race is ready to start! I'm so excited! ~ Bethany

God had touched Bethany's heart to do more than simply come and see Maisha Mapya. Since she returned from Africa to her home in Minnesota, she'd spent the last six months organizing a bike race fundraiser. Buying food for the starving children in our neighborhood brought her joy. Amazingly, this was happening in a small town on the outskirts of Minneapolis where so much unrest after the senseless, heartless killing of George Floyd upended America and caused riots in the streets. Now, something selfless and loving was occurring in that community because of Bethany's beautiful heart. And so, at 6:00 a.m. on a crisp, autumn day, thirteen cyclists woke up, put on their racing gear, grabbed some coffee, and pedaled and pedaled—some for one hundred miles.

I reread her text message. The time on my phone said I should be sleeping. Joe's gentle snoring said I should be sleeping too. But the jetlag was winning, and I couldn't nod off, even after three melatonin pills. Plus, I was elated at Bethany hosting our first big fundraiser without me being involved in it. So, I drafted an email to encourage the race team and volunteers and to express my gratitude. At the same time the cyclists were pedaling in Minnesota, I was typing in Kenya.

Imagine you're inside the locker room after winning the world championship game. Even though you are sweaty, tired, and have aching muscles, the smile on your face and satisfaction in your heart makes it all worth it. You look around the room and see your teammates in the same shape, exhausted after giving it their all. As your eyes connect, your smile gets even bigger.

Then the coach walks in. He hoists the trophy and says, "Congratulations, champs! You did it!"

Well, today, I feel like that coach, and I can barely contain the smile in my heart. I am so grateful for your time, hard work, and generosity. Thank you. You did it!

It's not just the players on the field who are responsible for the victory. All the supporters on the sidelines and even the fans in the stands make it possible. It's a collective effort. Together, we are loving our neighbors on the other side of the world by providing food at their moment of dire need.

I'm off doing my part too. As you read this, I am in Kenya to encourage our students, staff, and community. I will have the honor of distributing the food you made possible with them. I wish you all could be here with me. I'd love for you to feel their gratitude. Maybe next time?

Keep an eye on your inbox because, as soon as the grand totals are in, I will share how many meals you provided to the community. You'll see with your own eyes the impact you are making, and we can celebrate together.

As a donor to our organization, and a member of the Living Stone Global family, you're a part of something extraordinary—you're a part of our community. You make everything we do possible.

Thank you!

By the time the event was over, Bethany's team raised enough money to buy seventy-five thousand meals for starving kids.

With one last look at the email, I hit send. I adjusted my single pillow, scrunched up half the blankets, and snuggled them. They were a poor substitute for Kim.

I looked at the time; it was after midnight. Even though I'd just gotten here, being with a few old friends and feeling the pace of the city, I was settling in. But God sent me here to engage a new group, and I hadn't made a stitch of progress on that. With one day gone and no gang contact, I already felt the clock ticking. I checked my messages again. Nothing. I had to leave in twelve days.

I couldn't wait to see the school's leadership team tomorrow. I knew they needed comfort and reassurance from all they'd been through in rescuing Angel and coping with the gang killings. They are the ones who, day after day, are on the ground in Hilton making change happen. Plus, I love them. And I needed to hug them all. COVID-19 or no COVID-19.

Joe's rhythmic, gentle snore lulled me to sleep—finally.

THE PERFORMANCE

October 11, 2020

WHEN THE ALARM SOUNDED, my lovely bride wasn't at my side. Instead, my cold computer was still on my lap, trying to hide under a pile of blankets. I got up, smiled at Joe, and he smiled back. I showered and put on my standard uniform of tennis shoes, jeans and a Hilton's Heroes T-shirt. The shirt's logo is the winning entry from a design contest we hosted, which had over one hundred and twenty submissions. It shows an image of a child with his left arm raised and holding an adult's hand on the background of Africa's continent. It's not only on our T-shirts. The logo is on full display on our school's perimeter wall and marks the Hilton community entrance. You can't miss it. It's thirty feet tall.

Joe and I walked downstairs and startled the lone hostess as we pulled back the doors to the hotel's Sapphire Restaurant. She wasn't used to guests showing up promptly at the scheduled 6:30 a.m. opening time. Vacationers going on safari tend to sleep in, and business breakfasts start around 7:30 a.m. Expertly trained, she didn't miss a beat and greeted us like a long-lost friend. "Good morning Mr. Hatfield. How was your night?" she chimed.

Desperately trying to unglue my eyelids and clear my head, I moaned, "May I have some mixed tea? Oh, and good morning to you." While my body had been transported across continents, my manners were still somewhere over the Mediterranean. I blushed that I stated my need prior to returning her greeting.

Before I knew it, a piping hot mug of goodness warmed my hands. I love Kenyan mixed tea. It's a magical combination of one part tea, two parts milk, and twenty-three parts sugar—with an ample dose of caffeine. There's no need for a Starbucks Caramel Ribbon Crunch Frappuccino when you have the sweetness of Kenyan mixed tea in your cup. With one sip of the brew, I was home again. But it was incomplete because Kim wasn't enjoying the treat with me.

The server returned three minutes later. "What may I get for your breakfast?"

I said, "May I have a *whole pot* of mixed tea?" Joe grinned, something I learned he does a lot. His resting face might be a smile.

She looked at the cup in my hand which was only an inch from my lips. I could tell she was thinking, "Kind sir, you have tea in your hand," but her only reply was "Right away."

I'm not sure she understood I was still operating in the twilight zone, being transported across eleven time zones in a matter of hours. I hoped the caffeine would clear my fuzzy head. It is useless to plan as I did in my old Wall Street days when my Day-Timer was complete and open to tomorrow's page before I left my desk at night. I'd walk in the following day and systematically tackle every item one by one. The fluid nature of life in the slums only compounds the problem.

Now instead of a daily planner, I have a list of prayers and an expectation of watching how God will answer them. Sometimes I scribble thoughts on a napkin. Then ultimately, the napkin gets tossed out. And God makes beauty out of my surrendered heart.

God reminds me of the Scriptures that say, "Follow Me" and "My will be done." There is not a place in the Bible that says,

"Dave, I'll make a way for you to live out your dreams, just let Me know what you want."

With a fresh cup in my hand, I thought about how before COVID-19, the Sapphire Restaurant was a hub of activity. It usually was awash with people attending conferences at the hotel, tourists getting ready for a day of adventure on safari, and the movers and shakers of the Nakuru business scene preparing to fuel up and start their day at the bountiful buffet. But today there were so few guests that breakfast came as a set menu with few choices. Joe and I both got a good start to the day, selecting two fried eggs, breakfast potatoes, and fresh pineapple. I always like the pineapple. It's sweet, and they say it fights intestinal parasites.

As the meal arrived, Joe looked at me. The corners of his mouth turned up, and he bowed his head. As he prayed using Thees and Thous, it was apparent he is a reverent, kind gentleman. Joe isn't legalistic. He is respectful. Joe knows God is above all. God is sovereign. God is the Almighty. It comforted me to hear those words said the way he said them.

The charming server returned. "How did you enjoy breakfast?"

"It was amazing. May I have a takeaway of mixed tea?" I had a feeling I was going to live on sugar, caffeine, and the power of the Holy Spirit for the next two weeks.

———

Normally on a Sunday morning, I'd be on my way to church to hear Pastor Edgar preach. Maybe I'd even run into Wasili Wally and worship with him there. But God had something different in mind. Today's church was going to take the form of loving some Maisha Mapya students by watching them dance in the International Day of the Girl Child celebration at the Hyrax Museum.

It was quite an honor for our little school at the dump to be invited to such a prestigious event. The selection committee requested Maisha Mapya to take part because our reputation was growing within Nakuru. People were noticing what God was doing, and they wanted to be part of it. His favor on us is contagious.

I cared little for the pomp and circumstance. My heart only cared about seeing the kids I love so much. God also wanted the children to feel special that Daddy Dave traveled from America to watch them dance.

Our group had hired a choreographer who taught them every step, every beat. The children, both boys and girls, prepared for weeks. I envisioned them training like the opening scene from *A Chorus Line.*

Joe and I arrived early. Presentation tents, giant speakers, and food booths were being assembled on the dew-covered grass. We rolled up our sleeves and joined in. As we helped set up three hundred plastic chairs, I imagined the kids' excitement waiting for their ride to show up at Maisha Mapya.

The plan was for the performers to wear their cute school T-shirts sporting a caped superhero cartoon giraffe on the front. As the children lined up to receive their T-shirts, the staff made a discovery. During the several months of COVID-19–forced school closure, all the kids had grown! Most couldn't even pull the shirt over their heads. Even little Bridget giggled when her shirt was stuck halfway on. Auntie Maggie rushed to the market so the kids would have something to wear that fit them. "You guys go. I'll meet you at Hyrax," she said as she vanished.

We rented three matatus so the children could ride in a van. They'd watched motorized vehicles of all kinds pass in front of the school, but for many, this was their first time inside, feeling the exhilaration of accelerating on a straightaway and the g-forces from taking turns too fast. New experiences like this help expose them to life outside the slum. It is the soil where seeds of dreams are planted. The kids hopped in the matatus, left the school, and headed to the festival. After the ride, more than one of the boys wanted to be a race car driver.

Maggie returned as quickly as she left with two dozen brand-new, highlighter-yellow T-shirts, enough for everyone. Jumping kids with outstretched hands calmed themselves, formed a line, and claimed their prize. Receiving new clothes is another rare experience for our students, and they couldn't tame all their giggles and wiggles.

They didn't see me sneaking up on them, but once they did, their eyes grew big, and they rushed over and mobbed me. I could barely contain my giggles and wiggles too.

In the distance, two young adults raced toward us. The girl was outpacing the boy. As they neared, I knew exactly who it was. I'd watched these two grow up since they were little kids. I knew their walk, their run, and when they lowered their masks, their smiles. It was Lucy and Martin, whom Kim and I have sponsored since our first trip to Kenya. They were little children in primary school when we met them and fell in love in 2007. They were now fully grown.

Kim felt God's pull toward Lucy in an explanation-defying way. When she first met this quiet little girl who just wanted to silently sit next to her, Kim struggled to find words to say. We had two sons of our own, but there was some unspoken, unexplainable connection between Kim and this tender soul who would become our daughter. Pastor Bill's wife explained that many of these children have been through so much trauma, you don't have to say anything. Just being near is enough conversation. Lucy was one of these children.

School was challenging for her, but with grit and determination, Lucy became the first in her family to graduate from high school. We found out later she endured beatings under corporal punishment, which still occurs because those in authority look the other way. Some of the worst was administered by the self-righteous forty-five-year-old female headmaster of the school. It serves as a constant reminder for me in creating the culture at Maisha Mapya to always value our students as precious children made in the image of our amazing

God. Love and nurturing are above academics at Maisha Mapya.

When we met Martin, he was a sweet second grader. He was the boy who steered away from trouble. Maybe that's why he connected well with our sons. They'd play futbol together and relax as one under the shade of some trees at Martin's school.

Now, Martin is a gentle giant standing over six feet two inches tall. He is brilliant, consistently scoring at the top of his class. Being smart has its consequences, though. After taking the national eighth-grade exams, the Ministry of Education moved him to a remote city to attend a government school to groom him to be one of Kenya's best. We had no way of knowing where he was, and no way to contact him. Kim and I were heartbroken that we could only send a faceless monthly check to assist him financially. We knew the money was important, but being a sponsor means more than money to a child who needs love.

Four years later, we received a text from him out of the blue, thanking us for all our support and that he could never have graduated high school without our help. He also aced the high school national exams and was accepted into Kenyatta University, the Yale of Kenya. It's quite a feat for an orphan who grew up on a farm and was raised by his grandparents, his school fees paid for by an American. Martin dreams of becoming an engineer. Even though he's well-educated, hardworking, and a man of excellent character, he still has a tough time finding employment during school breaks. Even before the economic devastation of COVID-19, jobs were scarce, no matter your abilities.

Lucy and Martin call Kim and me Mom and Dad. It used to make me uncomfortable, but I've learned to understand it means you care for us, nurture us, sacrifice for us, and are like parents to us. We do our best to meet them every time we are in Kenya. Because that's what moms and dads do.

I got lost in the conversation with all my kids and overlooked the festive setup's completion. Banners, booths, and tables with fancy cloths graced dignitaries sitting behind them and made the scene look like a state dinner.

It was time to start the show. Joe and I were ushered to the front of the stage and placed at the head table. Visible seats of high honor don't hold me too long. It was a kind gesture, but I'd rather be in the middle of the mosh pit jumping around with our kids.

In her best boxing announcer voice, the MC cried out, "Let's welcome Maisha Mapyaaaa!"

The choreographer waved the kids into formation. Sixteen girls and four boys sprinted to him and stood at attention. Only Salome was lagging. She started to move with the group, but then scurried to the side of the stage. Her sad eyes called me to come.

"Daddy Dave, where's Angel? She's missing." Angel is Salome's best friend.

"She won't make it today, sweetie," I said. "You go and have fun. Make her proud." I wondered where Angel was too.

Salome sprinted back to join the group, and like a Broadway show, a composed line sidestepped to the middle of the arena. They paused, placed their arms at their sides and bowed their heads. With the first beat, they popped, arms and legs spread in an X. The crowd clapped, cheered, and shouted. The children's smiles grew larger, but they never broke form. They set the place on its ear dancing to "Superwoman" by the Tanzanian All-Stars. The song was a perfect choice to kick off a celebration for young girls on their way to becoming super women of Kenya.

The children nailed it, every step, every beat in unison. Well, almost. One poor little guy looked sort of like me, half a step behind and occasionally wandering in the wrong direction. At the last beat, my standing ovation sent them the love of a proud papa. My shouts of "Wow! Wow! Amazing!" most likely could be heard in Ethiopia. Spinning around inside the tent, my joyfulness encouraged the others to holler and clap. The distinguished guests obliged and cheered like their team had just won the World Cup.

The dancers ran off the assembly ground, formed a tight

circle, and hugged and bounced with glee. I snuck out of the dignitaries' tent and hijacked Joe to come with me. We joined in the jumping jubilee. If I headed to the airport and returned to America at that moment, my heart would have been full. Seeing our children, who the world cast aside, filled with such joy had my adrenaline pumping.

The MC grabbed the microphone. "Let's hear it for the super women and children of Maisha Mapya!!"

The crowd erupted once more.

She continued, "All women are superheroes. Who else can bleed every month and survive?" *What? Where did that come from?* Her directness and drastic change of topic caught me off-guard. Our kids on stage are seven, maybe eight years old. Without flinching, she talked about menstruation and the necessity of sanitary pads for girls. Some of our little ones looked inquisitively at each other. Whispers circulated. Now I was getting it. It did not embarrass the MC to talk about a subject that often causes shame for school-age girls experiencing the natural miracle of puberty. In our neighborhood, girls as young as nine may begin their periods. The woman was setting the tone that this was not only a day to sing and dance, but a day to address real-life issues, come together, and support one another.

Many girls won't go to school during their cycle because they cannot afford the ten cents a sanitary pad costs. Ridicule and teasing from schoolmates, teachers, and even administrators make it unbearable for them to attend, so they stay home. Or worse, some sell themselves to sexual predators for ten *bob* (about ten cents) to purchase a sanitary towel and maintain dignity at school. What a tragic exchange.

It's a genuine problem for hundreds of girls in Hilton. We've worked on this issue for over a year. Maisha Mapya has a dispensary of free sanitary towels for neighborhood girls. And we're exploring what more we can do to help.

"Let's hear it one more time, Maisha Mapya. I'm a Superwoman!" the MC shouted.

The crowd roared, and our burgeoning superheroes ran out, danced, and enjoyed their first curtain call. Before the day was over, they performed their routine three times. It was a day of celebration, but more importantly the event laid the groundwork for these young girls to learn to navigate some of the challenges in front of them.

For some of the kids and the staff, it was a perfect day. One they will never forget. For me, it was a wonderful way to spend a jetlagged Sunday, except a few things weren't quite right. Angel should have been there right next to her friend Salome, laughing and dancing, not hidden away fearing for her life. Kim should have been there too, not sick and alone 9,500 miles away, worrying about her husband. I also could not stop my anguish over Mama Amon and what she might be planning. Was she recruiting more police to be her enforcers?

As the day went on, I noticed our staff was spread out, gathered in small groups. Dan, Mary, and Maggie sat together. Our new teachers formed a clique. Nia and Nafula were off on their own. The teachers who had been with us over five years didn't even bother to show up. *Something wasn't right.*

THE WHY

October 12, 2020

MY EYES WERE open most of the night, and visions of gleeful kids dancing filled my head. The chorus "I'm a superwoooman" played on an endless loop in my head. The other constant was tossing and turning over the reason our Angel had missed out on the celebration. No matter how much I tried to momentarily ignore the violence in the community, it always crept into my consciousness.

At 5:30 a.m., the alarm went off. I greeted Joe and jumped into the shower. By the time I got out, he was already dressed proudly displaying a Hilton's Heroes T-shirt. I wondered if the morning routine would get repetitive like the movie *Groundhog Day* with Bill Murray. The plot focuses on when the alarm clock goes off, he wakes up, gets dressed, and every day's the same, until one day it's not. I was wondering if a different-feeling day would ever come.

Today's scene was: Alarm. Shower. Dress. Elevator. Arrive at the Sapphire Restaurant before they open.

Right on schedule, we entered the restaurant three minutes before they opened. The hostess station was vacant. A polite, distant voice from the kitchen greeted us, "Good morning."

A server, looking like she was trying not to run, burst out of the kitchen, straightened her face mask, put on her nametag, and greeted us once more. I asked for mixed tea, then added "Good morning" quickly, mentally chastising myself for putting my selfish need ahead of honoring the person with a greeting once again.

Two minutes later, as she placed a steaming cup of tea in front of me, she asked, "What would you like for breakfast?"

Glancing at her nametag I said, "Ayanna, may I have an entire pot of mixed tea, please?"

"My pleasure."

Joe smiled and ordered two eggs over easy on whole wheat toast, along with bacon and mango juice.

As our breakfast arrived, Joe glanced at me and lowered his head. He has a cute little thin spot of hair right on top. Hands folded on the table, his eyes turned up. It was a cue that it was my turn to pray, making a silent agreement to alternate the honor of giving thanks for our meals.

My prayers are more in the language of the Message version of the Bible rather than the King James. "Lord, thanks for the gift of this day. Thank You for the safety of this place. Give us the stamina to make it through the day. Thank You for being with our wives. Keep them safe. Let them sense Your presence. May we be a blessing to all we encounter today. Thank You for the way You love us. Lord, teach us to love like You. In Jesus's name. Amen."

His answering amen complete, Joe tucked in to his breakfast. On his plate were four eggs fried hard, two pieces of white bread, two slices of brown bread, roasted potatoes with peppers and onions, bacon, and half a grilled tomato with a rosemary sprig. Joe giggled and shrugged at the feast before him.

"Well, Joe, they must have thought you were too skinny," I laughed. "Actually, it's all you can eat, and they want you to feel like you're getting your money's worth."

"I can't eat all this, and I don't like wasting food." The way his voice softened told me there was some deep connection between Joe and throwing away food. Now it made sense why he was a director of Kapu with its mission of feeding hungry kids all across East Africa. Wasting food hurt his soul.

After breakfast, the server asked how my meal was. I replied, "It was great. May I have a takeaway of mixed tea?"

Sugar and caffeine Kenyan style—hot and tasty—keep it coming.

———

Wasili Wally lived up to his promise and was perched outside the hotel door promptly at 7:30 a.m. "*Twende kazi*, Wafula. Let's go to work."

It had been seven months since I was on the school grounds, and I was fired up to see all the staff, including the five new members. They were living with a fearful combination of COVID-19, economic devastation, and unprecedented violence. I knew my presence would calm their nerves and lift their spirits. Hillary, the security guard, dressed in his uniform and cap, stopped us at the gate. He motioned to the handwashing station. After I sanitized my hands, he pointed a temperature gun at my head, showed me the readout, and said, "Karibu Maisha Mapya, Daddy Dave. Welcome. Welcome home."

I rushed to meet anyone and everyone who was on the grounds. It was like Christmas morning with the anticipation of bright, wonderful presents to meet. Each one of these people is a precious gift to me.

The first group was our teaching staff. In preparation for the trip, I'd asked head teacher Mary to invite them to return to school so we could do something I'd wanted to do for a long time: to make my dream a reality by creating a Christian character curriculum that had the heart of God and the collective effort of our teachers all in the cultural context of Hilton.

Too often, students merely memorize and regurgitate Bible verses with little understanding of what they mean. Too often, materials are either too legalistic, too Anglo, or too outdated and are just words to the students. They are lifeless. If we're going to restore the fabric of this society, we need to raise a generation well-grounded in the Word of God. God must form, grow and mature the children's hearts. They need to learn and comprehend the principles of forgiveness, kindness, and peace all wrapped in love. It's the only way to turn the tide on the violence permeating our culture. I didn't want more catastrophes like Angel's and the poor guy who was stabbed fifty-three times. I didn't want more people to live with the guilt and shame of doing those atrocities, either. God's story, written through our eyes, in our voice, for our students, with actual situations they face would bring life to the kid's lessons. We were going to make it so when the kids heard these stories, they would experience Africa, Kenya, Nakuru, Hilton, and Gioto. The children would see themselves in these stories. And they could learn who they truly are in God's eyes.

I burst into the grade four classroom and exchanged a range of handshakes, fist bumps, smiles, and verbal greetings with the teachers. We milled about the class and enjoyed some tea together. Then I floated the idea of creating our curriculum.

"Let's start with a virtue you all do so well—compassion," I said. "I know you'll do an outstanding job. Here's the template. I'd like you to meet every day this week and make something great." Then I entered unknown territory. "I don't want to see any blonde-haired, blue-eyed Jesuses who look like the King of Norway on any of the pages. No stories of a mzungu being the savior." It got nervous laughter as eyes darted around the room. Without further instructions, I flashed a smile, set the book on the desk, and walked out. I wore my grin all the way down the hallway to the admin office.

This is the school's command center where our young global leadership team (GLT) makes magic happen. It's usually a hub of activity. Kids shuffling in with scraped knees needing a bandage, student athletes bouncing over asking for a soccer ball, worried parents requesting a slot for their kid to come to school, or community members discussing a sensitive topic can fill the office at any given moment. None of that was occurring now because COVID-19 had the school closed. Dust had built up on the reception desk.

Today was a family reunion, just me and the team—Dan, Maggie, Mary, Joel, and Nia. We embraced each other like veterans returning home from a victorious battle. After the high fives and hugs, we broke the huddle, and everyone settled into their workspaces.

I followed Dan, the head of everything at Maisha Mapya, into his office. He waved his hand for me to close the door. Before I could sit down, he whispered, "Dave, there's an issue with Nia."

Oh, no, I thought immediately. *Is she stealing? Lying? Is she two-faced and putting on an act for me? I've already been through enough of that in this country.* I had been spending five hours a week the past several months with Nia on Zoom calls trying to bring this place into some sense of order. I hadn't detected a single thing wrong.

For him to mention it though meant in Dan's mind, there must be a genuine issue. When he's happy, he calls me Daudi. I return the banter by calling him Danny. When something's bugging him, he calls me Dave. When he blatantly complains, which happens once every ice age, it means we've got a real problem.

"Oh gosh, really, Dan? I'm sorry. Is it okay if we talk about it later? Right now, I'd like to get the whole team together and start our meeting on time."

Leaving Dan's office, I smiled at Nia. Her well-organized desk was just outside Dan's door. She seemed exceedingly competent and hardworking. As I passed by her, I couldn't help but wonder what was the matter.

The GLT is a young and talented group with a willingness to attempt anything, but most of them were inexperienced. Dan, Maggie, Mary, and Joel were in their twenties. Their energy was wonderfully electric. Kim and I like to think we are hip, young peers, but in reality, we could be the staff's mom and dad. (We're grandparents, for goodness' sake. I've got the aching joints and gray hair to prove it.) Only Nia, in her mid-thirties, possessed specific training and real-world experience in her field. And we could be her mom and dad too.

I love each one of the GLT members dearly. I marvel at the way God has assembled us. I'm reminded of how Jesus gathered His disciples. He chose fishermen, tax collectors—ordinary people, maybe even a few scoundrels. When they encountered Jesus as Lord and Messiah, it placed a deep calling in their souls. Each one had a specific reason for leaving the life they had been living, setting down their nets and following Him, learning to become fishers of men. The GLT is the same. Each has their own reason why they follow me as I follow Jesus.

August 27, 2019

Kim and I invited Dan, Maggie, and Mary to the best hotel in town, had tea in the courtyard, and introduced a concept famously presented by Simon Sinek called *Start with Why*. His TED Talk has been viewed over fifty million times in forty-eight languages. Sinek's key idea is "People don't buy what you do; they buy why you do it." It's clarity and optimism have been an inspiration to me. I thought exploring this would help the team learn about each other and themselves.

"Today, we are going to share why we are part of this movement called Maisha Mapya. I'm not talking about 'because I get a paycheck' or 'because I want to make a difference in the community.' I'm asking *why* do you want to make a difference in the community? What brings you here? Is there something about you or your past that makes helping little kids who live in a dump so important?"

I didn't expect it, but silence was their first answer. Every eye looked down solemnly. It was as if they wanted to disappear. I didn't know that answering would mean ripping the Band-Aid off their hiding place of pain. It would take courage to bring to light their innermost hurts and wildest dreams.

My eyes were down too, but it was because I was praying, asking God for Kim and me to be a place of refuge—a safe place to discuss history's deep wounds, which we all shy from uttering out loud. Their pain was too great to bring them to life.

Often, we bury our hurts, hoping to render them powerless, only to find the opposite happens. The devil stores them in the recesses of our minds, poised to discourage and shame us at any moment. It was time to have the boldness to look directly into the source of our torment, trust God, and open up so the things inflicted upon us, and even things we've inflicted on others, could heal.

As the team sat motionless, Kim and I sat in reflection, giving them time to muster the courage to start. Our tea got cold.

Finally, I detected the softest voice imaginable coming from Maggie. She was perhaps the most natural leader on the team and blessed with incredible instincts.

"Um, okay." She looked up for a split second. Back down. And halfway up again. "I grew up thinking being a Christian was about being kind, not getting into trouble, going to church, singing in the choir, and being on time. Ever since our first walk through the dumpsite, seeing the people's conditions and witnessing how to love a person, I wanted to know how to do that. When Roberto asked for some help with his house, which was only a lean-to covered with paper and plastic, Maisha Mapya helped him. To hear his desperate cry to Jesus to remove the alcoholism, to see you all comfort him, accept him without judgment, and pray with him changed my life. You welcomed him amid his filth and brokenness. He is the least of these whom Jesus talks about. Right then, I knew this was a place where I could serve my God."

Her eyes glazed over with deep reflection. I got the sense she wasn't through, so I waited before saying, "Good job." She was peeking into those dark corners of her mind where she only went to in the middle of the night. Maggie sat up straighter, raising her chin. God strengthened her.

She paused, absorbed in memory, and started slowly. "Okay, I grew up in a house where I didn't know my father. My mom tried to raise me, but she was always having a struggle with money. So, I lived with my grandparents."

Her eyes welled up. She forced the words out, daring to enter into vulnerability and defeat the ghosts that, at times, rendered her paralyzed.

"There wasn't much love in the house. I went to public school, and you know how that is. There's no love there, only discipline and fear. I grew up without love." I could see her battling the protective numbness she so carefully built over the years.

"When I see these kids at Maisha Mapya and know where they come from and what life is like for them, I just have to be here. There is no other place. I want to be the love for them I never got. This is my home." The conviction in her voice made this an anthem echoed by the resolve on her face.

Maggie's strength to step into her hurt and her desire to conquer it was one of the most admirable things I have ever seen. She took the risk to talk about her greatest sadness. Having experienced a similar upbringing and then bravely dealing with the memories the schoolchildren's suffering digs up made Maggie a hero to me.

My tears rippled in my cup of tea. I could relate in a small way to growing up in a house where love was lacking. My mom's bipolar-fueled rants and "you were a mistake anyway" reminders were always on the tip of the devil's tongue to inflict pain.

I meant to speak at full volume, but in nearly as soft a voice as hers when she began, I said, "Thank you, Maggie. You belong here. You are home. We love you." Kim scooted over and rubbed Maggie's back.

Dan gathered himself and started. His words came out quiet. "My Dad passed when I was two."

He'd never divulged that to me. Not in three years. It was like a rhino stomped on my chest. I wasn't sure I could take another heartbreaking story.

"My mum had so much on her plate. With all my siblings, we couldn't afford school fees. So I just spent time in the community, and sometimes well-wishers and neighbors helped. I was a community kid."

He said "community kid" as though it was a title. Without question, it was a label. Did it mean being a tossed-aside child and raised by anyone in the neighborhood who could care for him? Is that why Dan was so sensitive to disappointing anyone?

"I was a talented student, got good marks, and got a chance to have a sponsor send me to school, even college." (Dan graduated from Egerton University with a double major in chemistry and physics.)

"But I was a community kid." I could see him picturing the Maisha kids in their homes. "So when I look at all of our little guys, I know just how they feel. I want to make a difference in their lives. I just love the kids so much. I want to be like their big brother or uncle and be there for them. I just love them so much. No one was there for me. I just love them so much."

With that, he sat back in his chair and folded his hands in his lap. He kept it brief, perhaps because he had been with us longer than Maggie by a few years and was already in the healing process. He truly is the kids' uncle in spirit. He is known as Uncle Dan to a few thousand kids in the community too because his heart has grown around all "those little guys" to protect and nurture them. He truly does "just love them so much." At times, I'm astonished Dan has all this pain bottled up inside him because laughter lies just underneath his skin. He's a fun-filled, joyful guy who loves to laugh and make others laugh too.

Mary looked away and remained silent the entire time. I could see her wheels spinning, trying to figure out how she could say anything or maybe, just maybe, how she could get out of it.

Mary had only been a classroom teacher with us for one week

when the school's head teacher texted us he was not coming back to work. Then he vanished without a trace. When the education ministry officer learned we didn't have a certified head teacher, he threatened to close Maisha Mapya if we couldn't find a qualified replacement immediately. We were in a jam. For our kids, no school means days spent back in the dump.

Only one person on our staff had the credentials, the coveted P1 designation, necessary to be a primary school's head teacher. It was newcomer Mary. Out of desperation, we offered her the job even though she had no administrative training or experience. I wasn't even sure what grade or subjects she taught. All that mattered was keeping the school open. I knew nothing about her personal background, work history or certifications, or what she must have been thinking of this twist of fate. Mary took a day to pray about it. "The kids need me. I'll do it," she said.

Since then, she has proven herself time and time again, meeting every challenge put in front of her. I've never regretted the decision, not for a second. What seemed like dire straits now seemed like providence.

Mary is always eager to learn and fearless to try. Voicing her "why" was no exception. However, it might have been the biggest challenge I had seen her confront. It might be easier to take on the unknown of more responsibility on the job than to come to grips with the deep wounds of one's life.

Ever poised, her petite frame sat tall, and she held her chin high. She addressed us in her characteristic, "Hellewww." Usually, we laugh, but this time everyone remained dead silent.

She paused, raised just a bit more, and set her shoulders back. "I grew up in a family where . . ." Pause. Head up. Shoulders back.

"My mom . . . my dad . . ." She surveyed the team seated around the table and tried to speak, but no more words were uttered.

I wanted to say, "It's okay, Mary, you don't need to share." But then I recognized she might need to release her pain more than I needed to rescue her from taking it head on.

"My mom became pregnant in her second year of high school. The man didn't marry her. She married someone else. And that man never accepted me as his own."

It amazed me that her expression didn't change because my nostrils were tingling and the corners of my mouth were quivering.

"He treated me differently than his kids. He always belittled me, sometimes never fed me, even when my siblings got enough food."

I wanted her to stop. She never flinched. Her emotions had been crushed to the point of numbness.

"He said, 'you'll never be anything. Never. Women are only good for one thing. You will never be anything! Do you hear me? You're nothing!'"

That's when her tears began. Mine had already started. My heart sank further as she said, "I don't know why I have tears. I've learned not to cry, no matter how much he hurt me. I cry inside my heart, never outside."

"I told him, 'Daddy, I want to be a teacher.' 'You'll never be a teacher. Never. Never. Forget that. You will never be a teacher. You will never be anything,' was all he ever said. And he repeated this over and over."

Like a porcelain doll, her face never changed expression. Head up and shoulders back, a steady stream flowed down her cheeks.

"I still hear those words. They haunt me."

She squared up once more, and with a penetrating stare, she turned and faced me. "I will never let you down. Not ever!" She gathered herself again and proudly stated as if her stepdad could hear, "Now, I'm a teacher."

"And a good one, Mary. Even more than that, you are our head teacher! Two hundred beautiful kids can attest to that," I said.

I got the sense this may be the first time she verbalized what motivated her. She ventured into the graveyard of her long since buried public cries of pain. And with her new family surrounding her, she dared to trust them with her secrets. They were off her chest now, out in the open, where light and love could bring healing. God was making Mary who she was born to be.

"If you allow, I'd like to share" were the words escaping from my mouth. I didn't intend to say anything. I was there to support the team and do the whole Simon Sinek thing. My wounds were going to stay hidden, where they belonged. But God had different plans.

"It might surprise you that I wasn't born into a Christian home. My parents never took me to church as a kid." Then I blurted it out. "I don't even know if my mom and dad ever loved each other. What I do know is they didn't want me."

Maggie's jaw dropped. Mary's eyes widened.

"My mom was forty when I was born, my dad forty-six. He drank too much. My mom was manic-depressive; it's called bipolar today. When she hit menopause, her tirades were epic. She was always angry, and I never knew why. I just knew it was my fault. All I remember is her calling me a swear word I will not share, but she called me it so often I responded to it and even believed it was my name."

Kim knows the name and the pain it causes me.

"For over two years, she never got out of bed. She would just summon me in to stand at the foot of the bed, and then curse at me at the top of her lungs. Over and over it was, 'You were a mistake!' I'd turn to leave the bedroom. 'Get back in here, [expletive], I'm not done! You are a mistake!' My mom didn't want me. My dad didn't know how to deal with her, so he stayed out as much as he could. I tried to get away too but couldn't escape. I didn't belong in my family."

I wanted to spare the team from any more details, so I switched the tone to how I tried to fix the problem.

"Maybe if I was rich and accomplished, I could win the

affection of my mom. I buried myself in chasing success. I was good at it. I was the youngest stockbroker to go through training. I made lots of money. I partnered with my best friend. We made even more money. After thirteen years, he walked in one day and said, 'I'm taking the business from you.' With those words, everything collapsed. My income. My identity. The entire kingdom I had built around myself to protect against the hurt of being a mistake. To me, my success proved I wasn't a mistake. It proved I was better than you. It proved I was better than everyone. But it all disappeared in an instant. Wall Street wasn't my home either."

Dan's pained expression looked as if he had just lost everything too.

"Kim and I took our kids and moved to a small town. I walked into a church for the first time and heard the gospel. I got baptized. Seven months later, the Lord sent me on a trip here. I saw the kids in the dump and thought maybe I was here to help these kids. Maybe I wasn't a mistake. We started a school with a Kenyan partner, you know who they are, and it was stolen from me just like my Wall Street business. To me, it was a sign that maybe I never belonged here either."

"So how did Maisha Mapya happen, Daddy?" Mary asked.

"God told me to start over. At first, I told him, 'No, find someone else. I quit.' I gave all the money in the foundation away to help others except for $273. Yet God insisted. He made a promise, 'Do it again. Kids will be in school in three months.' He said to me, 'You won't be alone. I'll be with you.' So I did. I told my pastor, the man who discipled me for seven years. Every week for three hours, he poured into me. I was his Timothy. He was my pastor, mentor, and friend. I told him of my heartache of losing the school. I told him about the burden God gave me to do it again. I was obsessed. God made me a prophet with a message the church needed to hear. Only my pastor got to a point where he didn't want to hear about poor kids in Kenya anymore. So much so that one day, he told me, 'There's no place for you to use your gifts in my church.'"

Maggie and Mary shook their heads. Kim grabbed my hand and placed it in her lap.

"Being kicked out of church hurt more than my business partner stealing my livelihood. It hurt even more than my mom calling me horrible names and telling me I was a mistake. If your spiritual father kicks you out of God's family, where do you go? What do you do? I didn't belong there either. I felt like I didn't belong anywhere. I was super angry again."

I took a deep breath and continued. "Then God placed me here to create a place of belonging where everyone who doesn't belong anywhere belongs. Everyone is welcome here at Maisha Mapya, whether a drunkard, prostitute, abuser, gang member, washed up stockbroker, kicked out disciple, or whatever. Maisha Mapya is where I belong. It's my home on earth too Maggie."

We all sat for a bit, exhausted from the emotional marathon. We each had shared a few of our deepest secrets. I'm sure there were more we kept hidden. But the facades we'd so carefully constructed and maintained experienced their first strike.

Psalm 56:8 says Jesus collects all our tears in a bottle and that He records each one in His book. Enough tears streamed down my face to fill a jerrican, and Jesus wrote several chapters about tears that day. One thing was clear: each of us had encountered Jesus. And God was building a team from ordinary, broken people of immeasurable value to love other broken people in this small corner of the world.

THE START

October 13, 2020

GROUNDHOG DAY. No sleep. 5:30 a.m. alarm. Joe smiles. Head downstairs to breakfast.

Ayanna was poised, standing at her station. She escorted us to our table near the open window. The cool fresh air, lush green garden, and singing birds welcomed a new day.

Joe ordered, maintaining direct eye contact and employing a new strategy. "I would like . . ." His speech was so slow I wondered if he guzzled some Benadryl while I was showering. "Two eggs, over easy." He raised two fingers like a peace sign and smiled for confirmation. "Not well done," he said, slowly shaking his head. Next, he made a level gesture with a flat hand. "On brown, wheat toast." Peace sign. "Just two slices. Some bacon. And mango juice." Vigorously shaking his head, he added, "Noooo tomato." One final smile and Joe added, "Thank you."

With all these hand signals, it looked like he was a third-base coach telling the server to lay down a bunt. Even I was confused about what he wanted. Ayanna must have been thinking he had a speech impediment. I couldn't wait to see if it worked.

His order came complete with two eggs, two pieces of brown

toast, bacon, sausage, a pancake, and of course, a grilled tomato with a rosemary sprig.

"Progress, Joe, progress, but you must still be too skinny."

"Not according to my belt," he said, patting his tummy.

I got three pots of mixed tea. And a takeaway.

Wasili Wally was in full engagement mode and right on time, 7:30 a.m. He was enjoying being overpaid by 50 percent every day. And he was happy to milk the cow a bit more. Plus, I think he enjoyed being around people who appreciated him.

He shouted, "Wafula! *Twende kazi.* Let's go to work!" We sped off to Maisha Mapya in his shiny pink car.

Each day upon arriving at school, I try to greet every staff member. If there are visitors or parents on campus, I enjoy welcoming them too. My sweet wife taught me to do this. She said it was a loving thing to do.

I always begin in the kitchen. This was in a separate building from the rest of the staff, and they often felt neglected. Florence is our head chef. She is emotional, joyful, worshipful, and best of all, knows what every kid likes to eat. Cooking is not a job to her. It's a chance to love the neighborhood kids who need food. During the month-long breaks, she insists on coming to school and cooking. "What else would I do, Daddy Dave? Sit home and wait for school to open again?" Even though we're only a few years apart in age, her affectionate use of "Daddy Dave" conveys her respect for me as being the father of this place.

When we opened our first school together over ten years ago, Flo's entire kitchen consisted of a small wooden shack with one dented five-gallon aluminum pot balanced on three rocks with a few smoldering sticks as fuel. The fumes, backbreaking work, and sparse kitchen never stole her joy as she prepared meals for her neighbors' children.

Today, she has a bright, modern space with ample pots, utensils, and three giant, shiny steel *jikos* that sit on the floor and are waist high—everything needed to feed one thousand hungry people in a single sitting. Flo and her crew have served over one million meals since 2014. She's earned the title of "governor"; more specifically, "the governor of the stomach." She and the crew dish up the tastiest food in town, whether it was a simple mug of *uji* (porridge) or a robust plate of beef stew, shredded cabbage, carrots, boiled potatoes, and *ugali.*

Flo was born in Hilton and has lived here all of her fifty years. She's seen Mama Amon rise to power and become an agent of fear. Five days after the gang attacked Angel and the Shosh, she stumbled upon the two bloody corpses lying in the street on her way to school. She couldn't even talk about it except for a few murmurs. "I don't know what's happening, Daddy. Sometimes I'm scared to leave my house." It was almost beyond what she could bear.

From the first day Maisha Mapya opened, she has brought her son Rooney to school. The cute pint-sized two-year-old wearing a fleece beanie tied under his chin was our unofficial school mascot. Now he's one of the tallest children in our grade-one class. When he turned four, he put on a school uniform and became a student at Maisha, and like Linus with his happiness and security blanket, Rooney kept his trademark cap for a while. The massive smile on Flo's face seeing her youngest boy in the school gear meant there was a chance for a better life for Rooney than she had.

Flo's lifelong best friend, Ruth, got the job to assist in the kitchen. Ruth can chop a head of cabbage like it's nobody's business—and without a Ginsu knife. She is quiet at times, which only makes her more dangerous because she's a little prankster. She is the main instigator to live out the Kenyan tradition of "washing" a staff member on their birthday. She uses Flo as a decoy who engages the victim in a conversation and then sneaks up behind them and dumps a pail of cold water on their heads. It doesn't matter if it's inside their office or not. If it's your birthday, you're getting "washed." I always keep an eye on her when on campus on July 6—my birthday.

Our third member of the kitchen crew is James Wafula. If the name sounds familiar, it's because that's where the "Wafula" in

Daudi Wafula Kamau originates. He is a young, strong, and gentle guardian of all the kids in school. He loves being called Uncle Jemo. He's a good sport and allows me to joke, calling him "Chakula Wafula" since he works in the kitchen (*chakula* is Swahili for food). Jemo lives in a small house on the property and is our gracious, friendly, campus host.

I walked upstairs and poked my nose into the classroom to see how the teachers were doing with the Christian virtue curriculum assignment I laid in their laps. Collins, one of our new teachers, was at the chalkboard outlining the lessons. The other teachers were surveying the board and offering suggestions. I wiggled my eyebrows and smiled. They wiggled and smiled back at me. I pulled my nose out of their business and rushed to the hall to meet the GLT.

At 8:00 a.m., the team filed into the hall and got right down to business. We pounded out some refinements in our accountability chart. I knew the topic was dry, but I may as well have been talking to myself. In place of the usual playful banter was dead air. The tense atmosphere in the room was communicating more than any of the five people sitting around the table. They barely acknowledged each other.

I tried to refocus them on something important. Something that bound us together.

"Any word from Angel?"

"No, Dave, nothing."

It was the strangest, most disconnected time we'd ever had together. When the excruciating hour was over, we adjourned the meeting, and it was time for Dan and me to meet with the Chief.

The Chief strode in, dressed in slacks and a sweater instead of his combat fatigues. When he dresses in camo pants, forest green shirt, knee-high boots, beret, crop, and is flanked by police officers, people fear unknown consequences. The show is meant to intimidate, and it works. Even when he's not wearing his military uniform, he casts a presence. He strutted past reception, Maggie's office, and Nia's desk, and sat down in Dan's office without saying a word.

I wasn't sure this was the perfect moment to launch the dream God placed on my heart three years ago. With all the violence and economic devastation happening in Nakuru, maybe this was, in fact, the worst time ever. But with only nine days until my flight left and having the Chief's attention, I went for it.

Since that first trip in 2007, I've watched people with good hearts reach out to help the community. But mostly, their approach had been the same. An endless series of one-off acts of kindness, like sponsoring a child to go to boarding school or helping a grandma see the doctor. It's a loving gesture and makes a difference to one person at that moment in time. It is a good thing. But it doesn't change the overall staggering conditions of the slum. And usually, it flows through Mama Amon's sticky fingers, watering down the effectiveness. People have been living in this dumpsite for over sixty years, and there are more people here than ever before.

Every chance I had the Chief's ear, I'd cast the vision of forming a community council that would identify and address our problems, explore solutions, and access resources with a focus on resolutions coming from within the community. The community members themselves needed to attack the mindset of despair defining our people.

Introducing a new entity was going to be tricky. Two sets of often conflicting authorities were already in place. One formal— the existing government. The other an informal, complex hierarchy of influential individuals and elders. The government may mandate an action, but if the community doesn't agree, nothing gets done.

The council would be solely community-driven. There would be no government involvement, no officials, or their surrogates sitting at the table. In the eyes of many residents, nothing but empty promises and a twisted sense of justice had come from the politicians. They feared the brutality corruption brought. Shosh not getting the time of day at the police station was a shining example. Plain and simple, if anyone outside the ordinary, unconnected, resident was involved, many people wouldn't trust it. But we had to thread the needle of not upsetting both sets of power. We needed a system where the entire community would buy in for it to rise to the level I dreamed of.

A part of the Chief is always curious about what God will do through Maisha Mapya. There's an attraction to the goodness that radiates from Maisha, thanks to God's anointing. But there's another side of having the love of 15,000 of the most unruly people in Nakuru that put Maisha Mapya in a potentially threatening position to those in power. We have influence. But I knew if the area became more peaceful, prosperous, and loving, it would make the Chief's life easier. Also, the transformation would take place under his watch. The Chief would build a powerful legacy.

I swallowed, asked for God to pave the way, and said, "Chief, if you allow me, I think it's time to form the Maisha Mapya Community Council. I wanted you to know I will take the team, go into the community, and have them select their representatives."

He didn't change his expression.

"I also want to meet with the groups causing the violence." I made sure not to use the word "gangs." Still no reaction one way or the other on the Chief's face.

"These past few months must have thrown so many challenges at you. I can't even imagine." I was alluding to the murders that had taken place—of course, without using the words "murder" or "gangs."

He folded his arms across his chest and slouched. "Yes. We have encountered a few, some small problems."

Small problems? I would hate to know what he considered big issues.

The Chief slapped both hands on his legs, sat up, sighed, and said, "Well, I guess that's it." He stood and strolled out of Dan's office. We followed his lead. As we walked past Nia's desk, he stopped, turned around, and tapped three times on her desk, and pointed at her laptop. "I need one of these."

You've gotta be out of your mind. My mouth calmly said, "Well, I could draft a proposal and present it to our Board of Directors for approval. Because these laptops aren't mine, they belong to the organization. And as you know, the mission of Living Stone is to help the people in the dumpsite. I'm not sure providing a laptop to a government official would be within their mandate, but I can ask."

He responded, "Oh, it's not for me."

I tilted my head and furrowed my brows.

"It's for my daughter."

I repeated the same story.

He paused for a moment. When the stalemate ended, he walked out—sans laptop.

It was a huge victory. Oh, not a win in the chess match over a laptop. I had permission to do what I needed to do—meet with the gangs, organize our council, and have free rein to roam the community and do what I do, which is to follow Jesus wherever He leads.

We met for a quick GLT session to set goals for the term and year. Instead of dreams, the only thing that was set was the team, into their various cliques. The three musketeers, Dan, Maggie, and Mary, sat so close they were almost in the same chair. Joel placed himself around a corner next to them. And Nia was off in exile. A full seat and a half between her and the rest of the team marked the border. Dan's comments of "there's an issue with Nia" had been ringing in my ears. And now seeing them this way was stinging my eyes and beginning to break my heart. It may have seemed like a small thing. But when there is a fissure in the family dynamic, dads notice.

The session was scheduled to discuss forward-looking dreams, but my goal focused on God revealing what in the world was going on with my beloved staff.

Lord, give me eyes to see the raging invisible battle and the wisdom to know what to do about it.

I did more listening and observing than I did teaching during the session. I think we were all glad when the meeting adjourned.

At 11:00 a.m., we ended the meeting. Dan, Joel, Smiling Joe, and I prepared for our first journey into Gioto to get buy-in for the community council idea.

Gioto is a Kikuyu word meaning "a place of garbage." For those residing outside Gioto, the definition includes everything there, the trash, medical waste, broken glass, raw sewage, wild animals, grandmas raising orphans, young widows with nowhere else to go, predatory men, and even the little children. The stigma of calling Gioto home is crushing. I am dead set on changing that. The people who live in the dumpsite are made in God's flawless image and are dearly loved by Him and by me.

People in Nakuru avoid going anywhere near Gioto. The severity of the conditions is scary. But it's the area's reputation for theft, drug abuse, prostitution, and muggings that build a moat of fear around the castaways in Gioto and the civilization of Nakuru. A recent TV spot stated Al Shabaab terrorists had a hideaway there, including a video of a friend of mine as the ringleader. The day after the broadcast, he saw me at the dumpsite and greeted me with laughter, "Daddy Dave, did you know I'm Osama bin Laden's cousin?"

Now our neighborhood was infamous for murder. The victims' blood still runs in the streets. There was no reason to ever go there in the first place. And now with people fearing for their lives, would anyone ever come to help? Or was it truly up to us?

I've discovered a surprising beauty lying within the dumpsite community. I've witnessed the most unbelievable acts of generosity between members. People with one scrap of food will tear it in half and give it to a neighbor who has none. Maybe they do it because each one knows what it means to be without, so if they have something that can help someone else right now, they will give it.

Often, they live out the story in Luke 21 in a most beautiful way when the poor widow gave only two small coins to God. To outsiders, the gift looked inconsequential. But it was everything she had. Jesus looks directly into our hearts and says the widow had given more than even the rich people who filled the collection plate out of their surplus. She gave her entirety.

So why do I hoard things? Why do I feel that I do not have enough—yet? What am I waiting for before I have the generosity equal to that of the poorest among us?

Unified by their struggle, the dump residents are the most harmonious group around Maisha Mapya. Maybe it's because in your desperation, you reach a point in your life where you have hit rock bottom and have nowhere else to go. And you end up living in a dumpsite, realizing not one single person on earth cares about you. Everyone around you is in the same boat, so you come together as a family. Then the community accepts you, and you are not judged. It's a place, although unbearable, you feel belonging. It serves as an inspiration to me and confirms the importance of creating a place of belonging for everyone. That concept is at the heart of Maisha Mapya.

Preparing to visit our friends in Gioto again, Hillary unlocked and swung the front gate open. A red tuk-tuk with a crumpled side panel and torn vinyl roof chugged up the cobblestone driveway spewing black smoke before it stopped in front of the hall. During the pandemic, the hall served as a storeroom for vast quantities of food purchased from Joe's organization, Kapu—just under eight tons a month or about eighty thousand meals.

Joe wasted no time tossing more than his fair share of twenty-five-pound sacks into the teeny three-wheeled bucket of bolts.

Yesterday, Joel informed the community about this meeting. We've learned if we announce a meeting over forty-eight hours in advance, they won't show up. To them, life is one long emergency, and they focus only on what is immediately in front of them, whether it be food, a health crisis, or a community gathering.

I hadn't been to Gioto since Kim and I left on February 18,

2020, before COVID-19 locked everything down. As we passed through the slum and entered the dumpsite, the methane produced by the rubbish had self-combusted and was on fire again, and the smoke burned my eyes. It always does. Over the years, I'd grown accustomed to the stench of the trash, and I didn't notice it anymore. Only when I was in a different area of town, maybe the Rose Diamond or Java, after having been in the dumpsite all day did it come to my attention. I didn't smell it myself. I was made aware of it by the disgusted looks I got from others—like I hadn't bathed in a month. All over town, I got literal stink eye from everyone.

Today, I was on a mission to introduce the idea of the council and win their participation. Passing out food was a means to get them to gather. It shocked me to see how thin my friends were. The men were always wire-thin and strong from the combination of manual labor all day, followed by consuming near-lethal amounts of alcohol each night. But now there was no meat underneath their skin. I could see their ribs outlined through the worn cloth of their shirts. I thought the three-quarters of a million meals we provided since March would sustain them, but obviously it was not enough.

One hundred twenty people greeted us, including two men in their seventies dressed in tattered sport coats, along with a forty-year-old dude wearing a baseball helmet. Not one person wore a mask. Unlike the rest of Nakuru, no protocols or restrictions were enforced in the slums. Lack of education and resources, like masks, soap, and water, leave them vulnerable to whatever disease is raging, not just COVID-19. Since most in Gioto earn a quarter a day, why would they spend money on a mask when they don't have enough money to afford rice and beans?

Joel addressed them, speaking Swahili at such a pace I lost track after he said, "I'm Joel."

The translation happening in my head said, "How exactly do you form a community council? Why would they listen to me? Who am I, a white, former stockbroker, to do something like this?

Is the reason no one else took this approach because it doesn't work?"

Joel took a step back, placed his arms at ease and turned to me. "Daudi." It signaled, "You're up!"

Two quick blinks and a look skyward. *Words, God, give me words.*
"Give them your heart," was His reply.

As I looked at them, all gathered orderly and fully attentive, I saw hope.

My eyes connected with a gentleman with gray hair, just like mine. I asked if he would pray to open the meeting. He smiled, as though given a great honor, removed his faded Cleveland Indians baseball cap, bowed his head, and spoke to God.

Simultaneously, I was silently asking Jesus for the words to say because even though I'd dreamed about this day for years, my mind was blank.

"Thank you for meeting with us today. You know we love you." Joel translated for me.

"We love you too," was heard at various volumes from a few in the crowd.

"God has sent me here to bring us together as one community. He wants me to tell you something, down deep, you already know, but don't want to hear: a handout big enough to feed all of you, house all of you, educate your kids and grandkids is not coming. It's not coming. A handout big enough is not coming. It's not coming from the government. It's not coming from us at Maisha Mapya. It's not coming. A handout big enough is not coming."

A few glanced at the tuk-tuk full of Kapu food knowing it might keep them alive for a week, but not forever. They knew of the broken vows from the politicians who always promised things would get better in exchange for their vote. They also knew that Maisha Mapya didn't have room to educate all their children.

"Many of you have been here for a long time. You've seen how things go. People come and make promises and never follow through. Or handouts go through people who take the biggest portion for themselves. Then what little is left over is given to the rest of you." They knew exactly who I was talking about.

"Plus, I know you don't want to live off handouts. You want the satisfaction of providing for your kids. You want dignity. You want respect."

The gray-haired gentleman stood at full height and filled his lungs.

"Also, violence has increased so much and you know the government can't keep you safe either. It's time we made things better ourselves. We've gotta do this ourselves. And we have to do it now. This is our moment! We want to gather everyone— everyone from the six communities around Maisha Mapya—and decide what kind of society we want to be. Next Tuesday, we'll have a meeting with representatives from each neighborhood. We'd like you to select an elder man, an elder woman, a younger man, and a younger woman to represent Gioto and have a voice at the table."

They erupted into applause and roared, "Yes! Yes!"

One of the old men in a sport coat turned, raised his arms, and addressed the crowd. I'm not sure of all he said. But they all shook their heads to agree. Then he said a word I knew, "*Tuombe*," which means "Let us pray." Every hat came off, some brought praying hands to their faces, others folded them or placed them behind their backs, and every head bowed. He led his community in prayer for God to bless this council and make it happen.

God had not abandoned me. He hadn't abandoned my friends. He filled their hearts with His Spirit and longed to hear from them.

As we left, the dude in the baseball helmet cruised up beside me. He lifted his T-shirt to show me the homemade knife he had fastened around the waist of his sweatpants.

He said, "We all have something to stab you. Knife. Pangas. It not safe for us. We always attacked. We job dumpsite have a few coins. We all have knife to stick you. Everyone come for us."

Now the baseball helmet makes sense. These people are in a war.

We walk another ten yards, and I hear a familiar sound.

At about one hundred decibels, loud as a freight train, "Da-OOOOO-dee!!! DAUDI LONG TIME!"

It's noon, and Biggie is drunk. It's always uncanny how he can crawl up inside my ear and pound "DAUDI!!" on the drum. Sometimes he follows me for forty-five minutes and repeats the same thing over and over and over. "Da-OOOOO-dee!" Rather than coming to rescue me, the GLT members usually laugh and shake their heads at the game.

"I'M HUNGRY!"

No Biggie . . . you're drunk. And hungry.

Biggie is only "big" because of his voice. He's about six inches shorter than me and fifty pounds lighter. He's lost a frightening amount of weight since February. The sight of his baggy pants barely staying on his bony hips imprinted deep within me. *My friends are starving.* And it's more important than ever to come alongside them. When you see someone you love hurting, you want to help.

Biggie has a special place in my heart because he is always kind to me, despite being really loud. We have a unique relationship. He can suck the life out of me after a three-quarters-of-an-hour walk together with his constant demands at HIGH VOLUME. But in some strange way, I miss him when he's not at my side in the dumpsite. We walked a few yards. He staggered left, split off from me, and headed toward his home, reciting his happy "Daudi is here" cheer and pumping his fist in the air.

Ten minutes later, and back at Maisha Mapya, I enjoyed my three-minute lunch break. A grass-fed Slim Jim and an RXBAR —no mixed tea this time. Either I'm getting adjusted to the time, or the adrenaline was kicking into overdrive and there was no need for a caffeine boost.

Joe ate the same meal Florence prepared for the students— ugali, cabbage, and beans. I envied his iron stomach. Between bites, Joe said, "Remember when I toured Gioto with the Kapu team last year and asked how you got the people to embrace you? Now I get it. You treat them with dignity. You treat them with respect. You love them, and they love you back."

Before I could respond, my phone rang.

Then my heart stopped, and the room faded to empty as I recognized the caller ID. It was the same number who messaged me days before. It's Anonymous! Clicking accept, I heard the voice for the first time. A raspy, masculine voice talked over the pandemonium in the background. I heard some Swahili. Maybe it was a mother tongue. "Daudi, guys heard Mama Amon was back and without guards. Seventy grabbed pangas and went after her. Somehow, like vapor, she vanished."

Before I could respond, he hung up. I wanted to call him back and ask, "Can I meet you? Can I meet the gangs? Are you going to come out of the shadows?" But I didn't want to spook him.

Mama Amon is like a ghost, only creepier. How was all this commotion going on when I was just there? I can't believe she's flying around on her broom still taunting everyone.

All I knew was my plane was leaving in nine days and I was no closer to helping anyone. All afternoon I wondered if I came all this way for nothing. *Am I too timid to not call Anonymous back?*

At 5:15 p.m., it was time to head to dinner. Wally pulled the car in front of Maisha, and Joe and I rushed to Java to meet Kelsey. Joe was really in for a treat tonight. He was going to hear things that only happened in movies.

Hempstone, with menus in hand, led us to a table outside. I hoped the dust and car exhaust wouldn't be too overpowering. Soon after we sat down, Kelsey and her nine-year-old daughter Kat, which is short for Katie, joined us. Kelsey is another of my heroes. Plus, she and Kim are best buds and have a lot in common. Both are faithful, bold, beautiful daughters of the King.

Hempstone returned, twirling a pen between his fingers while holding a tablet of paper.

"What's on the menu tonight, Wafula? Grilled chicken breast, white rice, steamed veggies, and a double masala tea?"

"Perfect, except no tea, please. I think I've stolen all the caffeine from Nakuru already. Make it a *dawa*, kindly." (*Dawa* means medicine in Swahili and deliciously combines hot lemon juice, fresh ginger, and a healthy dose of honey.)

"Two or three scoops of ice cream?"

Now he was just teasing me.

He turned to the others and took their order, not writing a single word. Then repeated our total order back to us perfectly. He walked away, writing it down to hand to the kitchen.

Joe did what Joe does. He sat with an engaging smile as our conversation began.

Leaning on the table, I wasted no time. "Kelsey, I want to meet the gang leaders."

Without hesitation and with a simple nod, she said, "I think we can make that happen."

Joe's mouth opened wider and wider as he looked around to see if anyone else heard it. The idea that a white woman with a daughter would know how to contact gang members, let alone get them to meet me, blew his mind. Joe must have thought she was a member of a crime task force or something. He jumped up from the table. "May I take a picture? I've got to remember this moment."

I wished I could have gotten a picture of *his* reaction. Like so many things, memory will have to do. But in an instant, hope ignited!

I did not know how a mom who was my wife's friend would contact a gang and convince them to meet me either. I was excited the wheels were in motion. And I couldn't sleep a wink. Nine days to go.

THE TRIANGLE

WHY WOULD you sleep when you could toss and turn and relive the first time you encountered a street gang?

There were many firsts for me on the initial mission trip with Cornerstone Fellowship in 2007, but meeting a street gang may have been the topper.

January 2007

Andrew, our thirteen-year-old son, and I drove three hours every other week for three months to Cornerstone Fellowship in Livermore for training sessions. Linda, an old pro at taking mission teams to Kenya, led the ninety-minute meetings.

We enjoyed spicy masala tea and *chapati* (round tortilla-like Indian flatbread made of whole wheat flour and cooked on a griddle). Chapati was brought to Kenya during the colonial period when the British government imported Indian laborers to build railroads throughout East Africa. Linda said chapati is a delicacy and is the highlight of the Christmas dinner celebration. It tasted like a dry, super-dense tortilla to me. When I think of a Christmas meal, I envision honey-baked ham, twice-baked potatoes, scalloped potatoes, cherry pie, pecan pie, ice cream, red and green

M&Ms, chocolate chip cookies, and eggnog. I guess that was the point.

We studied the Kenyan culture, learned a few Swahili words I still struggle to pronounce correctly, and practiced formal introductions. We learned to sing "Hakuna Mungu Kama Wewe," meaning "There's No One Like You, Lord."

We learned games the Kenyan school kids play, like "Have you seen my goat?" To begin, everyone in the group sits in a circle, just like musical chairs. The person who is "it" is in the center of the ring and asks a question to the group beginning with, "Have you seen my goat?" and adds made-up descriptors about the goat that apply to people in the circle. If you wanted to pick on a particular person, you could call their name, like, "My goat's name is Andrew." The person who is "it" must find a seat, and everyone who matches the description must switch seats. It's bedlam. Of course, no one called out "Andrew" because he was thirteen, fast, and enthusiastic. He'd catch you every time. The game usually ends when people get bored or something, or someone, breaks.

We also had handouts, homework assignments, and all sorts of stuff. Mostly we were learning to bond as a family, preparing for an unknown adventure to a faraway land.

One session focused on what life is like for some students at the school. Most of them came from poor rural subsistence farming families. Many had parents who did not survive the global HIV/AIDS epidemic in the '80s. Some children experienced significant trauma from abuse or neglect. Linda mentioned something about a dump, but I never gave it much thought.

Another potentially dangerous visit would be going into the inner-city areas of Nakurutown where the street boys hung out. We'd essentially do the same thing we did in other places in Nakuru—introduce ourselves, sing, share a Bible verse, and eat together. It sounded easy enough.

We seemed ready, but no amount of preparation would have

been adequate for this former stockbroker and Little League coach—some things just have to be experienced.

———

February 16, 2007

Two safari vans were waiting in the Kunste Hotel parking lot for us after breakfast. The team wandered out and scattered, talking in groups of two or three, some scanning the trees looking for the birds with the strange call.

Linda, all five feet of her, stood at full height and called out, "Today, we're going into town to visit some street boys." She explained that gangs are territorial and fight for and defend their turf. The central meeting place for a gang is called their base.

We broke off into two teams of six people, each escorted by a couple of Kenyans experienced in dealing with street gangs and boarded the vans for the ten-minute ride to town. Driving on the wrong side of the road like the Brits is confusing in the best of circumstances, but it can be downright disorienting with streets packed with pedestrians and vehicles. Navigating the roundabout nearly gave me vertigo.

Our van managed not to run over anyone. We parked outside the Elim Curio Centre, named after the oasis where the Israelites stopped during their Exodus from Egypt. It is a place of plenty representing the natural blessings of God, with twelve springs of fresh water and seventy date palm trees to provide food and shade.

The faded green and white awning provided shelter from the blazing sun but made it so dark inside you could barely see. Squinting, I squeezed through the doorway into a dusty room overflowing with stuff displayed on tables and hanging from walls. Once my eyes fully adjusted, I saw a menagerie of wonderful things. Colorful handwoven baskets, Kenyan national flags, African fabrics, each in any size you desire. Brightly painted soapstone plates with the Big Five—the lion, leopard, rhino, African elephant, and Cape buffalo—etched into them filled three giant tables.

A tribute to the Maasai's rite of passage, where teen boys must go into the wilderness and kill a lion with a small club to signify they are now a man, is on display in the corner.

I picked up a black wooden carving of a rhino. "That's ebony," the shopkeeper exclaimed. "Very rare and very, very valuable." So, I set it down and rubbed the black paint off onto my pant legs.

Eerie African masks filled an entire wall. I swear their glares followed me wherever I walked as I made it to the back of the shop into Pastor Bill's "town office." I considered it a victory that I hadn't knocked anything over on the way there.

Pastor Bill and two guys from the shop led us out the secret rear exit. Single file, we tiptoed past a pit latrine with raw sewage splattered about, through the kitchen of a restaurant, and into the streets of Nakurutown. Again, my eyes had to adjust; only this time, it felt like staring into an oncoming car's high beams.

Open-air shops selling everything possible lined the streets. There were shoes, clothes, furniture, newspapers, magazines from the 1990s, watches—anything and everything piled high on top of one another. It was as if the Kenyan version of Walmart had exploded and was lining the streets. Somehow, the merchants could keep track of every transaction writing nothing down. One guy was welding a bedframe using a car battery and some wires. Sparks flew everywhere. I pictured Andrew teaching his little brother how to do it when we got home.

Every eye stopped to stare at the *wazungu* who dared to venture into real Nakurutown far away from the touristy curio shops.

The buzz of the crowd three times as dense as what was in front of Elim Curio Centre made it hard to hear Pastor Bill's instructions. "Okay, here's where we split up. We'll meet up later." His group faded off into the mob to the right.

Our young guide put his hand up and pointed to the left, "Let's go."

We cut across Stage Base, home to one gang. It was a plaza created by a collection of four-story buildings—the tallest buildings in Nakurutown forming a square about the size of two football fields. We walked past our other team already engaging with a group of street boys.

We entered the open-air food market, with mounds of cabbages, maize, avocados, watermelons, and mangos piled six feet high. The countless produce was only outnumbered by the swarms of flies.

I ducked and missed *all but one* dead chicken hanging from the ceiling. While removing goo from the poultry parts out of my hair, Andrew and I fell forty yards behind the group before losing them altogether.

My heart immediately doubled its beat. So did my steps.

"Dad, do you see them? Do you see them, Dad? Where are they? Dad? Dad?"

No, no, no, this isn't happening.

My head was on a swivel. Only an ocean of vendors, their stacks of produce, and busy shoppers as far as I could see lay ahead. I got pressed up against a lady with a large sack of dried beans balanced on her head, trying to cut through the masses.

"Fresh mangos for you and your boy, sir?" one merchant said politely.

Paying no attention to him while waving my hand, "No, no, not now. Thanks. We're in a hurry."

"Your friends went that way, sir."

I looked toward his pointing. Thankfully, I'm taller than the average Nakuruan, and it's easy to spot a herd of white foreigners among a few hundred, maybe thousand, Kenyans. We ran to catch up.

About fifty yards from the gang base, I saw two guards standing at attention like Army MPs flanking the entrance. A bridge made from a wooden door stretched across a ditch full of raw sewage. The guards were muscular, but as I got closer, they got smaller. I realized they were kids, maybe thirteen years old, the same age as my son. They didn't acknowledge us and kept staring at each other as if on duty.

While their behavior said, "'We're soldiers," their uniform spoke of the despair of their lives—a ragged tank top, filthy jeans, a flask tucked in their pants pocket, and armed only with pangas.

The guards pulled the bridge up behind us as we crossed. The message was clear. Nobody was going on or off this island without their permission. There was no escape, no turning back. All of Africa, which seemed so huge on a map, was reduced to a small cement triangle with a deep culvert full of sewage on one side and tall building on each of the others. We were trapped on Triangle Island.

Twenty unruly street kids of various ages and sizes moved in all around us. There were sixteen boys. Every child, except one, had a bottle of glue in hand and would huff it every few seconds. The one who didn't have a bottle in his hands had a bottle shoved in gaps he had in his two front teeth, making it so he could huff glue and have his hands free to do whatever. *I think Linda said something about it in training, but why are these kids sniffing glue?*

I looked at Andrew and then down at my pants and shoes. We were in khakis and golf shirts, looking like we had just gotten off the links. *Why did our leaders make us dress like this?*

The group's biggest guy was sitting on a ledge with one leg still on the ground. His half-lidded eyes moved only slightly to acknowledge us. He looked about thirty. The scars on his face told the story of battles lost. His position in the back of the crowd, surrounded like a lion by the only females, told of his victories.

Outwardly, he looked like he couldn't care less about having us there, but my spirit was telling me to be careful. The smallest little thing might set him off. *Was he sizing me up because I was the largest guy in the group besides him?*

One guard, now with his panga shoved in his waistband, marched in front of the gang, faced us, and said, "I'm Gideon.

Welcome to the triangle." He turned his head to the guy sitting on the ledge. "That's Rambo, the general."

Rambo's brown teeth kept smiling at his ladies, and he might have been making faces; I couldn't tell.

Our leader, also dressed in khakis and a golf shirt with a smile on his face, started clapping his hands and singing, "What a Friend We Have in Jesus." It wasn't even the song we practiced.

Rambo looked down in complete defiance. He didn't even mouth the words to save face.

I clapped and played along, wondering if Andrew and I could make it if we tried to jump across the ditch in case things got out of hand.

We sang a couple more songs and shared a Bible verse. We tried to connect with the kids without success. They probably wondered what we wanted from them. The older the child, the less they engaged with us. It was as though they were too involved in their way of survival to risk something new. Did Triangle Island hold them captive too? Or maybe they were simply imitating their leader?

I didn't know what to do. I felt they didn't know what to do either. So, we passed out some bread and milk. The only girls never moved farther than an arm's length from Rambo. Two of them were breastfeeding their babies. We gave them extra bread and milk.

One more song and a prayer, and it was time to go. Gideon, which means warrior, and the other guard grabbed the bridge, lowered it into place. Single file, we crossed into safety. My heart returned to its regular beat; only it was aching much more than when we first arrived. We waved goodbye and scurried away.

As we were walking back to the town office, one leader named Eddy from Elim Curio saw a kid passed out in a heap of rubbish on the side of the road with a flask still stuck under his nose. He reached down, grabbed the plastic bottle of glue, crushed it in his hand, and threw it as far as he could. Eddy was shaking his head the whole time. I could see the tension between his disgust, heartbreak, and inability to do anything lasting for these children. A few yards ahead, I saw a lady with a child strapped on her back with a big jug of glue pouring it into another street boy's flask.

"What's going on there, Eddy?" I asked.

"She sell *gum* (glue) to *chokora* (street boys). She knows it bad, but what can she do? She need to feed her own kids. It's hopeless."

Later, I asked Pastor Bill why the street kids inhaled glue. He said it was to help satiate their hunger. They could spend the four shillings (less than a nickel) and buy glue, which gets them through the day, or they could buy one piece of bread, which staves off the hunger for only thirty minutes before their stomachs are rumbling again. Plus, it's part of the social interaction of the boys. It's like guys who go to bars. Everyone is hanging out and drinking, so you hang out and drink too. It helps get them through the day, endure the chilly nights, and do the things boys have to do to keep alive on the streets.

"It can't be good for them," I said.

Pastor Bill replied, "Oh, it isn't. It destroys them. It's an organic solvent that dissolves their brain. The kids who are on the street for even six months get permanent brain damage. It weakens their immune system, and most don't live past their twenties." *Brains dissolved by poverty—literally.*

I wanted him to stop talking because each additional word stomped on my heart. One more syllable and I thought I'd start crying tears of blood. But I wanted him to continue so I could better understand the life of these kids and figure out how to help them.

I looked over at my son Andrew, thought about Scott and Kim back at home. *How could I not know about any of this? When I hear of issues in Africa, why do I only picture starving, crying children with flies on them? These kids are God's children, too. Doesn't He care?*

Why do I care so much about what golf score I shoot? Why was it so important I replaced the carpet in our house with hardwood from Brazil? Why was I so much happier when I BBQ'd a ribeye rather than a New York steak?

Why did I look at the stock market and my bank account every day? Why am I not doing anything about this? God was infusing a burden into me.

My heart ached to help them. The shocking image of a ten-year-old child with yellow eyes and a bottle of glue under his nose melting his brain away replaced my eyes' lenses. The vision became ever present. Surely there must be something more we could do than simply fly by, sing some songs, drop off some bread and milk, and be on our way?

It turned out we could. God used that ordeal and thirteen years of devotion to start and grow our ministry. He used it to keep me up for hours tonight. I know it will linger tomorrow. It does every day.

_____

October 14, 2020

I looked at my phone. Two a.m. *Has it really been four hours?* Joe was breathing rhythmically, probably enjoying a peaceful dream.

Even though my body was dead tired, my mind was still spinning. It's a familiar place for me. It's how I know God is about to share something with me. The busyness of my life can drown out His voice. He will wait until I exhaust myself trying to fix it alone or convincing Him of my point of view. I'm thankful I never exhaust Him. But once I surrender relying on my intellect or experience, He will talk, teach, and guide me. It's often in the middle of the night when I'm captive and done doing *my* thing that I quiet down and am ready to listen.

Finally, after tossing and turning and focusing on engaging the gangs, I settled down and prayed.

Lord, is there something you want to tell me? Why can't I sleep?

The trauma of remembering Triangle Island and expectations of Kelsey connecting me with the gangs was drowned out by Dan's warning, "There's a problem with Nia," and the GLT silently yelling at each other. "Get things right with your family first. You're their dad. Lead them. And I'll lead you" is what God put on my heart. The inner demon of division infiltrating my Maisha Mapya family had me poring through His Word the rest of the night preparing for the battle to come. If we couldn't have peace within our own family, how in the world would we establish peace with the thugs outside our gates?

THE MELTDOWN

October 14, 2020

I DID my best not to wake Joe with the sound of the thin paper pages of my Bible turning and the glow from my iPhone flashlight. *How could I have missed the squabbling among the team? Are people that good at concealing things?*

We seemed connected through constant video calls since the beginning of the pandemic. On Mondays, I'd meet with Nia for ninety minutes. Tuesdays it was with Dan for an hour. I'd teach Bible study on Wednesdays. I did not require the GLT to tune in, but they never missed a session. On Thursdays, the entire team assembled for the GLT meeting. And on Fridays, I alternated between community care meetings with Joel and sponsorship meetings with Maggie. Everything was going fine. Problems were getting solved. We'd joke and laugh and get business done. *Was our ability to flourish during a pandemic just some utopian dream in my head?*

From looking at the interaction on the calls since March, there was no sign of trouble. But, seeing the team in person around the table this week, in their cliques, eyes darting around, waiting for the meeting to start so they didn't have to engage certain people, made me wish we were back on the screens. Warning lights on the dashboard of my heart were flashing red.

It might seem strange that I would be so emotional about this division in our team given the severity of events happening around us—children's lives threatened by glue addiction, starvation, disease, and murder.

The fact is I love these young people. They are more than the leadership team of a small nonprofit. They are my family. If the devil can destroy Maisha Mapya and everything it represents, he can further kill the community's hope. *Lord, please do not let this happen. Show me the verses. Have Your wisdom burst forth. Don't let this team destroy each other.*

My Bible is a tale of two cities. The pages in the back, the New Testament, are full of handwritten notes and are soft and worn. The pages in the front, the Old Testament, are mostly crisp and clean. Some are even stuck together.

In the very back of my Bible is this thing called the concordance. For the longest time, I thought it was the *concourse*, like in an airport terminal, which never made any sense. I've always wondered why they don't call it an index like in other books since it's an alphabetical list of important words and where you can find passages on the topic.

I searched for the term "division." It pointed to a verse on page 2190, Galatians 5:15 (NLT). "But if you are always biting and devouring one another, watch out! Beware of destroying each other."

It was as if the author of Galatians had been sitting in our meetings and wrote those words of wisdom directly to us. In reality, the Apostle Paul penned those words over 2,000 years ago. I guess division among people is nothing new.

I stared at the words again. "But if you are always biting and devouring one another, watch out! Beware of destroying . . ."

My alarm sounded and scared me to death. Another night over. Another day ahead—5:30 a.m.

Joe woke from his slumber. He sat up 90 degrees, stretched,

and said a spry, "Good morning!" He looked closer and saw my red eyes and dark circles. It only made his eyes soften more. He didn't say a word. A reaffirming glance conveyed, "I'm here if you need me."

What I needed was a therapist, and some sleep. I'd settle for some mixed tea.

Fortunately, as soon as we entered the restaurant, there was a pot of tea on the way. The sleep would have to wait. And I'm only kidding about the therapist. I took comfort in having the best counselor ever, pouring wisdom, truth, and empathy into me during the night. He fully armed me with the Word of God to take on the day's battle.

We sat at our garden side table for two. Joe folded his hands under his chin, smiled at me, and joked, "Wonder what's on the menu today, Daudi? Maybe I'll just have some cereal?"

He again ordered, using the two-finger, peace sign strategy to denote two eggs, two pieces of toast, and two slices of bacon. Joe was now on an adventure. His curiosity was piqued, wondering what would arrive on the plate.

Like the animals on the ark, items on his plate returned paired two by two—two eggs, two toast, two bacon, two sausages, two pancakes, and of course, two grilled tomatoes, each with a lovely rosemary sprig garnish.

"Still too thin, Joe. You're still too thin."

"Well, my weight is about right if the scale reads the same and I'm six inches taller! I can't eat all this."

"I'll help, Joe. I'll help."

I ate three-quarters of his breakfast and grabbed a takeaway cup. Wally was already waiting.

"Twende kazi, Wafula."

Yep, Wally. Let's go to work.

———

I greeted the kitchen staff. I think they heard me coming because they weren't working as I burst in the door. They were standing, heads tilted, grinning, anticipating the joyful rhythm of my love for them.

Next, I trotted upstairs to meet the teachers. They were giggling, already at work on the compassion curriculum. It appeared they were really enjoying the assignment.

"Daddy Dave, kindly, can you get Teachers Sharon and Charles from their class?" I might have detected a snicker from the teacher with her head down.

"Right away." And down the hallway I hustled toward the fourth-grade classroom. Twenty feet from the entrance, I heard the sound my heart missed so much, the murmur of little children.

My walk turned into a trot, and I poked my head into the doorway and saw a sea of shining faces beaming with glee. I shouted, "Hey! Oooh, I love you!" My arms spread wide as I stood in the middle of the room. "I love you. I love you."

The kids couldn't help themselves. They all sprung out of their chairs, jumping up and down, cheering, "Daddy Dave! Daddy Dave!!" Their poor teachers, both of whom are new to the school, repeatedly instructed the kids to sit down. It was no use. The swarm got tighter and the shouts louder. Most of these children have known me for six years. We have skipped rope together, played tag together, laughed at puppet shows together, and comforted each other through the difficult things in life. The love was overpowering. The teachers surrendered trying to keep order. Now, they were smiling too. Teacher Sharon added a few dance moves for flavor.

Seeing the students looking smart in their blue and white school uniforms, back at Maisha Mapya where they belong, was sweeter than any cup of mixed tea I could ever drink. It increased my resolve to make Maisha Mapya the place God wanted it to be.

"Why are the kids here?" I asked.

Apparently, even with the pandemic raging, the Ministry of

Education issued an order for grades four, eight, and twelve to report to school immediately. Who knows why they picked only those grades. Maybe because they are the ones that the country does national testing on. The reason didn't matter. My heart overflowed with joy. And so did all of theirs.

Having created an ample amount of havoc, I danced out the door so the students could get back to their lessons.

I flew down the stairs to greet the GLT. Seated the same way as all the previous days, in their factions, their expressions were respectful but as cold as ice—a striking contrast from the fourth-grade class's exuberance. That was it. I couldn't take it a second longer. I was in a riptide of heartache, disappointment, bewilderment, and anger. I wanted to scream, "What the heck is the matter with you? Knock it off!"

I looked around one more time and began to speak. I felt my frustration build, then I held up my index finger. "Excuse me. I'll be right back." I turned on a dime and bolted out the door. *Lord, please, please soften my heart. Give me eyes to see. Give me words they need to hear.*

Running upstairs into the admin office, I pulled the large canvas pictures off the walls; each told a story of its own.

I grabbed the bright, beautiful photo showing Teacher Faith at the head of her class with captions reading, "passionate," "dedicated," and "hardworking." I took a heartwarming print of our children dressed in their uniforms with the most welcoming smiles you'll ever see above the words, "We love our neighbors." I could not leave behind the closeup of one of our young girls during an assembly, head bowed, hands folded, the heading, "We love Jesus," on the print. And just for good measure, I snatched another impactful photo of two of our little ones at the dumpsite on a Saturday, stooped down, writing in their composition books surrounded by trash. The caption read, "Education goes with you, no matter where you go." A touching photo of Teacher Richard assisting a student with their classwork. "We are generous." A colorful, fun photo of the entire staff gathered on the staircase, relaxed and smiling. "We are family."

I took them all.

As I sped to the hall, the core values my team helped create from the beauty of the deepest part of their hearts flashed through my mind.

- We love Jesus and live out His love in all we do.
- We are passionate, dedicated, and hardworking.
- We are compassionate and treat everyone with dignity and respect.
- We love our neighbors as ourselves.
- We are generous with time, talents, and resources.
- We are not just a team; we are a family.

And now, the authors of those words could barely look at each other without an undertone of a scowl.

Arms full, I entered the hall and set the canvas prints face up on the table behind me. The GLT members watched my every move. Dan leaned over slightly and whispered something to Mary. Maybe they thought more beautiful artwork was coming? Nia stared straight ahead.

I stood at the whiteboard for the first time all trip and looked around for something to write with.

"May I assist, Dave?" Nia said as she handed me an erasable marker.

Joe sat smiling, waiting to see what I would do.

The GLT shifted in their seats. I drew a box and made a bullet point list.

While my left-handed block printing resembles a preschooler's, my place at the top of our organizational chart declares the significance of my position. It wasn't the scribble that mattered; it was me standing at the board in full authority, scribbling anything at all.

Inside the box were my five primary responsibilities at Maisha Mapya.

- Culture Creator
- Passion Provider
- Major External Relationships
- Fundraiser/Speaker
- Vision Creator and Champion

"These things on the board are my responsibility. Without me doing these, our organization would have a major void. Just like if each one of you isn't doing what's inside your box."

Every head shook in agreement. Class was in session, and the students were taking notes.

"Culture, passion, and vision. The way being part of Maisha Mapya makes you feel, how we treat each other inside and outside the organization is my responsibility. Right now, our culture stinks." I could feel the intensity of my stare.

Their eyes all widened. Maggie dropped her pen. While I had been busy getting mad at the team, God pointed out that they weren't the only ones who were falling short. I had failed too.

"I am letting you down. I've allowed us to lose our heart, forget who we are and how we love each other. How we do things is as important as what we do. The secret sauce of the loving culture at Maisha Mapya has spoiled. It's rotten mayonnaise."

I picked up my Bible and headed to the part I knew well, the back. Words from 2 Timothy 4:1–2 (NLT) flowed through my lips. "'I solemnly urge you in the presence of God and Christ Jesus, who will someday judge the living and the dead when he comes to set up his Kingdom: Preach the word of God. Be prepared, whether the time is favorable or not. Patiently correct, rebuke, and encourage your people with good teaching.' That's what we will be doing today."

They looked shocked to hear uncharacteristically harsh words from me. I sat next to Joe and looked at each family member. "I'm dying. I am watching us dig, undermine, divide, and devour ourselves. I've seen us respond so beautifully to ambushes from the enemy. The devil cannot destroy us. When the devil attacks us and a five-month-old baby dies, we mourn together. When five-year-olds are sexually abused, we seek justice together. When gangs threaten to cut our children's heads off, we circle around the kids, rescue them, and stand together. But what I see here is something that will break us down and rip us apart. A house divided will not stand. The only thing that can beat us is ourselves."

It started with an observation and ended with a plea.

"Galatians 5:15 was written for us at this moment. 'But if you are always biting and devouring one another, watch out. Beware of destroying one another.' We have to stop biting each other. I may not be in charge of much around here, but I am in charge of our culture. We created this set of values not for just how we act, but for what we are inside. When we interview people, we stress our values repeatedly so when the right person hears them, they feel, 'Oh, they are just like me. They think like me. They love like me. I must work here.' That's how God has made this place such a shining light in the community. It's because of who He has made us to be—from the inside out. They are drawn to our love. Since we are all, in our core as believers, full of His light and love, the darkness around us doesn't stand a chance."

I reached behind me and set the first photo on my lap so everyone could see it, the one with Faith addressing her students. "We are passionate, dedicated, and hardworking. We are all of these things now. We are passionate. We are dedicated. We are hardworking. But we are also mean, petty, and divisive."

Conviction ruled over their faces.

As my voice softened, my eyes moistened.

I picked up the next picture, which reads, "We love our neighbors." I took an extra long look at it before turning it around to show the team. It's a photo from two years ago of our joyful kids smiling in the hallway. In it, some of the children were barely older than toddlers. Now they can read, write, tie their shoes, use a toilet, and do so many other things we have taught them. Loving them, nurturing them, and giving them a chance at an abundant life fuels us.

"Aside from being at home sleeping, where do you spend most of your time?" Their heads tilted as they considered the question.

"Who do you spend time with?"

It was strange they were thinking hard about it since they all spend most of their waking hours at Maisha Mapya.

"Isn't it the people to your right and left? They are your closest neighbors. We love our neighbors outside these walls well, but how are we doing with loving the people in this room?"

A couple of heads went down, others crumpled in a full-body slump, and Nia's eyes were leaking.

My face contorted in an effort to hold back tears. All I could see was the entire thing falling apart. My place of belonging was being ravaged.

I picked up the last picture and could hardly get the words out. It was the photo of the entire staff, the GLT, teachers, caretakers, cooks, even Kim and me, standing casually on our colorful stairway. The letters spell out, "We are family." It's short for our expression "We are not just a team; we are a family."

"We're not even a team right now, let alone a family."

Streams of tears flowed from all our faces as my heartbreak became contagious.

Joe was still sitting quietly next to me. I didn't look at him, not even once during my oration. This was a time for a dad to address his kids and say, "Knock it off. Stop it." Nothing else mattered. No one else mattered. This was a family matter.

And just like the God who loves us doesn't just rebuke us and leave us to flounder, I rounded the corner with the team.

"With God's help, we can do better. God has wise words for this too."

I turned to the words of encouragement God had given me throughout the night. I knew them well because I depended on them to get through the hurts of my past.

People can be so vicious. But God, who created everything and everyone, knows the human heart better than anyone. And He has words of wisdom that resonate. It was time to teach them to the team and see if we could repair the fabric of our family.

Colossians 3:12 (ESV): "Put on then, as God's chosen ones, holy and beloved, compassionate hearts, kindness, humility, meekness, and patience."

1 Corinthians 1:10 (NIV): "I appeal to you, brothers and sisters, in the name of our Lord Jesus Christ, that all of you agree with one another in what you say and that there be no divisions among you, but that you be perfectly united in mind and thought."

1 Corinthians 3:3 (NIV): "You are still worldly. For since there is jealousy and quarreling among you, are you not worldly? Are you not acting like mere humans?"

Philippians 2:2 (NIV): "Then make my joy complete by being like-minded, having the same love, being one in spirit and of one mind."

One by one, I held up each picture again. "How are we doing on these values?"

My eyes surveyed the room; a penetrating stare connected with each team member. "Does anyone have anything they'd like to say?"

No one said a word. Not one peep. Not one decibel of noise.

Five minutes went by.

Ten minutes.

I was about to say something because my mind flashed a scoreboard. Devil 1. God 0. We continued to bite each other. This time through silence.

I was failing again.

Fifteen minutes.

At the twenty-minute mark, I could see them settle into their seats like *I will not be the first one to speak. I can sit here all day.*

During this whole thing, I'm pretty sure Joe didn't even blink.

He sat with his arms folded in his lap—waiting, watching, and learning. I'm certain he was also deep in prayer.

I broke the silence. "Okay, Maggie, what do you have to say?" I chose Maggie because she's always the first to speak and answer honestly with more than a single word.

She addressed the issue with a broad statement. "We need to do better."

Well, at least she said something. But we had to get specifics on the table.

Nafula spoke up timidly. "Once you hired me, they did not give me a tour of the place. I didn't know where anything was, not even the bathroom."

I tried not to shake my head and yell, "What is wrong with you people?"

She went on. "I lined up with the kids and used the students' little toilets for two months because I didn't know there was a bathroom for adults, a staff toilet."

The more she spoke, the more her shoulders hunched. Her gaze became distant. Everyone could hear the embarrassment in her voice. She wrapped her arms around herself and rocked back and forth. "I want to create an orientation manual so new staff won't have to go through what I did."

Her shame was palpable. All I could say was a soft, "I'm sorry, Nafula." I was ashamed I'd let this happen.

Nia gathered herself, straightened the already neat stack of papers in front of her, and started. "Dave, if you allow me. It may take a while."

Oh boy, she's gonna let people have it.

I nodded, yielding her the floor.

"I first met Dave and Kim when they were staying at the Rose Diamond where I worked for the general manager. They were staying at the hotel longer than any guest ever had: seventy-one days. My boss asked me to figure out why they were staying there for so long. My job was to find out about them. We thought if we could figure out why they were staying at the Rose Diamond for so long, maybe we could find similar guests. The next day, my boss asked me, 'What did you discover?' I said, 'They are white.'"

Everyone around the table chuckled.

"You know, Dave, one of the core values at the Rose Diamond was to make money, and nobody had ever stayed at our place that long. The second day, my boss asked for more information. 'What did you find out about them?' I said, 'They're married.' The third day during our meeting, my boss asked again, and I responded, 'Mr. Hatfield wears a tourist bracelet on his right wrist.'"

The GM wanted to find out more, so he took on the task himself. One night at dinner, prominent Africans from all over the continent filled the dining room. Kim and I were there too. We were dressed in casual clothes, still smelling like we had been at the dump all day because we had been. The GM introduced himself, waved his arm across the room, and said, "These people are here from St. Andrews at Turi. It's one of the most prominent international schools in Kenya, where the dignitaries send their kids. They come here every term to meet with their children."

"Oh, that's wonderful," I replied, "We have a school too."

"Really, a school in Nakuru?" He was probably expecting it to be an upscale academy too.

"Yes, it's at Gioto in Hilton."

"Gioto?"

He was probably struggling to process that I just said the Kikuyu word for "the place where waste is dumped."

"Yes, the dumpsite. It's just about a five-minute drive from here."

The GM's reaction was priceless. He cocked his head, raised his eyebrows, and crossed his arms. "Dumpsite? Gioto? That's why you're here?"

I could see the wheels of curiosity turning in his head. *Why would these people come all the way from America to help people right here in my backyard, a place of poverty I don't even know about?*

He left us to return to work, attending to his important guests; however, before parting, he waved his index finger and muttered,

"I need to know more about this." That simple meeting spurred a friendship between me and the GM.

Nia went on. "One day all the leadership from the Rose Diamond went out to Maisha Mapya, but I had to stay behind to hold down the office. They came back and were so excited, raving about the impact Dave and Kim were making. I felt left out of the excitement. But it piqued my curiosity. If I ever had the chance to see Maisha Mapya, I would certainly go. When I saw an advert on Facebook for a receptionist position at Maisha, I reached out to Dave. I asked if there was a conflict of interest in applying because I knew him. He said, 'No, please send in your resume.'" She paused for a moment. "When I was called for the interview, I set foot on Maisha Mapya for the first time. And the interview process was so unique and welcoming. You people really know how to do it. I've been involved in hiring people for over five years and have experienced nothing like it. It was a great, great memorable day. As I stepped outside the gate to leave, and I'll never forget this, I turned around and looked at the glorious place and didn't want to leave. God spoke to me, 'Nia, this is your home.'"

She turned to me. "Dave, I would've accepted the job if you had offered me one shilling."

"At my former job, I was told how to stand, how to sit, how to speak, and how to breathe. But at this place called Maisha Mapya, there was truly new life. The way the staff interacted. It was just so full of joy. Everything in me cried to be a part of it."

She paused, turned, glared at Dan, Mary, and Maggie, and paused again. She pursed her lips. "You never let me in. And. I. Tried. But you never let me in." Her voice trembled. "And I am angry with you!"

I appreciated her candor. I'm not sure I would have been well enough in touch with my feelings and articulate enough to say them so clearly.

But all it did was unleash a tidal wave of others piling on complaints. "You said this, and you said that." The dam of manners burst, and insults flew. Deep-seated hurt was given words, sharp ones intended to inflict pain.

There was no inkling of an apology from anyone. They even brought up tribal differences, as we had Kikuyu, Kalenjin, and Luo in the room. These tribal divisions are ingrained in the culture. They run deep. Inequity of access to resources and opportunities has occurred since Kenya's independence. Only a few tribes in the past sixty years have held office and received all the benefits that result from political power. Someone blurted, "When some team members from the same tribe speak in their mother tongue the others couldn't understand, you just get the sense they're talking about you."

Our meeting had started three hours earlier and things were still a mess. We were still biting each other. My breaking heart had reached its limit. I couldn't believe they were so spiteful. I was too tired and too emotionally crushed to play games. "I'm going to leave now." That comment sucked the oxygen out of the room.

"I'll be back tomorrow morning at eight o'clock. For those of you who want to be a part of what we do here and how we do it, you're welcome to join me. But if you can't, I would request you give us thirty days' notice, of which I'll give you five days off to interview for other jobs. I'll write a glowing letter of recommendation for each of you. I'll give you a thirty-day severance. And you can keep your company phones."

And then I said, "I've started over before. And I'll do it again."

I wasn't sure I meant those words even as they came out of my mouth. I was tired, burned out, and hopeless once again. I did not know if I had the stamina to start over or if God even wanted me to. Maybe this was it. Maybe everyone was right. Maybe we were done.

I turned to Joe, and we walked out together. I left, not knowing if I'd see or hear from any of them ever again. The scoreboard in my mind still showed defeat. Devil 1, God 0. I didn't know if it was the end of the first quarter, or the end of the game. Maybe the season was over.

———

I texted Wally. "Kindly pick us at Maisha now." When he arrived with his jovial, "Where to, Wafula?" my lifeless, blank stare said it all. Wally turned and looked at Joe in the back seat and waited. Joe looked at me and back at Wally.

"Wallace, would you take us to the hotel, please?" Joe said.

Not another word was spoken. All I saw was a mushroom cloud of despair hanging over Maisha Mapya. I didn't even want a cup of mixed tea. I wanted to go home and be with my wife.

Images of past times together with the GLT, people I love so much, played like a slideshow in my mind. Even though I said I'd start over again, I'd probably quit. I've quit before. I wasn't sure I had the inner strength to go on. Or maybe God wanted to pull the plug on this.

Joe just did what Joe does. He was present, and he made me feel okay.

We got to the hotel, and I lay on my bed and stared at the ceiling, empty. When I closed my eyes, I saw the same void. *Was the only place I ever really belonged going to be taken away?*

It could have been five minutes or two hours; I don't know. I finally sat up on the bed and looked for Joe. I hadn't even realized he'd left to go downstairs to talk with his wife on the phone.

Bzzt, bzzt. A message on my iPhone, and a flash of hope across my heart. Maybe it's the team! *I knew they'd come together! I knew this wasn't the end for Maisha!*

The guys are excited to meet you but uncertain of your intentions. ~ Kelsey

You've got to be kidding, Lord. Now? Now is when you have the gangs reach out to me?

My phone interrupted my thoughts again. Only this time, it was a call from Dan. He said the team wanted to meet at Java at 4:00 p.m. I asked them to come to the Rose Diamond instead. I did not know who was coming or what they would say. Joe and I surveyed the hotel looking for a quiet place for a confidential meeting. Finally, I asked the concierge. She led me to a private conference room on the second floor.

Joe and I went downstairs. Everyone—Dan, Maggie, Mary, Nia, Joel, and Nafula—were there to my great surprise. Everyone! Praise the Lord!

As we headed up to the conference room, I asked if anyone would like some tea. Politely, they replied, "No, thank you, Daudi." *Hmmm, they rarely miss an opportunity for a treat.*

We filed into the beautifully appointed conference room. As the team sat, the former rivals sat next to one another, their heads up and hands folded on the table. They thanked Joe and me for meeting with them. They told us they had been at the school this entire time, from 11:00 a.m. to 4:00 p.m., airing out all of their grievances.

"There were lots of tears and lots of forgiveness," Dan said.

They had sat down and apologized to one another, some with specifics they did not share with me. I could see the healing with my eyes and feel it with my soul.

Maggie wasted no time, "Maisha Mapya is my home. And this is my family." She turned and looked at each person sitting at the table. "I want to water the vision you have set out, not burn it down."

I was already watering it because tears of hope dripped from my chin. *It's my home too, Maggie.*

Each member of the team shared. They were holding hands. My heart wove between their intertwined fingers.

"You know, before COVID-19, we used to hold hands and pray together every day. We hadn't done that in so long, until this afternoon. We drifted. We are sorry."

The team pledged they would remember this day. This team wanted never to have to go through this again.

My joy, like the Apostle Paul's, was made complete.

Then Nia gave everyone a tour of her former workplace, the gorgeous Rose Diamond: the restaurant, the conference rooms, and the new, sparkling pool. Maggie modeled the modern lounge chairs and enjoyed sunbathing for a few brief moments. Dan tested the water with his fingers, dreaming of diving in. There was lots of laughter and talk of having everyone for a pool day at Rose Diamond if Nia could arrange it. The ladies on the team made a FaceTime call with Kim back in the US. There was beautiful healing. It was springtime.

The scoreboard changed: Devil 0, God infinity. His victory is eternal. He is Jehovah Sabaoth. He is always there to defend us, fight our battles, and win our wars. He had not forsaken us. There is no enemy God cannot defeat. It a good thing because we were going to need Him.

THE MEET

October 14, 2020

DURING THE MAKEUP session with the GLT, I was having a mini text fest with Kelsey.

The guys are excited to meet you but uncertain of your intentions. ~ Kelsey

What a great question. *What are my intentions, Lord?* And I wondered if any place was safe for a meeting.

Where should we meet? ~ me

They say the social hall. ~ Kelsey

The social hall seemed like one of the riskiest places. It's an abandoned government project where everything inside has been looted, even the water pipes. What remains are shards of glass from the broken windows, a few piles of ashes where people have burned trash to keep warm, and the echo of the past. The most abundant thing is the graffiti all over the walls. Drawings of pangas with red blood dripping from them with "K2 hate poliz" and some profanity only made the social hall feel more threatening. Plus it was secluded behind seven-foot-high stone walls. I couldn't think of a more vulnerable rendezvous spot. Joe and I had toured the place yesterday, and I thought of what a waste this expansive structure was and what great things we could do for the community if we owned a facility like this. And who or what is K2?

They saw you there yesterday with a short mzungu. ~ Kelsey

Wow. I can't go anywhere without being seen. Since nowhere was truly safe, and only eight days before I had to leave, I agreed to meet them there. They immediately changed their mind and said it would be dangerous for them to be seen with us at the social hall. Were they playing a game with me? Kelsey said the rival gang, known as the Kenya Killers or K2, considered it their turf. If they found out we were there, they might think we were up to something and come and attack.

They want to meet at Maisha. ~ Kelsey

I reacted like the Chief was trying to take another laptop. *Are you out of your mind? NO!* I am not bringing death squads into Maisha. No way! But in my desperation to connect and before I could chicken out, I replied.

How many want to come? ~ me

6 ~ Kelsey

OK, that seems reasonable. When? ~ me

Tomorrow at 10 ~ Kelsey

Sounds good. 10 a.m. tomorrow. ~ me

With just over a week to go, what good can really happen? I might even make things worse.

———

October 15, 2020

I slept through most of the night with only the occasional plea to God. *What are my intentions?* I got a strange sense that I might experience what Peter, James, John, and Andrew did in Mark 13:11 (NLT), "Don't worry about what to say—just say what God tells you to. Then it is not you who will be speaking, but the Holy Spirit." At least that was my hope.

Groundhog Day. 5:30 alarm, Joe's smile, and three pots of tea. "Twende kazi" from Wally, and greetings to the kitchen staff. The only change was that Joe got the breakfast he ordered.

The spring was back in my step. It's funny how that happens when God doesn't allow your family to fall apart. On the way into Maisha Mapya, I even got a bonus text encouraging me.

THE CHIEF TOLD MAMA AMON NEVER TO SET FOOT IN GIOTO AGAIN. SHE BRINGS TOO MUCH TROUBLE. SAME FOR HER PASTOR FRIEND. ~ ANONYMOUS

What took you so long, Chief? She's caused chaos for over a decade. I wonder how serious you are about this and how long it will last?

Maybe the tide was turning on Mama Amon? They burned down her house, she got arrested, seventy guys chased her with machetes, and now one of the most powerful men in the city who used to be her friend, banished her. Would it finally be enough to rid the community of her?

I greeted the GLT who was seated side by side ready for the day's session to begin. There wasn't an inch of daylight between them. "Boy, am I glad to see you guys." My exhale of relief put an exclamation point on it.

Sheepish grins and a chorus of "We're happy to see you too, Daudi" rang out.

Nia shared that during the night, God placed on her heart the vision that we were a living example of the parable of the prodigal son. The GLT had returned from their straying and were glad to be home. I felt like the prodigal's father. Little did I know, I had been running after them ever since I boarded the flight several days earlier. Before making the journey, I wasn't sure of all God had in store for this trip. Now, I knew one reason He had brought me to Kenya was to restore unity among His family.

The aura of yesterday's triumph and today's harmony filled the hall as we moved on to talking about building a better Maisha Mapya. I posed questions to the team: "What do we do better than anyone? What is our niche?" I was looking for something tangible and specific.

"We have a great school."

"Yes, we do. But lots of schools could say that."

The team gave sporadic answers from around the table. "We serve lots of meals." "We love the kids more than anyone." "We love our community."

"True. True. True. But what do we have that no one else does? What makes us special?"

I was thinking of the meeting that was to occur in just a few minutes with the gang members. What makes something like that happen?

Maggie spoke up. "We know this community better than anyone."

Dan added, "We have great relationships with the people."

Yes! That was it! We knew the community better than anyone. We had a permanent presence there. We employed the community. They built our buildings. They volunteered at the school. They are us and we are them. And when other organizations in Nakuru wanted to help the people in the dumpsite, they came to us for guidance and expertise.

Just last month, the Nakuru Rotary and Gilani's Supermarket

wanted to donate food to the community because of COVID-19. Who did they come to? Us! They asked us to distribute it to genuinely needy families. The Lions Club came to us to deliver masks. Springs of Hope came to us to help identify suitable candidates to be beneficiaries of their ministry and learn how to sew. More and more groups were realizing our unique role.

"We connect people who want to help with people who need help. That's our niche. It's time for us to dream and dream big! What do you see us looking like in ten years? How many students will we have? Will we be in multiple locations? How many staff members will we need? What will our budget be? How are we going to do this?"

Mary said, "Daudi, if I may, I dream to keep educating the kids all the way through high school."

"Well then, we're gonna need more land," I added.

"And lots of it," Joel said. "Enough for all the students, plus a sports field and *shamba* (farm) with thirty chickens, five goats, and three cows."

I laughed because I sensed this wasn't the first time he'd thought of this.

"How will we get the kids there?" I asked.

Dan laughed. "Joe can drive the bus!" Dan's always wanted a vehicle.

Joe gestured as if turning the big steering wheel of the bus and honking the horn. The team cracked up as he smiled and waved at the make-believe passersby.

Round and round we went, images, ideas, and emotions filling the air. Nia did her best to jot everything down, but the ideas were flowing faster than the ink in her pen. I knew she would assemble these random ideas into a well-knit PowerPoint presentation at the first opportunity.

It was a fun exercise and created a buzz because we were moving forward together. God was not finished with Maisha Mapya yet. Throughout the Bible, you see those to whom God gave much were expected to do much. God had given us a lot, including the gift of every person in this room. We needed to do the most with it.

My right knee started bouncing up and down. Maybe I'd had too much tea, or perhaps I was excited, or nervous, about meeting "the boys"? I remember reading that our bodies produce the same chemical reaction for excitement as nervousness. Olympic athletes translate the feeling to excitement. Those who sit in the stands think it's nervousness. I was opting for excitement, believing God was on the verge of doing something great, and if I came across as being nervous, the gang would smell it a mile away.

"Well, guys, would you pray with me?"

"Yes, Dave, we will," replied the GLT in unison.

They probably expected a request for prayer for blessing our long-term vision or something. Instead, I asked for wisdom and protection for the next meeting.

"Thanks for a great time. I love you all. Have a wonderful morning. I'll see you in a bit." I left the table and entered the unknown.

The concept of a street gang coming to Maisha filled my mind with images of the feast in Luke 14 where it says when you throw a banquet, invite the poor and guests who can't pay you back. If you do, it says God will bless you—would His blessing be peace?

We set out our best spread. The kitchen staff beautifully positioned a table on the school lawn under the shade of two one-hundred-year-old trees named Adam and Eve. The white tablecloth and teacups had an air of sophistication about them. An arrangement of queen cakes was placed in the center. The last thing I wanted was for these guys to be on edge because they were hungry.

The GLT headed off to do their other duties for the day, but some never made it all the way upstairs to the admin office, choosing to stop in at the kitchen for some tea of their own. Some thirty yards away, I could see them taking turns peeking around the corner hoping to get a glimpse of our guests as they arrived.

I set only two rules for these gangsters to be allowed on the property. First, they had to be sober. Second, they had to leave their knives, pangas, booze, weed, glue, and whatever else at the gate with our security guard when entering. We'd give it all back, even a rocket launcher, on their way out the door. I didn't care.

As the gang members entered, I didn't check to see if they handed anything over to the guard or not. I didn't want to know. I sat at the table, pretending to be calm, and waited for them to approach.

Kelsey, who somehow arranged the meeting, her daughter Kat, five men, and one woman passed through the gate. A woman? I didn't see that one coming. And I recognized her. I didn't see that coming either. Three of the men were older than I had imagined. A couple of other guys were muscular and looked like they knew how to handle themselves. One was big as a volcano, with long dreads and a distrustful squint in his eyes. Most looked worn out.

As they approached, I stood, introduced myself, and extended my hand. It wasn't a formality. It was an icebreaker. I shake so many hands during each visit to Kenya, it always results in a trip to the dermatologist's office to get whatever starts growing on my hands frozen off. It's happened so often that when I visit my doc, he simply asks, "How was the trip?" A fifty-dollar co-pay and a few scars are a small price to pay for the dignity it instills in whoever's hands are attached to the people God puts in my path.

When they sat down, I couldn't tell if they were comfortable or apprehensive. The youngest one sat at attention. Another had his head lowered, but eyes tilted up in a deep study of the white man sitting across the table (me). One avoided my gaze at all costs. Others slouched with legs wide apart.

I took a deep breath. "Thanks for coming. I heard you want to know what my intentions are. So, I'll tell you."

I put my elbows on the table and leaned in so far that my chest touched my fists and said the only words God gave me. I felt a calm wash over me as my lips parted. My eyes softened.

"My intention is to love you."

They all focused their attention on me, and I made eye contact with each person.

"And to have you love me back. That's it."

And I sat back in my chair and folded my hands in my lap. Of course, I couldn't see them, but I knew my eyes were twinkling. No one snickered. No one pulled a knife. No one got up and walked away. They just looked at me like those words were what they had been longing to hear their entire lives.

I leaned in again. "Let me ask you this, do you guys know me?"

Every head nodded up and down, even the one guy seated at my immediate left with gray tips on his short Afro. "Of course. You're Daddy Dave. Everyone knows you. You're a man of peace."

How in the world did they know who I was well enough to know me as Daddy Dave? I thought that moniker was reserved for our students, staff, and a few close community members. But the familiarity put me at ease.

"Thank you. What's your name?"

"Dembe."

"Thank you, Dembe. Now let me ask you all this. Do any of you have any issues with me, personally?"

A few shook their heads, but all said, "No."

"Well, that's good." I let out a nervous laugh. "If you ever do, this is how we're going to settle it. Just like we're doing now. We're going to sit down, have some tea, and talk about it. There's no need for violence. I'm a peacemaker. My deal with the community is that I'm going to love them and they are going to love me back. Just like it's going to be with you guys. If you've got an issue, we can always sit down and talk. Just like this. I don't fear our community. We love each other."

There was a silent, total agreement. Since ground rules were being established, I kept going.

"Now, let me ask you another question. Do you have any

issues with any of my staff members? Any of the eighteen people who work here? Not their brothers, or aunts, or cousins, but these eighteen people. Are there any issues at all?"

A resounding no.

"Good. If you do have a problem, we're going to sit down and talk about it. And maybe have some tea. There's no need for violence."

All looked like they were okay with it.

"Let me ask you one more question. Do you have any issues with any of our students?"

I was thinking of our poor, terrified, four-year-old Angel, still in hiding, who we had to rescue from being beheaded.

"I'm not talking about their families, not their brothers, sisters, cousins, aunts, uncles, just the kids themselves. Do you have any issues with my two hundred kids here in this school?"

Now I was really testing the waters. They looked around the table, taking inventory of any hidden acts of revenge in their hearts before letting out a chorus of no.

"Good. If you do, we're going to sit down and talk about it. And have more tea. There's no need for violence. And just to let you guys know, we don't have to have issues to sit down and have tea. We can just sit down and have some tea and talk. We're neighbors."

Then, I went for it.

"What this means then is hands off my staff and hands off my kids. Agreed?"

They all nodded. One said, "Hakuna matata." Another responded, "No problem."

My heart was instantly relieved. Mission accomplished. Our kids would be safe! I could have folded up my tent and gone home.

Yet I continued. "I'm sorry for the problems happening in our community. Everyone is on edge. This COVID-19 thing is impossible. It's caused so much violence." They grumbled in full agreement. "Can I ask you guys, do you want revenge or do you want peace?"

Now I knew I was in the deep end of the pool. It was one thing to probe about issues with children and staff. I mean, who really has a problem with any of our sweet kids or kind teachers? But now I was asking them about their hearts, their motives. And this was happening with temperatures running high and young men in the morgue, one with fifty-three stab wounds.

The guy who was as big as a Coke machine with dreads that had a long history growled, "We want peace." He grabbed his head with both hands as if to drown out blaring music. "We want peace."

When all the rest joined him saying they wanted peace, I knew there was hope.

I asked the big, brooding guy, "What's your name?"

His eyes slid across his face toward me. "Samson."

"Awesome, Samson. I want peace too. God sent me here this week to help bring peace to the people and community I love."

Our conversation opened up. They introduced issues plaguing them. The biggest one appeared to be the young people sitting around without jobs, with nothing to do, without hope, stealing things to sell to get money for drugs and alcohol. It confirmed the famous proverbs: "Idle hands are the devil's workshop" and "Wickedness loves company—and leads others into sin" (Proverbs 16:27-29 TLB).

They started complaining about the police and politicians. How when bad things happened in Hilton, no one cared. And when the cops showed up, they wanted bribes and they dished out brutality.

"Sometimes we end up in cells even when we haven't done nothing," Dembe said. "They want us to pay. We have no shillings in our pockets so they lock us up. I'm not a thief. I'm poor."

"The police don't stop crimes. They commit them!" Samson added.

Emotions intensified. One guy leaned in, placed both hands

on the table, and raised his voice so much, he almost stood up. Nostrils flaring, he screamed and shook the table, "K2 stole my kid's PlayStation!" It ticked everyone off, and they started arguing among themselves about who could ever do such a thing and that they must pay for what they did. So much for peace.

It caused such commotion that, like in a cartoon, one after another, the GLT's heads poked up, Dan's out the kitchen door, Mary's just above, and Maggie's head on top. Nia peered out the admin office. Their eavesdropping had now turned into a full wiretap.

Insults were flying around the table. To me, a PlayStation seemed like a minor issue, but I quickly thought of how some people blame their divorce on their impossible spouse leaving the cap off the toothpaste all the time. It revealed there was a deeper problem.

Seeing how quickly this spark set off the tinderbox of rage made my heart race, but I sat silently. If they felt this was an issue, then it was an issue. The glare in his eyes and veins in his neck didn't want peace. He wanted his kid's PlayStation back. And he wanted revenge. Thankfully, having vented his anger, he sat down.

The second guy on my left, named Balozi, was maybe five feet five, looking all rasta, complete with dreads and sleepy eyes. He started talking about how he didn't understand why the government had spent so much money to tarmac the roads around Hilton. He said they should've spent the money on a recycling machine to put in the dumpsite and create jobs.

"There's a machine the Germans make that's 120 million Kenyan shillings ($120,000 US dollars), and they could recycle the metal right there. Why do we need to be sending glass to China or plastic to Nairobi when we could recycle all of that right here and make good jobs?" he exclaimed.

I wasn't expecting to hear about a business structure and strategy from these guys. I was expecting monsters. I knew I wouldn't remember all the details, so I wanted to record it. I asked Balozi if he would mind repeating it so I could video and share it with people in the US. He said, "No problem." I got my tripod and iPhone and made a three-and-a-half-minute recording of this guy talking about his idea.

I wanted to be able to show others in the US that the people caught up in this conflict aren't dumb thugs. They even have some sound ideas. To me, it cemented the concept of the community council being the experts on their community—even if they were gang members. By allowing me to video him, Balozi revealed his trust in me.

We ate queen cakes, finished our tea, created a bond, and fostered hope. Dembe shared that his son gets angry sometimes. Balozi looked like he just wanted to sit and talk. Samson sneered. The other two guys spoke sparingly. The lady never said a word.

Kelsey sat quietly through the whole thing. Her wide eyes and continual looks around the table to see if others saw what she was seeing communicated amazement for the entire hour-and-a-half meeting.

I learned guys in a gang aren't "gang guys." They are people with names like Dembe, Samson, and Balozi. They are men with kids who like video games, just like my kids do. I learned we could sit down with people who are struggling, even people who only know one way to settle disagreements, and listen, learn, share a meal, and become friends. Then we can discuss our issues and agree on a way forward.

The group headed out, making a stop with the security guard on the way out to collect their things. I turned to Kelsey and said, "That seemed to go okay."

The word "amazing" and shaking her head were all she could come up with.

Joe and Kat skipped out of the kitchen onto the field and played catch while Kelsey and I talked. Watching them reminded me of Kim's dad throwing the baseball around for hours in the backyard with our son.

Nia on her tiptoes waved at me from the top of the stairs. I think she was relieved her boss was still in one piece.

My boldness increased. "Kelsey, see what you can do to set something up with their rivals. I want to meet them. My plane leaves in seven days."

"I'm trying," she said in a manner conveying, "I'm doing everything I can, and I really want you to meet them too." Then she called to her daughter, "Let's go, Kat."

Kat turned around, hugged Joe, and ran over to her mom. Then Kelsey and Kat skipped out the gate together.

I breathed. It had already been a full day, and it wasn't even noon.

———

My watch read 11:30 a.m., and Joel, Dan, and I needed to rush to Hilton to talk about forming the community council. Joe tagged along. It was my first time in Hilton in seven months. As we climbed the steep hill and entered the slum, the commotion intensified. Several hundred people hanging out in the makeshift bars were last-call, closing time drunk. And it was still morning. It was heartbreaking. There were maybe eight times as many people crowding the area as there were last February, including lots of high-school-age girls and older men. It made me feel dirty.

One girl, a senior in high school who we know well, walked alongside us as we made our way to the gathering place in an open field in Hilton. Her eyes were glazed. Her mouth relaxed.

"Where is Mommie Kim?" she asked.

I explained she was sick and couldn't make the trip this time. The girl moved in closer and closer, conveying with her action, "No, that's the wrong answer. Where is Kim? Go get her. I need her." She rocked back and forth while rubbing her hands across her arms and confessed, "I wish she were here. I'm backsliding. I'm drinking alcohol." I feared she was doing more than that in order to pay for her addiction.

As I took a few steps, somebody whispered in my ear that this girl was always at the bar and she served drinks. She was maybe fifteen. I couldn't imagine how painful life was for her. She'd suffered so many things in her young life, including sexual abuse leading to suicidal thoughts. God put Kim in her path to listen, comfort, and counsel her so she could make it through another day. But in this moment of need, Kim was too sick herself to be here to help.

On my other side, Luis, one of the more vocal leaders in Hilton, came to escort me. Even dressed in his current unique combination of a green Croc on his right foot and a pink, furry slipper on his left, he was physically strong and powerful. He put his arm around my shoulder and greeted me like we were long-lost friends. Unlike almost everyone else, he didn't reek of alcohol. Luis never drank—he was just outgoing.

He had assembled a group of maybe eighty people. I gave the same speech as I had to the Gioto family two days earlier: no handout big enough is coming, we've gotta do this ourselves. I urged them to select leaders and come meet next Tuesday at Maisha Mapya and have a voice in the council.

Some in the crowd had their necks cranked toward me and their eyes fixed on me the entire time. Others focused on Joel as he translated my foreign English to Swahili. Still, others held court of their own, off in some intoxicated world, rambling, partially echoing my words.

The Hilton community was more like a drunken island of misfit toys than a desperate, scavenging dumpsite community hanging on for dear life like Gioto. I hoped my sober message got across.

As we headed back to school, I got a text from Kelsey about the gang we had met with earlier in the day:

Can you meet them tomorrow morning at their place? ~ Kelsey

Sure. ~ me

Where is their place? I've never seen a group gathered in Hilton like the guys on Triangle Island. All afternoon I wondered where "our place" was. But the first meeting had gone so well that I was happy to meet them anytime, anywhere.

———

Wally had the engine running at 5:15 p.m. when Joe and I walked out the Maisha gates for the short ride to the Westside Mall for a dinner meeting at Java.

"Guess who we're having dinner with, Wally?"

"With you, Wafula, I have given up. I do not know. Who? The governor?"

"Haha, maybe he's tomorrow. But tonight, I have someone better."

"Really?"

"Yep. Your favorite pastor named Edgar and smooth-sounding George."

"Oh, I want to come."

"Maybe next time, Wally. Thanks for the ride. Can you pick us here at seven o'clock?"

"Will be waiting, Wafula. I will be here."

Joe and I got a table for four outside on the patio. I'd been longing to see Edgar. He's cool, has dreads, like Balozi and the boys, rides a motorcycle, and has the best Kenyan-English accent. His skin is dark, really dark, and he jokingly calls himself the blackest man in Africa. I don't care about his accent, or curls, or color; I love him for his heart for Jesus.

I met him a few years earlier when he was a guest preacher at Mavuno Church at Players Theatre in Nakurutown. He gave a stirring sermon on how we as Christians should help anyone in deep need. That God was not merely a genie waiting to grant our every wish and make our lives comfortable, but we were born on purpose and for a purpose. The thing I remembered most was his authentic desire to help the least of these.

We spoke after the sermon, and I asked him if he had ever been to Gioto. I was certain he had.

"No, I haven't."

"Well, then you must come. First, come to see our kids at school. They are amazing. Then we can visit where they live."

"I'll bring my team," Edgar said. True to his word, he and his team came to Maisha and made a day the kids would never forget. Worship pastor George, tall as a skyscraper at over six feet five, has a sweet voice straight from heaven. Edgar also brought a guy named Uber with him, a comedic entertainer who kept the children laughing for a full hour. He also brought balloons. Edgar knows how to connect with kids, even fifty-nine-year-old ones like me.

Then we entered the streets of Hilton together. The raw humanity overwhelmed my old friend. When we rounded the corner at the social hall and entered Gioto, with broken glass crushing beneath our feet, I think it broke him. Human beings rendered indistinguishable from the other things discarded there, walking like zombies through mounds of trash looking for food, seared an image on Edgar's heart.

In Gioto, just ten minutes from the church he called home, Edgar met the "least of these" that Jesus loves and talks about. Like so many of the caring disciples of Christ in this city of a million, the revelation that this place existed and they didn't even know it was there was convicting. The devil had done an incredible job disguising Gioto from the rest of Nakuru. It hid in plain sight.

Since that first visit, Edgar has had a special place in his heart for our young staff who faced those streets and loved the people so intensely it was humbling to know them. I felt the same way.

The COVID-19 shutdowns had affected everyone in Nakuru. Edgar's church met only online for a while, even though their meeting hall was not an enclosed building but a large open-air tent. When the violence increased in Hilton and the murders pierced our staff's hearts, I reached out to Edgar to console, mentor, and lead our Maisha Mapya family.

"I'd be honored" was his simple reply.

Edgar brought his team and buckets of chicken, mashed potatoes, and biscuits from KFC. (Yep, there's a Kentucky Fried Chicken in Nakuru now, at the same Westside Mall where Java is located.) They listened to my team as they poured out their fears and tears.

Tonight was my turn to provide some comfort food for Edgar and George.

We quickly caught up on the news of our lives, and then talk turned to Maisha Mapya and our surrounding community.

"Thanks for ministering to our team, Edgar."

"The pleasure was mine. They are an amazing group of people."

"They face so many things." Edgar, George, and Joe leaned in. "They need a spiritual leader to mentor them so they have the strength and wisdom to lead the community. They are hungry for a shepherd."

"Yes, Dave, they are. I see them, and I get exhausted thinking about their days."

I could see Edgar's own fatigue as he poured out, the wear of shepherding his needy flock showing. He looked at George. I intercepted their telepathic message.

"What do you think, George? Can we do more to help?"

"I don't know, Edgar, we're pretty maxed out as it is."

"Yeah, you're probably right."

A full conversation without saying a word.

"I appreciate all you are doing for us now," I said, "and I don't want to put any pressure on you, but would you consider meeting with our staff once or twice a month to encourage them? Please don't worry about the budget; we will raise funds to have some food and drinks for meetings. I'm just asking if you can squeeze them into your schedule."

He turned to his friend. "Let's see what we can do, George."

"Sawa, sawa (okay)."

Our meal came, and we continued to enjoy each other's company. I shared about the events of the day, the groundwork for establishing a community council, and, of course, my first engagement with the gang.

"And they want me to meet with them again tomorrow. But this time at their place, wherever that is."

Before I could finish, Edgar rested his utensils on his plate, stood, and placed his hand on my shoulder. We all bowed our heads. Hempstone, the server, moved in closer to be part of the blessing. Edgar thanked God, praised God, and asked for God to deliver a shepherd to Maisha Mapya. He prayed for peace and provision for the community and for God to use him in whatever manner He wished. He ended with, "Protect Dave as he engages the gangs. Give him wisdom, peace, and a supernatural covering from the attacks of the enemy."

Yes, Lord. Give me wisdom, peace, and protection. Amen.

THE BAR

October 16, 2020

GROUNDHOG DAY. 5:30 a.m. alarm. Morning. Grandpa Joe. Tea.
Twende. Greetings. Joe's breakfast ordeal was in the rearview
mirror. Two days in a row, items arrived as desired.

At 8:00 a.m., the GLT was around the table, wiggling in their
seats like puppies. God had restored *maisha mapya* (new life) to us.

We only had forty-five minutes before I needed to leave to
meet the gang, but since our time together was limited and
precious, I wanted to make the most of every moment. I was
already feeling pressure from so little time remaining before my
return flight to the States.

Our prior GLT meetings had focused on tightening up our
business operations and dealing with the unexpected event of our
unity crisis. Now it was time to ensure an extra measure of heart
was put in our process. The Traction management system we use
was designed for profit oriented companies. It focused on bottom
line efficiency and dollars and cents. But it was lacking when the
goal was to love a hurting population like ours. We were ready to
infuse our core values of treating everyone with dignity and
compassion into our much-improved operating system.

During Kim's and my COVID-19-inspired Netflix binge-watching, we saw a special by Brené Brown titled, *The Call to Courage*. It was so intriguing and informative, I purchased her book, *Dare to Lead*.

Brené labels herself a shame researcher. Hilton is a shame crucible.

While our Hilton community struggled to obtain even the bottom level of Maslow's hierarchy of needs—proper food, water, clothing, and shelter—that wasn't their most significant issue. The biggest challenge was overcoming shame. Our friends are crippled by it. With seemingly no choice, many young moms sold themselves for a few shillings in order to buy rice to feed their kids. Preteen girls did the same in order to buy a sanitary towel and attend school without ridicule and embarrassment. Being a victim of abuse, or being the abuser themselves, many drown themselves in alcohol. To fix the problem for a moment only further makes life a dark, bottomless pit of despair from which there is no escape. The daily experiences of our community members create the shame that haunts them, saying, "You'll never be good enough. Look at what you have done. Look at where you live. You're not worthy of anything."

When I was waiting to board the plane for this trip, I again skimmed through the first few chapters of *Dare to Lead*. My copy of the book is getting difficult to read because there's nearly as much ink from my notes as from the original text. All it took was a glance to recall the content. I'd nearly memorized it. *God take these words and run them through Your lens; sift them, refine them, and have only Your truth make its home in my heart. Fill me with compassion, empathy, and goodness.*

I greeted the team and set the vision. "Today, we're going to shift our thoughts from what we do to how we do it. As I've looked at our community, I see the biggest problem we face is not lack of material resources, like food, education, jobs, or anything like that. It's not alcoholism, neglect, or abuse."

Maggie lifted her eyebrows. Dan turned to Mary. "What could it be?"

"Their biggest issue is shame. It's a powerful force the devil uses to bind them. He puts his voice in their heads and says, 'You're useless. You're worthless. No one will love you.' In Gioto, there's a megaphone blasting loud and clear, 'You'll never be anything but trash. NEVER!'"

"That's my stepdad's voice," Mary said.

"Oh, I'm sorry, Mary. I know it's awful, isn't it? And its evil claws pin our community to the mat," I added. She sat stone-faced.

Dan said, "Yeh, some just sit there with the door open and never try. They sit in the prison they make themselves." Mary released her memory, and her expression softened.

"Brené teaches we should not confuse shame with guilt. Guilt says you did something wrong. Shame says *you* are wrong. It says you, yourself, are so flawed you are not worthy of love or connection. It seems ironic, but the glorious thing is we have all experienced shame. I have. You have. Everyone in our community has too. Our shame connects us and allows us to relate to one another."

I let that sit. A few shifted in their chairs as they had visions of their shameful acts creeping around in their minds. Maybe they were even thinking of the things that came to light just two days earlier as we were biting and devouring each other.

"But God has given us the antidote for shame. I'll share it with you when I get back. I'm sorry, but I need to run to a meeting."

I stood, turned to Nia, and handed her my wedding ring, passport, and phone. "I'll be back in maybe ninety minutes." Her brow furrowed, and she pursed her lips. She looked as though she was trying to solve some great mystery. With an outstretched hand, she followed me toward the door. "Wait, wait, what about your hand sanitizer? Are you taking some with you?"

"No thanks, Nia. I'm okay." Protecting myself from COVID-19 was the last thing on my mind.

I looked to Joe for an affirming smile. He obliged. I headed out of the hall. Right on time, Kelsey, with Kat at her side, met me at the gate. Kelsey's a single mom and keeps a close eye on Kat while equipping her to become a godly young woman. Rarely do I see them apart from one another.

When she was a missionary in Central Africa, Kelsey was the victim of a sexual assault. This traumatic experience gave her the gift of Kat and a valiant purpose. She bravely shares her testimony with crowds of young girls who may be victims of similar things. She's so committed that she started a movement called #itisnotok to begin the conversation of sexual violence in a world that remains silent about it. Kelsey is amazing. I'm humbled she is my friend.

Kat is a beautiful young lady. She, too, is brave. She goes to lots of adult places with her mom, though not today. Kelsey gave her daughter a kiss and a hug, saying, "Go have some fun with Joe. I love you. I'll see you soon."

Kelsey made a left-hand turn out the gate toward a different entrance to Hilton. She's about a hundred years younger than me, fit, and used to the 6,200-foot elevation. I doubled timed to keep up. She was walking so fast I was huffing and puffing even before hitting the hills going into Hilton.

I'm still quite the sight walking these streets. It's rare a lone white guy walks freely through Hilton. A few years ago, I would get looks of, "what is that guy doing here?" and comments of, "Mzungu, are you lost? The game park is the other way." Others would size me up, seeing if I was a good mark.

Now I'm greeted with smiles and shouts from almost everyone. Shopkeepers cry out from inside their kiosks, "Daddy Dave, karibu. Welcome. Come, sit, have a Coke." Many of them, ladies, who on a good day make $2 or $3 and insist on me not paying. It's their way of saying, "Thank you for all you do for us." I always wrestle between accepting the offer, knowing it may take her only profit for the day, or declining it and possibly causing insult. If I walk past without saying hi, I usually have a Facebook message waiting for me by the end of the day: "Daddy Dave, why did you not stop in my shop today?"

My favorite part of the walk is when the children run out, grab my hand, and swing it like we're best friends as they escort me through the neighborhood. Sometimes there's a child attached to each one of my ten fingers. A few kids only travel as far as the end of their block, others continue on the entire journey. Somehow, they all wind up back at home by the end of the day. I love it. And it makes me wish I had more fingers.

It doesn't matter if I've been gone for one day or three months. The reception is the same. This time, it's been seven months since Kim and I last strolled these streets. The improvements surprised me. Before, you needed a four-wheel-drive or a safari van to climb the rocky roads through the community. Now, stone-lined trenches on the roadsides kept the raw sewage contained. These must have been the government improvements Balozi was talking about. While the waste would no longer be running in the streets, little kids now crawled into the ditches to play, splashing in sewage up to their ankles.

We strode past the tallest building in Hilton. The four-story commercial structure was nearly vacant. Rumor had it that a devil worshiper owned it, so it sat with ghosts as the only occupants.

We traveled further, then made an immediate left and stopped. "This is it," Kelsey said. I'd walked within fifteen feet of this gate a hundred times, never knowing the nefarious deeds going on behind it.

She pounded on a rusted steel door. I feared the echo would attract attention. Like my glowing white skin and gray hair already wasn't enough of a beacon. I wanted to be discreet, undetected. I felt out of place. How many stockbrokers had ever knocked on this door?

The scraping sound of the metal deadbolt sent a chill down my already on-alert spine. I didn't know if I was walking into a trap or if yesterday's meeting had just vetted me. I had a feeling I'd find out soon. The door opened, and we stepped inside. I stood in a covered space that was nearly pitch black at nine o'clock in the morning. I scrunched my face, eyes squinting to adjust from the bright African sun outside. We slipped down a narrow passage between buildings to a patio.

About a dozen guys mulled around in the makeshift room, some circling the prominently placed pool table in the middle. They all looked at me, but no one uttered a word. The only familiar face was Balozi's. He looked like he hadn't slept a wink.

Well-worn sofas, chairs, and bar stools lined the perimeter. Behind one row of chairs was a handmade wooden fence with signs nailed to it. I tried to read them, but the light was too dim. A gate at the left end with a padlock on it hung closed, but the latch was only on one side, so it secured nothing. I wondered what it was for. The cool, damp air reeked of alcohol.

I looked around for the seat holding the least honor. It was off to the side, and I sat in it. Balozi shuffled about, smiling and greeting all the guys. Then he sat at one end of the pool table like it was his throne, wiping the sleep from his eyes.

Within two minutes, there were about thirty people crowding into the club. Mostly young guys in their twenties. I didn't know any of them. As they filed in, each grabbed a seat as if they'd take roll call any second. I felt old enough to be their dad. The look in their eyes said they needed one. I silently prayed for an opportunity to introduce them to the best dad ever—God himself —but for now, I would have to do.

I got up from my spot on the couch and bumped into Samson as he was filing in. I tried to squeeze past and then yielded. I didn't want to struggle over such a small thing. He squinted at me like a guy who'd been burned before. I went around the room and shook each person's hand, making eye contact with those who allowed it. I smiled no matter the reception. A few more guys came in and hung out by the entrance.

"*Mambo*" (slang for a friendly hello, though you won't find that meaning in Google Translate), "thanks for having me in your place. I am honored to be here," I said.

Their faces brightened with anticipation. The guy to my left was biting his lip as he swung his leg back and forth.

"You're probably wondering what my intentions are."

A guy in the back quickened his pacing. Another crossed his arms. A few leaned in. One stood, placed a straight arm on the pool table, and glared at me.

"My intentions are to love you and have you love me back." My smile was still there, even though I was holding my breath.

No snickers, no threats. So far, so good. One guy grabbed his buddy's shoulders with both hands.

"Do you guys know me?"

"Yes," was the answer from almost everyone as they nodded. A few said, "Daddy Dave." Still others said, "A man of peace."

I asked them the same series of questions I had asked the six gang leaders the day before, "Do you have any issues with me, my staff, my kids?"

They said no to all three.

One guy was poking his friend, whispering something. The other guy whispered back. Balozi said, "Okay, most of these guys don't speak English good, but they understand more than they speak. Let me help them."

He interpreted so they could understand my English. Even my American accent can be challenging for a Kenyan who is fluent in the Queen's English. He also translated their Swahili or mother tongue responses so I could comprehend. As naturally as I could, I stood up, slid across the room, and sat next to Balozi like we were buddies about to watch a ball game on TV.

I asked, "What are some of your guys' issues?"

The first issue: the stupid PlayStation. *Really!*

Then they brought up the police.

"The police aren't my friends either. At Maisha, we abide by every law and strive to be the best citizens in Hilton, but the police can be so difficult. I have no sway over them. And I have just as many issues with them as you do. They love to intimidate. Do you want to know something?"

Their eyes got wider.

"If you were a police, and you saw me, what would you be thinking?"

"You are rich and white. I must get a bribe from you," Dembe declared.

"Exactly! You guys, their goal is to try to find some way to make me so uncomfortable that I'd give them money to go away."

They nodded.

"And I never will. So, it can get really stressful. But no matter what, there is tension. I'm a target for them. They don't see me. They see money. They all think I am money."

The group gently bowed their heads, still displaying sheepish grins.

They complained about the MCA (Municipal County Assemblyman).

I said, "Well, he's a politician. He's going to make promises and not deliver. He tells people what he thinks they'll want to hear."

I decided not to get too involved in that topic.

"How do you feel about the Chief?"

They rushed in on me, yelling and waving their arms. They all had something to say. I had struck a nerve.

I said, "Let me tell you, not everything the Chief has done is bad. He has done some good things. Do you remember when the schools closed because of the collapse in Nairobi? Remember Hopeland and Jireh schools closing because they weren't safe for our kids? Well, the Chief reached out to us to see if we could take all of those kids into Maisha. He was looking out for the kids."

It was just straight-talk with them, and they accepted it.

"You all think things are easy for me. I've had my problems in Hilton ever since I got here. Do you know that Maisha Mapya isn't the first school I've started here? I started the Jireh Preschool in Gioto, you know, the one that was recently called Joyous. Did you know the family we partnered with stole it from me?"

There was an instant uproar. "LET'S GO GET IT BACK!!

THEY STOLE IT. WE'RE GONNA GET IT BACK FOR YOU!"

I didn't mean to spark pandemonium, but I have to admit that storming the compound was a tempting thought. I put my hands up, palms out waving, "NO, NO, NO, NO, guys, come on . . . we can't do that. But if I did have it back, I'd put in a maternity center and a medical clinic."

This only excited them more. "A CLINIC! LET'S GO GET IT BACK!"

I started laughing. I loved their enthusiasm and desire to set things right. It's the tactic they'd choose I was worried about.

"No, no," I said, still laughing and palms waving. "If God wants us to have it back, He'll give it back. We won't have to take it by force. But I wanted you to know what happened with that place. They took the property and kicked out the kids who couldn't pay school fees back to the dump. That's why we started Maisha. The point is you guys think it's been all easy for me. I've got my issues too. You know that lady from the other side?"

I didn't mention her name, but they all knew it was Mama Amon.

"We know her," said the young man sitting next to Dembe.

"She hates me. In fact, I'm pretty sure she has a little doll that has white hair, and she's sticking needles into its hip and neck right now because those spots hurt me so bad."

They all laughed.

"She's probably roasting the feet right now!"

Their laughter broke into a roar. They were rolling around in their seats and slapping their legs. One guy stood up, covered his mouth with both hands, and jumped in circles. The looks on their faces conveyed it was probably true.

Their energy fed me. "The other day, when I was walking through Gioto, I walked past her compound. And someone had burned it to the ground—all to ash. Guys, I've repented of my sin, but I'm going to share it with you. I kind of smiled as I walked by."

Their eyes got huge, and they looked like they couldn't believe I was happy about it—that the man of peace had thoughts like that too.

"You know, this community is better off without her around. She has taken advantage of so many, especially taking her cut from well-intentioned people who give things to this community." I probably have only a small understanding of the depth of her corruption, but I had shared the truth.

A wire-thin guy in his mid-thirties named Damu with the sleeves ripped off his T-shirt had been creeping around the pool table in my direction the entire time. He took four steps toward me at once and was now only inches away. Two fingers on his left hand were outstretched and his thumb was up like a gun, he twisted his head as his eye bulged, and he pointed his index and middle fingers at my right temple. I sat there unsure of what would come next.

Damu blurted out with spittle flying, "Well, pastor . . . what do I do if someone comes at me with a gun and wants to kill me?" His fingertips pressed into my temple. I could feel his breath on my face.

I didn't panic, but I easily could have. I had nothing to say because the gravity of the response were so significant. All I could do was deflect. Jesus answered tons of questions by asking questions. Especially ones that shed light on the condition of the heart.

"Let me ask you this. Are you guys for peace or revenge?" As I scanned the room, Kelsey sat leaning forward with her hands folded and forearms on her thighs. I looked right past her. I didn't want her to respond. I was leaving in six days, and I didn't want her to have to own the consequences of their response. Those had to be on me.

Samson, Dembe, Balozi, and all the rest said they wanted peace—*every single one.* Samson's hands covered his ears.

My combatant friend holstered his fingers and backed away. His glare remained as he stood with one arm leaning on the pool table as he spoke. "We want peace. We sleep all day and stay up at night because that's when the gang attacks. They come fifty, one hundred, on bikes (motorcycles) with machetes and slash whoever they can find, looking for us. We live in fear. We want peace!"

It was abundantly clear fear was their master. Peace was their elusive friend.

"I want peace too. Why don't we come together to bring peace to Hilton? You guys can be known as Team Peace from now on."

"I like it," Samson said.

Balozi pointed to one member slumped on a couch six feet away on my right who was barely visible in the darkness.

"See this boy? He is only fifteen, and he wants to go to school."

I squinted so my eyes could focus on the boy. His eyes were glazed and yellow. His face relaxed. I knew that look. He was lost in the mental haze from huffing glue. I thought about it for a second. If I asked him a question, would he be able to answer or would I be dumping humiliation on his inebriated self? I took a chance.

"What's your name?"

"Mmmikey."

"Do you want to go to school, Mikey?"

"Yes."

"What class are you in?"

"Grade . . . five."

I turned to Balozi, knowing he might be connected to the guy who sells Mikey his drugs. Maybe his pusher was Balozi? Who knows, but most dealers will not want to lose a customer, so I needed to watch my step. "Do you want this boy to go to school?"

"Yes."

His response actually astonished me. And that surprise reminded me no matter how much I knew, or how much the men around me thought I knew, there was still so much to learn. I may have had the most formal education in the room, but each person there knew many things I didn't. They were experts on their community. I was not.

Seeing Mikey wasting away, destined for prison or worse, was a sight I couldn't bear. With every fiber in my being, I wanted to help him. I didn't want another casket, small or otherwise, to mourn in Hilton. So, I kept exploring.

"You know, we only have classes up to grade four at Maisha Mapya, but let me see what I can do. Maybe God can find him a spot in a school somewhere."

I immediately thought of reaching out to Pastor Steve and Terri back in the States to see if the Nakuru Children's Trust (NCT) would save this kid. I knew I would be asking for an exception because the youngest kids in their organization were in eighth grade. My faith is strong, and I believe in a mighty God, and I knew if I had the courage to ask them, maybe God would move in their hearts.

Balozi moved right on to the next issue. He pointed to another guy and said, "His motorbike was impounded, and they wanted fifty-thousand shillings to get it back. All he was doing was carrying an empty barrel across town. Do you know the MP?"

Uh, that's like a congressman in the US. So no. "No, but let me see what I can find out."

I could feel the "Daddy Dave, can you fix this" list growing with no end in sight.

"Well, guys, I've got to run and get back to work at Maisha. Can we pray before we go?" They all expected me to start, but I lowered my head and waited. After a profound silence, the quiet young man next to Dembe said, "I will pray."

I couldn't understand all the Swahili in his prayer, but I knew God did. He'd blessed the meeting and set the groundwork for more of His love and peace to reign here.

Dembe walked out alone. As he passed me, he said, "That is my son."

"Who?"

"The one who prayed."

I took a quick detour through the dumpsite on the way back to campus to see if things had calmed down. In the distance, I saw Mama Amon's pastor friend with an unsuspecting group of foreigners passing out vegetables to people in the dumpsite.The residents lined up and the pastor selected who received the supplies. I guessed his being banned from Gioto by the Chief was more of a suggestion than a rule.

Mama Amon's cunning has led her to the top of the heap in Hilton. She rose from the ranks of those toiling in the garbage for twenty cents a day to being the only conduit for outsiders to enter and help the struggling people in the dump. Even though she isn't physically in Gioto now, her accomplice was distributing cabbages from a donor. I've heard they take a cut, the majority actually, and dole out a pittance.

I haven't seen it, but apparently Mama Amon has a shop in Nakurutown and sells a considerable portion of anything given to her to distribute to the community. In all likelihood, the community knew the details, but if they protested, they would probably be cut off. And getting anything, especially fresh, whole, edible food, was worth allowing her to take the lion's share. If you looked up the expression "beggars can't be choosers" in the dictionary, you'd see my friends who live under her reign. I do know she dresses better than me most days, including wearing her shiny gold watch and jewelry, so the money comes from somewhere.

These Team Peace guys probably knew all this too. And I was also a gatekeeper to goodies similar to Mama Amon. I wondered if they wanted more than peace. Maybe they were telling me what I wanted to hear. Maybe they saw me as their road to riches.

THE HOEDOWN

October 16, 2020

THERE WERE ONLY three days until the first Maisha Mapya Community Council meeting. If we were going to have representatives from all five neighborhoods, we'd have to invite the rest of the areas today.

At 10:30 a.m., I hightailed it from the gang's hangout to Maisha Mapya. Dan, Joel, and Maggie were waiting to go to Guba to seek their community council participation. Grandpa Joe was watching Kat skip rope. He smiled and gave her a wave goodbye before joining our crew.

Guba is the neighborhood at the northernmost border of the Hilton slum, about a fifteen-minute walk from school. Just like Gioto carries its negative meaning, "a place of garbage," so does Guba. Stories say there was a man nicknamed Saddam who owned rental houses in the area. There were always fights there, and someone was killed on his plot. The death happened during the Persian Gulf war when Saddam Hussein was in power in Iraq. The locals associated Nakuru's Saddam with Iraq's. Since there's a town in Iraq named Guba, they dubbed this place Guba. This seems far-fetched to me. But that's the story. Saddam's houses and violence are long gone, and the plot has new, peaceful owners, but the name lives on.

The residents despise the name and are working to change it to *Umoja*, meaning "unity" in Swahili. With a heart like that, it seemed like they would welcome the idea of a community council.

Our shoes kicked up dust the last hundred yards as we moved from cobblestones to a dirt road. A gentleman gathered a small crowd of fifty people around him near the giant water tank which supplied some of the life-saving liquid to the community. I was happy to see they'd already assembled their leader. *This is going to be easy.* A few more steps and I recognized the man in the middle. It was Sam, the MCA! He was gloating over the new tank the government provided and how meters would be installed in the homes to charge for water.

The residents murmured, "Who can afford this? It is just another way the government takes money from us." But I was thinking, *I knew the government couldn't stay away from this council.* Sam probably heard about it and wanted to benefit in some way. There's too much potential for influence and for good things to happen that they couldn't keep their hands off it. There would also be money flowing, and they'd try to get a piece. Creating a collective voice and mobilization of fifteen thousand people was too tempting for them to ignore.

The presence of the MCA didn't deter me. God had given me a vision, and despite the obstacles, I was going to plow ahead.

Joel introduced me to the group in Swahili. I thanked them for assembling. I looked at the MCA and said, "Sam, if you allow, I'm going to speak freely. I hope that's okay." I didn't pause for an answer and turned to the people who were now in front of me. Some were standing, others sitting against a wall in the shade.

I said, "Thank you for meeting with us. I know it's hot. I will make this short. A handout big enough to solve all your problems isn't coming. It's not coming from us. It's not coming from the government. It's not coming from Sam." They knew it was true. Just like the water that was now available for the neighborhood, there was a price attached to it. Even though it was only fifty yards away, it was still unreachable for them because they didn't have the money to pay for it. Many would never get one drop.

I purposefully did not look at Sam so I wouldn't incite the reaction a Doberman has when you stare it in the eye. I simply said the words God told me to say.

Surveying the crowd, I said, "We have to do this ourselves. We have to decide what kind of community we want. Are we going to be idle, complaining, and waiting for others to fix our problems? Are we going to live in fear of violence? Or, are we going to come together and see what we as a community can do ourselves? This is our moment, and we are forming a community council where you will have a voice along with the others. Umoja between all our neighborhoods is what we want." With that, I invited them to Tuesday's meeting.

Finally, I turned, looked the MCA in the eye, gave him a two-handed handshake, and said, "Thanks, Sam. This is going to be great."

It was brief, to the point, and well-received—even by Sam.

We left Guba, walking for fifteen minutes on the dusty rock roads before reaching the paved sidewalk. This simple improvement marks the difference between neighborhoods. Dirt roads say "poor." Paved roads say "middle class." Just a few years ago, all the streets around us were endless stretches of dirt riddled with giant potholes. Slowly, the soil and rocks are disappearing, replaced by asphalt. During this period of transition, some destitute families remain. The road outside their dwelling may look new and suggest improvements have come, while the pots inside their home still may be empty. We have a few children in our school who reside on the right side of the tracks; however, the difficulty of their homelives tell a different story.

The team continued for another ten minutes before reaching the London neighborhood, the most economically prosperous portion of town. Besides litter free paved streets, the dwellings have stone walls, concrete floors, and iron sheet roofs. It is a drastic difference from Gioto. I've taken friends from Gioto in need of medical care to clinics in London and experienced the way the Londoners looked down their noses at them. Many would sneer, get up, and move further away from us because of the smell. I hope forming a successful council would encourage our neighbors to embrace one another.

Joel had arranged for the meeting to be in a church I hadn't been to before. The moment I walked in, I noticed something that always amazes me. Many Christian churches in Kenya do not have a cross or image of Jesus anywhere. You're more likely to see several giant glossy posters of a charismatic pastor and his lovely wife dressed in flashy outfits, sporting a grin like the Cheshire Cat lifted high for all to see. It conveys, "Hey, look at me. If you join us, you can be handsome, have a beautiful wife, nice clothes, riches, and comfort. You can be like me." There's lots of teaching on tithing and earthly blessings that will come, but very little, "lay down your life, pick up my cross, and follow me." Catching my thinking, I prayed, *Lord, forgive my judgment. Bring Your truth.*

This was—by far—the most well-off group we met with. We were in a cool, dry building with people sitting *in chairs*.

Sixty people graciously assembled following social distancing protocols and waited for us to start. Some wore masks. A few were on their cell phones. Joel and I shared the same vision as we had in the other neighborhoods and invited them to attend Tuesday's meeting. There was no applause, just a simple acknowledgment that they would have representatives there.

———

Our team headed back to Maisha Mapya. For the next sixty minutes, like a professor holding office hours, I met with any staff member who needed help, advice, input, or a shoulder to cry on.

The GLT was getting along with each other nicely, and the trainwreck of a few days before seemed distant in the rearview mirror. Still, I wanted to take some preventative measures and bond us even closer to one another and to the rest of the staff.

I like to plan a special event during each trip to celebrate all God has done. It's a fun time to invite the entire staff to be together as a family, not do any work, and enjoy one another. We've had raffles, white elephant gift exchanges, and staff appreciation meals. Tonight, we were trying something new. At 2:00 p.m., all the staff left to go home to prepare.

I love to watch movies. I'm one of those guys who quotes movies all the time, even from the 1980s. When I suggested a movie night to the GLT, they were all for it.

We Americans love to watch two- or three-hour movies. Apparently, that's a Western thing. We struggled to select a film interesting enough to entertain the staff but that was not full of sex, violence, or anything else that would make anyone blush. I suggested *The War Room*, a story illustrating the victory of taking our concerns to God in prayer.

The team looked it up on the internet and said, "I don't think we can do that one."

"Why not? It has good Christian content and a powerful message."

They replied, "It's two hours. Daudi, it's entirely too long!"

Who knew? I thought movie night involved watching a movie. For them, the film was an excuse to get together and socialize, to eat, laugh, and eat some more. We looked for the shortest piece we could find and settled on watching the first episode of *The Chosen*—it's under an hour and free. Thankfully, the app works in Kenya.

"What's the theme for the night?" the GLT asked.

That question surprised me. Wasn't watching a movie theme enough? Somehow, I could handle sitting and relating with a street gang, but planning a party for the staff was completely above my paygrade. "You guys handle it. Make it fun! I can't wait to see what you do."

Nia offered that we have a black-tie formal—you can take Nia out of the Rose Diamond, but you can't take the Rose Diamond out of Nia quite yet. Some of our more practical leaders suggested Western Night because everyone has jeans, and we can provide a 50-cent bandana for each guest.

Still, Nia had to put a special Nia spin on it. Red, pink, and white balloons, a few filled with helium, filled the hall. A banner hung from our window, held in place by rocks read, "Maisha Mapya Goes Country." And there were guitars. Nobody knows how to play the guitar, yet there were guitars. At three o'clock, three bales of hay arrived to add some authenticity and make the hall festive. After that, I was waiting for a pony. Thankfully, one never showed up.

By 4:00 p.m., staff members and their plus ones moseyed into the hall. It looked like the set of *Young Guns*. A couple of them may have been bowlegged like they just got off their horse. Taking in the sight, I wondered where half the guests got cowboy hats. Nia's had rhinestones that would make Dolly Parton proud. She grabbed the front brim and tipped it in my direction and gave out a big cackle. Mary and Maggie strutted in, looking like twin sisters in their blue jeans, denim shirts, red bandanas, and cowboy hats and boots. I sat there in my jeans and Maisha Mapya T-shirt looking quite out of place. Joe whipped out a bandana and then a cowboy hat he'd been saving as a surprise. He could have been a stand-in for Ben Cartwright on *Bonanza*.

We sat at tables of eight to ten people. The movie started. Everyone was attentive and quiet for the first two or three minutes. Then, like our PP1 four-year-olds, they started wiggling, whispering to each other, and looking around like, "When is this thing going to be over?"

They endured until the end—a whole fifty-five minutes. Directly afterward, they popped up and headed to the bountiful Kenyan buffet boasting chicken, beef stew, sausages, rice, cabbage, and *chapati*. There were even ice cream sundaes especially for me.

I sat on the edge of the stage as those gathered went through the line, some feasting on seconds. I soaked in their joy. My heart was overflowing. The only thing that could have made it better was if Kim was sitting beside me, holding my hand. I really, really wished she could've been there to experience it.

After the movie and meal, James, our caretaker, took over as DJ. Somehow, my entire Kenyan staff knows line dancing, Alan Jackson, and every word of "The Gambler" sung by Kenny Rogers. We'd come so far in a week. Gone was the animosity of petty differences.

The most beautiful part of the evening is that I, the prodigal father, got to throw a banquet for all my kids. We slew the fatted calf and celebrated each other and the God who binds us in His Spirit of unity. We may have been dressed in robes of the Wild West—denim, plaid, red and blue bandanas, and cowboy hats—but it was God's grace that covered us. Clint Eastwood had the good, the bad, and the ugly. Tonight I had the good, the godly, and the beautiful.

By seven o'clock, I was bushed. I turned to Joe, who was strumming a guitar and singing a duet with Nafula, and asked if we could bail. We two-stepped out the door singing, "You gotta know when to hold 'em, know when to fold 'em, know when to walk away, and know when to run . . ."

Wally picked us up and gave us a ride to the hotel. Now the poor guy has heard me sing, "I'm a super woooooman" and a couple of Garth Brooks's greatest hits. I learned that Joe could carry a pleasant tune.

When we got to the hotel room, Joe uttered a simple, "Good night, *pardner*," and hit the hay.

I slept off and on but couldn't stop thinking about meeting Mikey earlier in the day. His future seemed hopeless. His only crime was drawing life's shortest straw. Was there any chance to save him from accelerating on the inevitable downhill slide to disaster?

At an uncertain hour, I reached over to my backpack and grabbed my computer. I hoped the light and sound of my fingers hitting the keys wouldn't wake Joe. As I was typing away, my alarm went off. Once again, Joe caught me with red eyes, tears streaming, and dark circles. I had pounded out the following email to Pastor Steve and Terri in the US:

Hello Terri and Steve. I hope you all are doing great.

This time in Kenya has been like no other. I will share about it later in some emails. But I wanted to reach out to you with a plea from the center of my heart.

I've met with every neighborhood in Hilton, London, Guba, Kenya Meat, Siko, and Gioto. Right now, they are selecting four members of each neighborhood (elder man, elder woman, younger man, younger woman) to form our community council. There is no government involvement, and I even met with government officials to get the okay. These reps will meet at Maisha Mapya on Tuesday for the first time.

But the single reason I am writing is that I have also met with one of the gangs. I have one more to go. It will be trickier, as they are in hiding because the police want them. There was one kid in the meeting, a 15-year-old who has lost both parents and is living with just whomever will have him. He wants to go to school. The leaders of the gang want him to go to school. I am pleading with you to consider him for NCT. I know he is outside your mandate, and I respect any decision you make. But please, please, a thousand times please, let's save this kid. His name is Mikey, he's 15 and only in grade 5. We can make an agreement with him that if there are any disciplinary actions, he is out. He's just a lost kid caught up in the worst circumstances imaginable. I have nowhere else to make this appeal to except you and GOD.

I could meet with the director and Mikey at Maisha Mapya. No need for the director to get involved in all the other stuff. Or I could take him to town and meet at the director's office.

PS. Please be praying for God to bring peace, forgiveness, and reconciliation for my community.

God bless you. Thank you for walking with me as I follow Jesus.

Send.

THE PARENTS

October 17, 2020

Ten minutes after hitting send, God responded via an email from Terri, the Outreach Director. Her virtually immediate response meant more to me than you might think, especially after the meltdown of my team and feeling I'd have to start Maisha over again—without help.

> *Hi Dave. I trust your judgment. Please connect with our local director for his input. I trust him completely to be aligned with God's will for this young man. Blessings and protection for you in Kenya.*

And just like that, Mikey got a chance. God had not abandoned him—or me. Before I arrived yesterday, the locals looked at Mikey's situation as merely his lot in life. His cries for help only found ears of people who had no resources to assist him. Then God sent me, an unlikely outsider, into Mikey's world, broke my heart, showed His love, and answered my prayer.

God built the courage and compassion in me to stop avoiding tough places like this, to not judge Mikey by his worst actions, but to see him as precious and created in God's image. Not to see him as addicted, lost, and beyond hope but rather as beautiful, priceless, and full of potential. Redeemable by the blood of Christ. God wanted me to love Mikey by doing what I could and by sharing his challenges with others who had the resources and connections to help.

It made me think of all the times I had crossed the street to avoid someone passed out in the gutter or begging. I was like the pastor in the parable of the good Samaritan of Luke 10:25–37, who saw the battered man and viewed him as a problem, finally choosing to walk on. So many times, too, I have been like the temple assistant who was curious, crossed the street, looked closely, and then walked on. But now, through His love and compassion, God is patiently making me more like the Samaritan. Even though Mikey came from a different culture, even though he was addicted, abandoned, and lost, God had now made me into someone who stopped and loved my neighbor.

I am far from perfect. Sometimes I still walk past the hurting, too busy to stop and help. Sometimes I walk by because I don't know what to do or say or how to fix it. My pride still gets in the way. Sometimes I just get overwhelmed feeling like I can't help them all. But this time, I did stop, and God showed how truly loving He is.

In Mikey's case, the innkeeper, the one who would watch over him, was Nakuru Children's Trust. It used to surprise me that the two-thousand-year-old teachings of the Bible apply to me. Yet the more the Holy Spirit illuminates the lessons, the more contemporary they become. They truly are timeless.

Jesus did the same for me as He did for Mikey. My lot in life was being born into a family with a bipolar mom and a dad who drank too much. To cope, I turned to pursuing the American dream and became addicted to success, money, and status. In Jesus's own words, I worshiped the god known as mammon, as in, "You cannot serve both God and mammon" referenced in Matthew 6:24. Mammon symbolizes money and everything money can get you. It translates into comfort, pleasure, and status.

Mammon boosts our ego. It is one of the most powerful gods in America.

So, Mikey and I were no different. He had his addictions and sins. I had mine. The remedy is the same. We both need Jesus.

Jesus entered my world. He, the Son of God, forgave me for *all* my sins. And He offered help. Just like Mikey had to say yes to the opportunity of going to school, I had to say yes to Jesus to enter His kingdom. Who knows, maybe saying yes to Jesus is next for Mikey too?

———

The sun was rising, and Joe stirred in his bed. I had to share the good news in the email. "Joe, listen to this!" I read Terri's response, and now I wasn't alone in my tears of celebration.

It was time to get rolling. Twende kazi, and all that. Fortunately, it was Saturday, and we were getting picked up an hour later than usual to go to the school. The busy week and excitement of movie night and dancing left me wiped out. So today, I required *four* pots of tea.

Spot on at 8:30 a.m., Wally arrived and drove us to Maisha Mapya. We pulled out of the Rose Diamond, and the ordinarily crowded roads had some space for a change. Often, if a street is wide enough for three vehicles across, there are five. The cars and vans dance on the roadways with a rhythm that makes the whole thing work, but the threat of mutually assured destruction lurks should anyone miss a beat.

For the first time since we arrived, I rolled down the window, put my arm on the door frame, and rested my chin on my elbow. The air filling my lungs and tossing my hair about was crisp and clean. When we'd approach a plume of smoke, I'd roll the window up to avoid the distinct odor of burning garbage.

Nakuru is torn between two worlds. Fragile, stick-framed booths with people just as frail selling bananas, mangos, and avocados line the streets directly in front of modern office buildings where people dressed in suits and ties hustle in and out. The strain on people without adequate education limits their job opportunities and caps their earnings. Even the ones with degrees and professional positions find it difficult to support a family.

Advertisements in primary colors paint the city. Gold crowns on giant blue backgrounds with white letters reading, "If you like it, CROWN IT!" cover many of the city's buildings and stone walls. I originally thought this was an ad for Crown Royal Whisky. Something like "Hey, if you like it, raise your glass—toast it." It turns out it is for a paint company. By the number of these ads, I'm surprised they have any paint left to sell. Unmistakable, brilliant-red Coca-Cola trademarks with *"Burudika"* (Enjoy) painted underneath are on kiosks, billboards, and any structure where the logo can fit. Green Safaricom signs with "Top Off" are everywhere. And it seems like every fifty feet, Mpesa signs crying "Load Up Here" border every roadside. Mpesa is a digital payment system, much like Venmo or PayPal. It seems odd to me for a country where people have little money that Mpesa appears everywhere. It's useful but has a downside. The K2 gang has a vibrant network working to steal every single digital shilling they can get their hands on—and they're pretty good at it too.

All these things had been a blur this week. The simple, beautiful, ordinary things of life didn't gain my attention.

We made a right-hand turn at the Kobil Fuel Station onto our school's unnamed road. Wally got a Saturday blessing of a few extra shillings because I know he doesn't work on Sundays. He whispered a humble, "Asante, Wafula. Blessed day to you and Joe," and drove away.

We entered through the gate and went straight to the hall that could have hosted a rodeo the night before. Thankfully, the hay bales and guitars were gone. Two hundred blue plastic chairs, socially distanced, were arranged for today's meeting with our students' parents. Only a single red balloon resting in the corner, and wonderful memories, remained from Western Night.

Parents began arriving at 8:45 a.m. for the 10:00 a.m.

meeting, each one greeted at the gate by James, Ruth, and Mary. Once the parents signed in, they walked twenty yards up the hill toward the hall. Nia stood, hands resting in front of her, at the door. She gave each person a number before escorting them to their seat. It was as orderly as it sounds.

I love our student's parents from a place so deep within me that only God could have put it there. The moms inspire me with their ability to fight for their children. They may not end their own suffering, but if they can give their kids a better chance at life, they step up, sacrifice, and do whatever they are able to.

They can't believe Kim and I haven't given up on them like everyone else. Sometimes the echo of Pastor Bill's words are the only thing that makes me hang on. It's beyond their wildest dreams God would reach down and provide an opportunity for their children to be given a chance they did not have themselves. Getting a first-rate education might be the best pathway to escape a life sentence toiling in the dump.

While our parents do not have money for school fees, they do have time to offer. We introduced the idea of having them put some skin in the game by volunteering to help at the school. It would be their way to contribute, to be part of the Maisha Mapya family, and to give them value so they could hold their heads high knowing school wasn't a free handout. They were paying for it with sweat equity. Maisha Mapya was not only for their children, it was their home too. A bonus was getting them out of the darkness of the dumpsite and into the joyful haven of Maisha Mapya.

Initially, the staff pushed back at the idea of parents volunteering to clean classrooms or work in the kitchen. "Daudi, they'll never come."

"Let's give them a chance. Just like God, everyone wants to be known. This is a chance for them to feel known."

For some, any effort is beyond their capability at this stage in their lives. Life has crushed them beyond recognition. Shame has crippled them. We embrace them as any healthy member of our society. They too are created in God's image. We just need to love them to a place where they recognize it.

Even in a dumpsite, there are hierarchies. The evil queen at the top is Mama Amon. She had the biggest compound and a pantry stacked full of goods intended for her neighbors. Sodas stocked her shelves. Most living around her are surviving moment to moment—even grazing in the rubbish as they collect recyclables. Some people are so far down, when they look up, they only see the bottom. Alcohol gets them past their immediate need until it obliterates them, then they can't focus on anything at all. When sober, many reciprocate the love they feel from us.

Our volunteer program got off to a slow start. In the first few months, 50 percent of the children's guardians showed up. Some grumbled, "Why should we come and work when others don't?"

It seemed like a good question, but I replied, "God will judge us on *our* behavior—each one of us individually, and not by the behavior of our neighbors. Also, what kind of example do you want to set for your child? Do you want them to only view you as a taker, and then follow in your footsteps and become one too? Or do you want them to be the ones to change their world for the better?"

It doesn't take any special ability to clean our classrooms. We could hire outside people who might do a better job. But our parents are an essential component of Maisha Mapya. Having them here makes us complete. It brings them dignity, ownership, and pride.

Slowly, more and more parents chipped in. Some volunteered for extra things so they could be in the bubble of safety and joy of Maisha Mapya.

So when we gather as a group to discuss something, it's not a meeting. It's a celebration.

Today we were celebrating God getting us this far in surviving COVID-19. As each individual entered the gate, I couldn't help myself. I gave them the biggest greeting I could, including handshakes, hugs, and high fives. They all obliged, although most were still wet from the hand sanitizer at the gate. Let's face it, social distance isn't my thing. I'm a social closeness guy.

I spotted Angel's shosho at the gate. I had hoped we'd see each other since God forged our hearts together, battling the gangs to keep Angel and her sisters alive. I wanted to sprint to her, but I stayed at the hall door with my wing woman, Nia. Shosh signed in and huffed her way up the driveway. I whispered to Nia. "Watch this . . . I know she wants a big hug!" Then I took off running.

Nia's voice was growing faint with distance. "Oh, Dave, she does not do that! Maybe you are not aware that she is part of a Christian sect that does not do any physical contact with anyone."

Chuckling, I replied, "Oh yeah . . . she sooooo much wants a hug." With that, I spread my arms even wider and sped toward Shosh. Nia looked terrified. Shosh's smile escaped from her mask, and her arms were wider than mine.

"So good to see you, Shosh! How's Angel?"

Her smile disappeared. She looked down, rubbed her arms, and shuffled her feet.

"I do not know."

"Oh, Shosh. Would you like me to try to find out?"

"Yes. Yes, please. I have not heard from her."

"I will. She's gonna be okay, Shosh. God has her in His hand. May I take you to your seat?"

Nia shook her head at the miracle of love and said, "Dave, how are you able to do that?" She was referring to my getting a hug from Shosh.

"It's not hard, Nia. Hey, why don't you try this? When the next parent comes, put out your hand for a shake, say your name, and ask theirs. Then say, 'And who is your student?' When they give the child's name, say, 'Oh, I love them!' Watch and see what happens."

"English or Swahili?"

"You'll know, Nia. You'll know."

She shivered at taking the risk to make herself so vulnerable.

But when the next guest approached, I raised my eyebrows and nodded, signaling "your turn."

Courageously, she stuck out her hand. "Thank you for coming, madame. I'm Nia. Kindly remind me of your name?"

"Elizabeth."

Nia replied softly. "And who is your child?"

"Mary."

"Ohhhhh, I love Mary. She is such a lovely girl. Isn't she?"

Elizabeth put her arm on Nia's shoulder, and the two walked to her seat like they were best friends. Nia glanced back over her shoulder to me like, "Did you see that?!"

Yes, I did, Nia. Love is powerful, and no one responds to it like those starving for it—people exactly like our kids and their parents. Jesus knows all about them. Maybe that's why He loves the poor so much.

When it was time to start the meeting, one hundred forty-nine people were in their seats. One hundred forty-three women and six lone men. That tells you a lot about our community.

Two of those amazing moms, Zuri and Elizabeth (yes, that Elizabeth, Nia's new best friend), headed to the stage, grabbed mics, and led the rest of the parents in praise and worship. There is a distinction between the two in Kenya. Praise is acknowledgment and appreciation of what God has done for us. It is a way of giving thanks to Him through songs encouraging hand clapping and dancing. In a word—excitement. In comparison, worship is when we totally and humbly submit to God. Expressions are full of adoration and reverence. Worship involves an intimacy only reserved for God. When the two women left the stage thirty-five minutes later, every heart in the room was linked each other's and anchored to God.

Fresh off their command performance at the International Day of the Girl Child a week earlier, the dance troupe from Maisha Mapya took the stage. Proud moms cheered like it was 1964 and they had front row seats to see the Beatles. Once the sunshine-yellow-shirted bundles of joy started, I thought some moms might actually faint. The DJ blasted the "I'm a superwoooooman" song at full volume. *Oh no! There it is again! It's taken me six days to get that tune out of my head.* But it was totally worth it. The elation on the children's faces showered delight on everyone. A standing ovation saw the kids off the stage, a new endorphin-filled memory created.

Our GLT did what they are learning to do well. They led our community. Mary, all five-feet-two of her, took command. She paraded like a peacock around the stage in her four-inch heels. She congratulated the parents for the support they were giving their students.

She said, "These kids will have a future far beyond what we see today. Some will go on to excel in academics, some in arts, some in athletics. But they all will grow up to make their communities better. They will all love their neighbors along the way."

Maggie, as our child sponsorship director, stressed the importance of teamwork in growing a child into a healthy adult. "We do our part. We help give them a top-quality education. We feed them nutritious food so they can grow. We don't want them to struggle to learn on an empty stomach. We reinforce Christian values. We help them make friends. Our sponsors do their part in helping financially and writing loving letters of encouragement to the kids. And you do your part. You make sure their uniforms are clean. You help make a space for them to do their homework. You volunteer to help at school. You are the ones who stress to your children how important education is. We all work together to create a better life for these precious ones. Thank you for all you do."

I saw Dan and Joel were next. I knew they would do a great job, and I slipped out to pray about what God wanted me to share when I got on stage in a few minutes.

"Just go love them and be who I have made you to be," came His words to me.

The cheers from the parents as the leadership team left the

stage meant each member had shined with poise and presence. They were really coming into their own. It's hard to believe they are only twenty-somethings, and I can't wait to see the thirty-five-year-old versions of each of them. I'm so proud of them. They are exceptional humans.

It was my turn. *"Just go love them and be who I have made you to be."*

My fifty-nine-year-old body made it up the six stairs. I jogged across the stage, giving it my best strut. With my hands held high, I sang out, "I'm a superwoooooooman!" and did the kids' signature leg-throwing dance move.

The ladies roared. The six gentlemen shook their heads, a few covered their faces.

These people know I love them with abandon and want to cut their chains of bondage free. Free from sin and free from cultural norms saying you need to act in a certain, somewhat uptight way that is always being judged by others. I want to love them, have them love me back, and have them become who God made them to be.

I told them how great it was to see them all. How much I empathized and prayed for them during the oppression of COVID-19 and lockdowns. Seeing me alone on stage, they all sensed someone was missing. It was Mommie Kim. They missed her so much I could feel their heartache.

"Hey, let's send her a message!" I got out my phone and held it up to the crowd. Let's say, "Hi, Mommie Kim."

In unison, they repeated after me. "Hi, Mommie Kim." Then, "Come to Kenya soooon. We miss you. We love you."

I panned the room with the video. "Repeat after me, 'We hope Dave doesn't lose his phooone!'"

They laughed.

With my dance and icebreaker out of the way, I shared the vision for the community council, that no handout big enough was coming and if we wanted things to get better, we were going to have to make the changes ourselves.

I addressed the issues with the increased gang violence and

told them I had been meeting with some groups to bring peace. A few heads dropped with open mouths and eyes still fixed on me. I asked them to pray for God's wisdom, intervention, and protection. I kept it brief because this day was about celebrating each other and our God. It wasn't about stirring things up, creating fear, and being fixated on the butchery we all knew too well.

Flo and the kitchen squad made a feast for the crowd, enough for everyone and even a little takeaway. The word always gets out when we're hosting an event. The delicious aroma signals to the neighborhood something is happening at Maisha. Kids and even a few grown-ups show up at the gate, desperate for food, to see if they can get a meal. We always make extra.

Enjoying food with our community is a gift. It assures them a full stomach for the night and creates a casual atmosphere where people can be neighborly. People feel free to hang out for an hour or two or leave as soon as they are served. There is no expectation —only freedom.

By 2:00 p.m., Joe and I were trying to get out the gate. Wallace had the car tuned up and ready to twende. Some teenage boys were lined up at the gate petitioning for lunch. It was Mikey and four of his friends. Mikey was stumbling, hammered, and wreaking from the glue he'd been inhaling. His friends had to speak for him to greet me and ask for food.

Oh, Mikey, come on, buddy. You are going to have to get cleaned up before Thursday. Lord, help this child.

I returned to the kitchen, scraped every pot, and gave them all the remaining food, praying the entire time for God to do a miracle. Mikey was so smashed, and I knew he wouldn't remember a thing. I gave him a lackluster high five and sunk in the car with Wallace and Joe to head to our next meeting.

Have you ever had the feeling of having a hole in your heart? You know, the one coming from getting horrible news. That's what seeing Mikey in that condition did to me. I didn't have time to process it because we were arriving at Java to meet with another young man, Ace.

Ace is an interesting guy. We've had some great times together, along with a few challenges. When he heard I was coming to Nakuru, he texted me.

I must come to see you. We need to be together. ~ Ace

He made a half-day trip just to meet me for tea.

We sat at the same table where Joe, Kelsey, and I had met a few days earlier. Joe stared in the distance for a moment. I wondered if he was experiencing flashbacks from me saying to Kelsey, "I want to meet the gang leaders," and her straightforward reply, "I think we can make that happen."

Ace grew up in Hilton, scavenged in the dumpsite as a kid to survive, and received the break of his life when he got sponsored to go to school. He did okay as a primary and high school student, and now he is in his last year of college. His dream is to get a degree, become a social worker, and return to his birthplace and make life better there for kids. Two years ago, we spent a great deal of time together as he did his "attachment" at Maisha Mapya. Kenya has an interesting system: third-year college students put the theories they have been learning in the classroom into practice by "attaching" (volunteering) themselves to an organization doing the type of work they have studied. I love this practical approach to preparing young people for their careers. Ace and Maisha Mapya spent a few months in 2018 "attached."

Growing up in the community, Ace knew everyone. He was bold enough to bring up issues the residents were too shy, too ashamed, or too afraid to talk about with me directly. Many in our community had never spoken with a white man. Rumors about wazungu being this or that ran strong. Have you ever watched *Downton Abbey*? There are distinct hierarchies in place, "upstairs people" and "downstairs people" and all that. As a former British colony, Kenya remains a land of hierarchies. Locals often end up on the low end of the spectrum even though it is their native country. My engagement with locals has broken a lot of stereotypes. I'm approachable. I wear jeans and a T-shirt along with a smile. I'm vulnerable. I walk in the community alone. I'm here to love them, not exploit them. My model is Jesus, and I pray we bring His kingdom to Earth right here in Hilton.

During the fall months of 2018, when Ace was with us, he took me behind the curtain to shadowy places I'd never seen before. Ace may have been a third-year college student, but he had a PhD in the issues of our community. I learned so much from our time together as I spent seventy-one continuous days in the dumpsite among the people. We had tremendous victories and also devastating losses. But Ace got to see this mzungu loving the community and be a man of peace. Hopefully God would use what he saw to inspire him to follow through on his promise to serve his hometown neighbors after college.

I knew our teatime would be brief, so after exchanging greetings, I dove right in. "I've never seen my friends in Hilton so on edge. Everyone is armed, drunk, or both. It's just not a good combination."

"True."

I needed to meet with K2 as soon as possible. The progress with the Team Peace guys seemed to be moving along, but this other group was still in the shadows. The only things I knew about them were their name and a few of their heinous deeds. And time was running out.

"If you don't feel comfortable answering this next question, feel free to pass. Ace, do you think the guys in all the gangs know me?"

"Yes."

Really? How is that even possible?

I could tell Joe was expecting another doozy of a question. "What do they think of me? Are they okay with me?"

"They always see you as a good man. Some see you as a father, brother, and also one of the community because of the concern you always have for them. You are a treasure to them, Dave."

You are a treasure to them, Dave. That made my tea go down easier.

"Can you introduce me to someone from K2?"

"I can ask."

I figured he would if he could. We spent the next half hour reminiscing over a few of our stories from the years before. We laughed, shook our heads, and told inside jokes. Joe played along. I was waiting for Ace to ask either for some personal advice or for financial help. Usually, it's the latter.

It never came.

Finally, I said, "You know one of my kids' homes was raided."

"Yes."

"Do you know who did it? Do you know who wanted to kill my Angel?"

"I don't. I do not know."

THE REST

October 18, 2020

SUNDAY. Finally. A day to sleep in! And a free day for my mind to relax.

The extra thirty minutes of slumber was pure luxury. Joe and I headed to breakfast. I committed to having only a single pot of tea that morning. In the previous ten days, I'd already consumed a lifetimes's allotment.

When we got to the restaurant, the lights were on. Other guests were engaged in conversation and enjoying their meals. There was even a line to get omelets.

Joe and I enjoyed a leisurely meal too.

Speaking of Joe, I was learning Jesus had sent him as a gift to me. I wasn't supposed to go on this trip alone. God knew that. Originally, I thought Joe was merely an earthly acquaintance, but he was a divine connection. Every day and in every interaction, Joe was the perfect traveling companion. Starting with his first visit to Maisha where he said to his Kapu team, "I'll be back." And he kept his promise and returned. Joe lifted my load by making the flight arrangements. He was flexible and accommodating to my schedule. He honored every invitation and graciously skipped private meetings. Joe prayed with me. He let his heart feel my hurts. Joe bonded with the Maisha Mapya family, students, and parents. He packed tuk-tuks full of food and went to the dumpsite. Joe danced the two-step. Joe was a grandpa to Kat, an uncle to the GLT, and a friend to everyone. As I think through the Bible, He is a Barnabus named Joe.

Finally, I realized Jesus was rooming with me. He just went by the name Joe. He never forced me to do a thing, like take him to Lake Nakuru to see pink flamingos. He was simply a constant source of love and support—always available but never needy.

It was a glorious day, ideal for the forty-minute walk to Trinity Vineyard Church in Milimani, the richest neighborhood in Nakuru. Outside the gate at the Rose Diamond and up the hill, giant, manicured compounds with mansions line the streets. The governor's white palace is on the left and overlooks Lake Nakuru. Camo-clad guards make sure no one disturbs his excellency. Their machine guns give weight to the display.

A half-mile-long tunnel of jacaranda trees, their purple blossoms in full bloom, shaded us from the morning sun. Birds provided the first worship tunes of the day. Joe and I had little conversation. If I had said much, our words would have turned to wondering about Angel, connecting with the other gang, the GLT's ability to hold it together, and if we've done anything good at all. I wanted to exhale and have Jesus breathe His precious Spirit into my soul.

Trinity Vineyard is where Pastor Edgar leads his flock. Many of the missionaries in Nakuru attend Trinity. It's a comfortable open-air place. There are no walls, only a canvas top to provide shade from the hot African sun.

After a quick squirt of hand sanitizer and a temperature check, Joe wanted to relax inside the tent. Since I had been surrounded by crowds the entire week and needed some space, I searched for a place to be alone. An empty swing in the trees called to me, and I sat in the old tire serving as its seat. I can't remember the last time I was on a swing, but I was longing for the childlike freedom of kicking my legs and having the wind blow through my hair.

George, the worship leader who had dinner with us a couple of nights earlier, saw me, smiled, and invited me to pray with his team before they began the service. I hope our community feels similar hospitality at Maisha Mapya. It was nice to be asked and to belong. It was nicer to not have any responsibilities and to be in the presence of God in prayer with others.

I walked to the main tent and sat next to Joe. Kelsey and Kat were one socially distanced row behind us. The twinkling of Kelsey's eyes above her mask was a comforting greeting. I felt like we were co-conspirators in goodness.

After the service, Joe and I said our goodbyes to Edgar, Kelsey, and the crew and made our way back to the hotel.

I had a few minutes to do some personal chores. I washed my underwear and socks in the hotel sink. Hallelujah! I sent my jeans to be laundered by the Rose Diamond so they would be clean for the flight home. I like to be kind to my neighbors on the flight and leave the smells of the dump behind. Plus, I wanted to be as fresh as possible for my reunion with Kim, which was just four days away.

Early in the afternoon, Joe and I went downstairs to the hotel's garden courtyard. It's a peaceful place. I wanted some tea but settled for water instead. Balozi texted me a photo of a scrap of paper listing six kids' names, ages, guardians' names, and contact numbers.

can you help find these kids a school? ~Balozi

Unlike Mikey, they all were age appropriate for Maisha Mapya. Balozi is smart. And caring.

Let me check with our staff. I don't make any of the intake decisions, but I can have the team see what they can do. Can we meet tomorrow morning at 8? I've got some news to share. ~ me

Three minutes later, he sent a photo with two more names.
Three minutes after that,

cool dave can meet. ~ Balozi

Joe and I relaxed and decided not to head back to town and
face another evening at Java with the COVID-19 abbreviated
menu. We'd eaten every dinner there, and I was feeling for him. I
suggested we try the Rose Diamond. He had lamb chops. I had
steak. It was a most delicious meal. For dessert, I talked with Kim
for over an hour.

An hour later, Anonymous resurfaced with a text.

THOUGHT YOU SHOULD BE AWARE YOUR NEW FRIENDS ARE THE
ONES WHO RAIDED SHOSH AND ANGEL. ~ ANONYMOUS

It hit me like a truck. Why would Team Peace keep this secret
from me? Were they afraid that I'd withdraw my kindness and
love for them? Would they think what they did was unforgivable?
Did they fear I'd judge them and then believe what they already
believed about themselves—that they are worthless and the very
things they hate? If we were going to overcome this, we'd have to
address it. But first I needed to be a safe place to begin the
conversation.

*Why is it that whenever I try to escape, even for a day, someone always
reminds me why I came?*

THE QUESTION

October 19, 2020

THIS MORNING it was back to the 5:30 a.m. wake-up schedule and being greeted as I had been every day by Grandpa Barnabus Joe Jesus.

Sunday's slow pace had me rested, but some news over the weekend had filled me with anxiety. Anonymous knew something Ace didn't. *Your new friends are the ones who raided Shosh and Angel.* The thought that any Team Peace members were the beasts had me upside down. Shosh's response of "I do not know" when I asked, "How's Angel?" had left me empty. So, though I was excited to share the email response I got from NCT with Balozi and the guys about Mikey getting a chance to get into school. At the same time, I was distressed about Team Peace being the one who threatened Angel and stabbed her uncle. I could feel a bipolar pull happening in my head between rage and trying to hold together the beautiful relationship we'd started. *Maybe I was more drained than I thought I was?* I had a suspicion which member was sick enough to threaten Angel's head. But I didn't want to make any accusations to set them off. I didn't know how to approach them other than to make myself available to God and have Him sort it all out.

The last thing I needed was caffeine to add to my jitters, but I had three pots of mixed tea anyway. And a cup to go. Ayanna brought Joe's breakfast without him mentioning a word.

Wally dropped us at Maisha. I greeted the kitchen crew, then popped my head in to see the teachers still working on the virtues curriculum. They looked organized and were working diligently. I didn't disturb them other than to say, "Hi, I love you."

At ten minutes to 8:00 a.m., I handed Nia my wedding ring, passport, phone, and wallet. She figured out I wouldn't need the hand sanitizer until I got back.

Of course, Kelsey was already at the gate waiting to go. Kat ran to Grandpa Joe like they had scheduled a play date.

Kelsey soon took off, and I hustled to keep up with her all the way to Team Peace's base. Thirty guys stuffed into the space joked and greeted us, full of smiles.

"Sit down. Sit down, guys. I've got some news."

Immediately, I told them Mikey might get into school. Jaws dropped, then corners of mouths turned up, and gigantic smiles appeared on their faces. Except for one.

"Do you really think you can help this kid?" Samson asked. The effect of prior empty promises filled his tone.

"I can try."

Heads turned toward Mikey as if to say, "You just won the lottery, kid."

"We'll see," Samson scoffed.

"I set a meeting Thursday for Mikey to be interviewed about getting into school. I saw him on Saturday afternoon at Maisha Mapya. He and some friends came by after our event and got some food."

I looked at Mikey. "Do you remember?"

He didn't respond except to tuck his chin to his chest and slowly close his eyes.

"He was high out of his mind. If he shows up like that Thursday, he'll have no chance. None! Do you get that, Mikey?"

A soft, shame-filled voice breathed out, "Ya-yes."

"Mikey, do you want to go to school?"

"Yes."

"Then I need you to do your part. You need to be sober until Thursday. No chang'aa. *Hakuna pombe* (No drinking alcohol)."

A random voice in the background shouted, "That's easy! He doesn't drink!" Everyone laughed.

Like that was some kind of victory?

"Okay, no weed. *Hakuna bange.* No glue. *Hakuna gum kabisa!* Can you do that, Mikey?"

"Yes . . . maybe. Yes." Then he mumbled something I couldn't hear.

"I know you can. I believe in you."

I turned to the entire group and addressed them like family, pointing at Mikey.

"Do you love this guy?"

Almost in unison, they replied, "Yes, we do."

My tone intensified. "Really?"

"Yes, Daddy Dave, we do."

"Then, we will do what all good families do. We will support him."

Despite how dysfunctional they may have been before I arrived, they were all each other had. They were a family. Maybe not a model one, but they clung together and had each other's backs. I cemented the concept in their minds and made them commit.

"If you love him, there will be no glue, no weed, no alcohol. Only *chakula and maji* (food and water). He's gotta be sober on Thursday. This is how we love our family. When one guy gets a chance, we help him. It's up to you. This is on you!"

"We can do this, Daddy."

"I know you can. Let's see what God does too."

It amazed me at how open they were to band together and do something good, something foreign to the habits they'd developed. I knew if we, as a family, could do this for Mikey, we could band together and support everyone else in the room when they needed it. How could these men who wanted the best for Mikey be the same guys that terrorized Shosh and Angel?

I looked at Kelsey. She knew better than most how the gangs caused trouble. She couldn't believe what she just heard. To see them surround Mikey in his chance for something good and leave gang life left her speechless. I felt like wrapping up the meeting on this high note, but with only three days before my exit, I pressed on.

"Balozi gave me a list of kids in Hilton wanting to attend school. I don't do the intake at Maisha. So I make you no promises. Some of our classes have too many kids. But I'll pass the information on to our team and let them do their jobs. They will visit each home. If it's a genuine case and their families agree to do what it takes to be a part of the Maisha Mapya family, like volunteer work for the school and also make the community a better place, then there's a good chance *some* of these kids will get in. But they have to be a Team Peace player."

This was fine with them.

Balozi asked again about the dude's impounded motorbike. "What did you find out?"

"Nothing so far. Let me see where things stand."

Balozi is persistent but polite. The more we interacted, the more I felt we could do some good things together. We certainly had different spheres of influence, but I thought we could bring them together and see how we could help each other.

Damu, still without sleeves but with plenty of vitriol, slinked around the pool table as he stalked me. Ever hostile, he took the final few steps and stuck two fingers into my neck.

"So, pastor!" His neck contorted and the whites of his eyes grew. "If some guy comes at me with a knife and kills me, what do I do? Nothing?" Damu's head turned like he wished he could twist a blade into my Adam's apple.

Give me an answer, God. Now! In place of an answer, He gave me nothing. The last time I had gotten away with deflection, so I used it again.

"Do you guys want revenge or peace?"

"WE WANT PEACE! WE WANT PEACE!" They shouted as if I was a slow learner.

I could see it in Damu's eyes. Rage. Hate. The thirst for revenge. It made me think Anonymous's text could be true. Damu backed off and placed both hands on his hips.

I looked right at him. "You say you want peace. Why did you attack Angel's house? Why did you threaten a little girl's head?"

Right then, they learned that Daddy Dave knew a lot more than they thought I did. Now I was the one with the steeled eyes. Their secret was out in the open.

"That never meant to happen," Samson roared.

"Really? Why?"

"He switched."

Shosh's son had been part of Team Peace but changed allegiance to K2. He'd been seen running with Mama Amon's boys. Mama Amon was even seen trying to make friends with the Shosh.

Now it made sense. They viewed Angel's uncle as a traitor, and he had to pay.

While our relationship had made a lot of progress in a short time, we'd still only known each other for less than a week. I had to tread wisely, so I addressed their barbaric attack indirectly.

"Really? You want peace?"

"Yes!"

"Peace begins with forgiveness. It doesn't come from a place where everyone on both sides is suddenly okay with each other. One side has to be the first to forgive."

They were listening. Samson settled in his chair and put his hands on his lap. Even Damu reluctantly sat, his eyes demanding an answer.

"Are you ready to go talk with Shosh and ask for forgiveness?"

Most of the guys hid their eyes. Some shook their heads no. I pressed on.

"I only need *one* of you to come with me to ask for forgiveness for stabbing her son. I don't need everyone. If you all go, it will scare her to death. I only need one of you."

No one said a word. I could hear their thoughts. *How did he know we were the ones to attack Shosh? Did God tell him in a dream? We can't ask for forgiveness. Angel's uncle was the traitor.*

I waited and prayed silently. I waited some more.

A lone voice to my left said, "Yes. I will do it."

It was Isaac, Dembe's son. Isaac had said little for the past week but closed yesterday's meeting with a prayer. His voice was soft and gentle, a stark contrast from his reputation as one of the most vicious thugs in Hilton. If Isaac went unannounced to her house, Shosh would either have a heart attack thinking he would assault her or defend her place to the hilt. She might try to burn him down, fearing he was there to set her house ablaze. I wasn't sure of his position in the gang's pecking order. He seemed to be in the shadows. *Maybe some leaders operate that way?*

"That's good, Isaac. Let me check with the Shosh and set things up."

He smiled at the ground without uttering another word.

The entire group prayed for God to make a way, and Kelsey and I left. Outside Balozi's bar, I asked her if she could check with Shosh and set up the meeting with Isaac. Something remarkable was within reach—bringing peace to Shosh and Angel's home. Maybe it would make it safe enough for Angel to return?

Lord, You say "blessed are the peacemakers." Please bless this whole thing. Peace was on our doorstep.

Kelsey made a right and headed to visit the Shosh. I headed left and skipped to Maisha. *Isaac is gonna meet the Shosh! Isaac is gonna meet the Shosh!* I was like a first grader. I almost sang out, "Hi ho, the derry-o, Isaac is gonna meet the Shosh!"

THE PARTNERS

October 19, 2020

WHEN I GOT TO MAISHA, Maggie and Nia were in the hall exploring how we could improve our sponsorship program. It's a topic that occupies a special place in our hearts. Barnabus Joe took his unofficially assigned seat at my left.

I was there physically, but my mind was split between the victory of Isaac agreeing to meet Shosh and what I would talk about at tomorrow's community council meeting. I'd dreamt about the day for three years, but my dreams never made it past the concept of getting people together. I had no clue what to say or how to say it. I passed a note to Nia.

Please prepare the hall for the council meeting tomorrow. Make them feel honored.

She looked at the paper, typed something into her phone, and began the meeting. "Dave, we've made significant progress in our systems."

The systems she referred to are all the wonderful gifts provided by individuals and organizations to bring efficiency to a remote little place like ours. Gone are the handwritten scraps of paper and sticky notes comprising our record keeping. In their place are digital files. Google gave us the G Suite set of products free of charge. Salesforce donated their customer relationship management (CRM) system to us. Volunteers from the Taproot Foundation in California helped set up Trello and Slack. Donors provided smartphones for our GLT to have full capability in their pockets. Everything is in the Cloud, searchable, and accessible anytime, anywhere.

However, having access to technology in the developing world is one thing. Figuring out how to break out of old habits with state-of-the-art tech is another.

One issue we faced was something as simple as what name should we put in the student's contact record? If the child has a birth certificate, do we use that name? What if, due to lack of education, the child's mother spelled the name phonetically, like Petah rather than Peter? (In the British accent of Kenyan English, the "r" turns Peter into Petah.) What if the child is never called by their birth name so that when a sponsor sends a letter to Brian W., no one knows who it's for because he is always called Dubs? Like everything, it's complicated. (Don't worry, eventually Dubs will get his letter. It just may not happen as efficiently as Nia would like.)

Just having a birth certificate is a luxury for many of our kids. In our intake of eighty students in 2018, sixty-five did not have birth certificates. No birth certificate means the child was not born in a hospital—instead most likely near home at the dump—and was never given an official document. I know what it's like not to be wanted. I can't imagine what it's like to not even exist? Once a child is over six months old, it costs fifteen dollars to get a certificate—something families who make two to five cents an hour never have.

One way we love our students is to prove they exist. The Chief works with us to help each child secure a birth certificate. The document gives them a name, proves they were born, and allows them to access all societal offerings like everyone else. It may not seem like much unless, of course, you don't have one.

This is one small way our sponsorship program benefits the kids. It's true— for thirty-three dollars a month, a generous donor can help clothe, feed, educate, and nurture a child. For us, a sponsor program is not merely a way of raising funds to pay for our programs. It's a way of raising complete children. And it's not only a child sponsorship program. It is a development program for the adult sponsors as well. The kids need the sponsors. The sponsors need the kids. The sponsors may not recognize it, but once they engage in the life of one of our precious little ones, their life becomes richer too.

There are lots of organizations who use a sponsorship model to fund their programs. Some have millions of donors and millions of dollars to advertise for more. We're not one of them. Instead, our marketing strategy is to create a remarkable experience for the donor worthy of them sharing with their friends. And we do it the old-fashioned way: word of mouth.

Our challenge is to make the experience for both the sponsor and the student exceptional. That's why, in designing our program, we went to the source. I talked with friends who sponsor children through well-known programs and asked, "What do you like? If you could do anything you wanted, what would you do?" The resounding answer was they wanted the relationship to be more than a monthly debit on their card and a photo on their refrigerator.

The child's experience with their sponsor is of supreme importance. We wanted to understand how our sponsor kids feel, so we reached out to former sponsor children who were now adults. We interviewed over twenty, including our staff members Dan and Joel and our director, Dr. Liz, who were beneficiaries of sponsorship programs. We focused on the best parts and what we could do better than what they experienced.

We discovered the extraordinary place sponsors play in the lives of the students. For many, it is the only source of love they feel. Just knowing someone, somewhere, loves them and cares for them meant they were not alone. Not forgotten and not abandoned. Dan's eyes sparkled when he said, "My sponsor, he's my dad too, Daudi. He got me through."

A few times a year, a sponsor child at Maisha receives a physical letter written personally to them. Often, they include pictures from "Mom and Dad." I asked Dan, "Do you remember what letter day was like for you as a kid? How did it make you feel?"

"So many tears, Daudi. You're so filled with joy when you get one. Then you see your friend crying because he didn't get one. You hide yours in your pocket and later read it a million times. But you can't share it with your best friend who feels forgotten."

"Let's make sure that doesn't happen."

"Not everyone will write," he said.

Dan was right. Not every sponsor writes a letter every time, even if they mean to. The busyness of life runs us all over sometimes.

He suggested, "What if we have more than one sponsor per kid? Maybe at least one of them will write?"

Dan was on to something. So, we designed a multiple-sponsor model to increase the chances a child receives something conveying, "You are loved." Each of our children can have up to three sponsors. More sponsors, more chances of a genuine connection with a child. More love and prayers all the way around.

Nia pointed out, "How are we going to get that many sponsors?"

"We'll come up with something great. God will make a way. How can we make the relationship come alive and keep a safe distance for the kids and sponsors?"

Maggie added, "We need to put the sponsor in the story with us. Take them along on the journey."

I agreed. All we needed was the right host to play the interviewer, explainer, child psychologist, and playful photographer—you know, one of the fun ones who uses balloons and Beanie Babies to make kids laugh. Only one person entered my mind for this critical role. It had to be Maggie, a young woman with heartbreaks I'll never fully understand. She's a beautiful bud waiting to bloom. She's adorable, loveable, and brings out the best in the children. The kids know she loves them day in and day out, whether or not a camera is around. She's perfect for the job. She just doesn't know it, yet.

"Maggie, you'd be a perfect interviewer."

"Not me. No way. I do not like that side of the camera. I am trained in accounting. I will do that. Anyway, what would I say?"

All I could think of was I could find a hundred bookkeepers in about ten seconds, but I could never find someone with Maggie's tenderness, instincts, and appropriate reactions to emotional situations. If she would be brave enough to share her beautiful heart with people outside the Maisha Mapya family, then they would experience how God works through us. They would see how His love is at the center of everything we do.

"Is it that you don't want to do it or that you fear not doing a good job? I think you'd be perfect."

"I am trained as an accountant. I know nothing about this other stuff. Besides, what would I say?"

So, you're saying there's a chance. "I don't know anything about it either. We'll learn together. You won't be alone. I'll do it with you. Let's give it a try."

"If you will help me, I am in!"

I could already visualize our first "Maggie's Minute" video flooding our donors with all the feel-good hormones that genuine acts of generosity provide. And I hoped the videos would also help them learn about people on the other side of the world who might lack material goods and battle shame but who also have dreams, the desire to love, and overcome all while possessing the full beauty of being made in God's image by our all-gracious Creator.

Before we closed the meeting, we prayed about how we could communicate the stories of our children's lives and maintain the dignity of the kids, parents, and community while accurately providing the context of their lives and the incredible impact our donors and sponsors have on this area. Above all, we wanted to shower honor and glory on God.

I reached into my backpack and pulled out the large envelopes with letters from sponsors Kim had arranged alphabetically for each class. I spilled out the PP1 pile on the table. Right on top was Angel's envelope. My heart sank, and echoes of Shosh's response to my question two days ago rang in my ears.

"How's Angel?"

"I do not know."

————

Good thing I had those three pots of tea. It was only noon, and I was spent. There was no word yet from Kelsey about her meeting with Angel's shosho. That drew on my strength some more.

In April 2019, a gentleman in California who founded a ministry in Nakuru eighteen years earlier to help street children emailed me. He reached out to get to know us, our heart, and how things were going for us in running Maisha Mapya.

From the questions he asked, I guessed his organization was having struggles. Maybe they were evaluating their options? One possibility might be a merger with a like-minded organization like ours. Maybe merging with them would be an answer to our prayer for providing the land we needed.

We were dedicated to growing our campus, so that day, the GLT road tripped to check out this potential new property for Maisha Mapya's longed-for expansion. Half the team jumped in Nia's car and sped off. Joel pointed to a compact car parked across the street from Maisha.

"Let's go," he said.

Somehow, Joel, our Community Care Director, had acquired a car. *Where did he get a car? And why was I surprised he was behind the wheel?* It illustrated the resourcefulness of my talented team.

We drove across town for about twenty-five minutes to a rural area near the original Jireh School. It brought back memories of the good times from Andrew's and my first trip to Kenya where God initiated this grand adventure. If you had told me thirteen years earlier, I would be looking to expand the school God had placed me in charge of, I might have called you a liar.

It had been years since I had been in this area. I rarely travel outside of a ten-minute radius of Maisha Mapya. Pavement now covered many of the former pothole-riddled dirt roads. Bare fields were now planted and had some permanent dwellings. Things had developed, but not as quickly as closer to Nakurutown.

I also experienced sorrow over how the devil had destroyed something so beautiful as the love Jireh had spread to lost children at its inception. I'm not sure if the Jireh School exists anymore; last thing I heard was if you wanted to attend, you had to pay school fees. The children who couldn't pay couldn't attend, and that's how the Nakuru Children's Trust started. NCT is a remnant and still doing good and loving work. But, they are a shadow of the bright light of Jireh when it was running full steam in the 2000s.

We pulled into the new property, and it reminded me of the old Jireh School. Built in the same era, it had a royal gate declaring a prominent presence, though it was looking tired and in need of some TLC and paint.

I got out of the car Joel had procured. Nia, already waiting for us, cackled, gave me a stare, and said, "Beat you!" And cackled some more.

The local executive director greeted us and motioned to enter the administration building. A tarnished brass plate displaying the founder's name was on the door. I could feel his pain at the possibility of losing his once thriving school. It reinforced my resolve to create a healthy organization that would live on well past Daddy Dave being at home in heaven.

Standing there, I saw the loss of a dream, but also the possibility of a new one. The classrooms were empty. The dorms were empty. The sounds of children were missing. The property's five picturesque, flat acres seemed to go on forever compared to Maisha Mapya's .8-acre rocky hillside campus near the dumpsite.

Nearly half their plot was an active farm. Walking through the fields and greenhouses, every one of the GLT commented on how wonderful it was. There was something about getting to touch plants and tree leaves that connected with each one of them. I'd only seen the GLT in my world, the urban world of poverty that is Gioto. Teacher Mary surprised me most as we strolled through the fields and she named each piece of vegetation, also stating its use. It was no surprise that Joel had a conversation with a cow. He's a trained veterinarian. He told me what the swamp of cow poop was all about. "Daudi, that is a biogas plant."

The rest of the property was an undeveloped open field. Perfect for a sports complex. I envisioned a track for an upcoming Kenyan marathoner, a futbol field, and a swimming pool. There would still be lots and lots of fertile soil to create a luscious garden and forest.

We left the complex not knowing where all of this would head; however, the visit blessed and encouraged me. There was comfort that maybe, just maybe, there was a place of belonging for the children at Maisha Mapya beyond fourth grade. And a new dream of the joy a swimming pool would bring.

Nia hopped in her car and revved the engine. "Let's go, ladies. Let's race the boys to lunch!" Her crew shot out of the parking lot. All we saw for the next fifteen seconds was her tailpipe, dust, and her hand waving goodbye out the window.

The GLT picked a local place for lunch, a stone's throw from the culinary safety of Java. They all got fish, except Maggie, who ordered chicken. My guess is that she had a bad gastronomic experience with fish. Barnabus Joe, the grandpa with the iron stomach, was all in, enjoying ugali and fish using his hands Kenyan style—no need for utensils. I had a lukewarm Coke.

When the meal was over, I turned to Nia. "I'll save you a seat."

"Huh?" she said

"Let's go, boys. Let's show these ladies who can get to the school first."

With that, the gentlemen, who would have preferred to digest for a while, sprinted out the door. Mary just lowered her toothpick and looked around confused. I'm not sure she heard a single word.

————

We needed to rush back to Maisha for a 4:00 p.m. Zoom call with a preschool in California that wanted to mentor our teachers. I'd met the founder of their school through Cornerstone Fellowship. We are cut from a similar cloth. He founded a nonprofit for youth in Haiti, and God had me fall in love with kids in Africa.

I love to connect people. I especially love to connect people who love God and want to shower love on others. Sometimes it's not easy. Sometimes time zones get in the way. The Maisha Mapya teachers in Kenya stayed late for the afternoon call to start. The Celebration Center teachers in California arrived early at 7:00 a.m. for the same reason.

I huddled our teachers around my laptop like they were going to hear the secret to God's kingdom. To our displeasure, the rains came and created internet connection issues. After exchanging introductions and pleasantries, the team in the US asked, "How many students do you have in your classrooms?"

"Thirty-five to forty."

"How many teachers do you have in your classrooms?"

Our teachers looked at each other inquisitively. I'm not sure they understood the question because the answer was obvious. "One."

Our Brady Bunch-looking Zoom screen had faces with open mouths staring at us before we heard, "We have one teacher per ten students."

Our teachers giggled. "Why is that, Daddy?"

Like a proud parent, I couldn't resist showing off. "Mary, why don't you share what the teaching staff here did this week?"

"Thank you, Daudi. Let me say we designed a Christian Character curriculum for our students that is culturally appropriate. We want our students to see themselves in the illustrations and make the concepts come alive. This week we focused on the important virtue of compassion."

The teachers from the other side of the ocean turned and looked at each other. "Wow. That's incredible." Then they asked, "How do you discipline your students? Here, it almost seems like the children are in charge of the classroom. We can't do anything."

Once again, our staff looked at each other, not knowing how to respond. They looked at me. The concept of children being in charge of the classroom was completely foreign to our teachers— the lack of respect for authority incomprehensible. I just let it play out.

Every day our teachers face the consequences of our students' poverty. For many of our students, the only meals they may eat all day are the ones served at Maisha Mapya. For some, lunch on Friday is the last food they taste until porridge on Monday morning. Some are sexually abused; most are neglected. Some have parents in prison. Some have never seen their mom or dad sober. Some witness mom doing whatever she has to with whoever can pay in order to put food on a plate. Some will face that decision themselves soon.

The chasm between our classrooms couldn't be wider, but the distance between our hearts was shrinking fast. On both sides of the planet, it was obvious that God-fearing teachers are full of love.

By the end of the call, I could feel our teachers questioning the myth of how much better the schools are in America. It's not that they are better or worse. They are just different. While I believe foreign teachers should never teach full time in our school, I hoped we could partner to build capacity and skills.

Five minutes after the call, I received an email from the American team with some great questions:

- What does a typical day look like?
- Do they do centers? Recess?
- Do your teachers break up the thirty-five kids into smaller groups?
- Do you see any ADHD or special needs with the kids? Autistic kids?
- How are the assessments done?
- How are your teachers trained?
- Do students sit at desks? Tables?
- Is "play" valued as a means of learning?

There was a genuine interest in understanding the differences and learning from each other. It was like my first meeting with Balozi's boys enjoying tea under the trees at Maisha. We brought our curiosity to the table. It exposed and broke stereotypes and birthed a relationship.

Two minutes later, they sent this email:

Would you be willing to allow one or two of our teachers to come to visit your school? When would be a good time?

God had placed a desire in their hearts to connect more deeply. He does that with His family, whether it's the guys who hang out with Balozi, our GLT, or even preschool teachers on the other side of the world.

This exchange opened up a dialogue among Maisha's teachers. I asked them what issues they faced. Without exception, they said, "Helping our students to read."

"Why?"

"We do not have enough books."

Our head teacher's brow furrowed, but to her credit, she didn't say a word. She listened to her staff.

"What else do you need?" I asked.

"Can we get a projector so we can put some lessons up on the board so everyone can see?"

"Nia, let's see how much it is to get three projectors. What else?"

The most significant answer was always "*more books*."

"Okay. We will get you the resources you need to teach our children to read. But here is the deal. We will take a complete and full inventory of every piece of equipment we have, and you as the teachers are responsible for its condition. Can you set that up, Nia?"

She smiled as if I had accepted hand sanitizer from her on my way to meet a gang. Everyone filed out for the evening.

I didn't have the energy or appetite for dinner. I asked Joe if we could skip it.

"Hakuna matata. No worries." He's quite the Barnabus.

I got to the Rose Diamond, opted out of a shower, and flopped onto the bed. Tomorrow was a big day. I'd waited for three years to form a community council, and it was happening in twelve hours. *Lord, tell me what to say.*

THE COUNCIL

October 20, 2020

I USE this expression with our team all the time, "I love to wake up and see what God did while I was sleeping." It's an inside joke because they have seen me struggle time and time again, trying to make Dave's, not necessarily God's, dreams happen. It comes from my Wall Street days, making business plans, daily goals, and all that.

Last night was one of those nights when God was doing stuff. I didn't toss and turn. I left my worry about the council meeting in my prayers and slept well. I woke up with a smile and in total peace. It made my three pots of tea even more enjoyable.

Twende kazi, Wally. Come on, Barnabus Joe, let's go watch God work. Greetings, teachers, how's your compassion coming along? And a new text.

I'm off to meet with Shosh to see if she will make peace with the guys ~ Kelsey

Of course, Shosh will want peace. She'll be rejoicing with Angel in no time. God was on a roll, and with only two days left before I had to leave, everything was going to come together. I could feel it. Shosh was going to make up with the guys. The guys were going to experience how good forgiveness feels and want more. They were going to forgive K2. The council would come together. We would create jobs. Abuse and neglect would end. Peace would be our new culture. Angel and her sisters would come home. God's glory would shine. We would all live happily ever after.

In the meantime, at 8:00 a.m., the GLT gathered to see what we could do to help combat the shame our community faces. Shame causes so much pain and leaves you feeling helpless to do anything to ease it. Knowing how to respond when a young girl tells you she sold herself to the old man next door in order to get food or a sanitary napkin is delicate business. My first instinct is to fix the problem and stop the hurt now: to provide food and sanitary pads, to meet the physical need that is causing the act bringing shame. I was learning there's a time for that, but first, I needed to connect. I needed to hone my empathy skills.

Empathy is not connecting with the experience itself. It's connecting with the underlying emotions of the experience.

We all have shame. We do our best to bury it deep inside, hoping to suffocate it. Or we throw ourselves into our work and accomplishments to prove that the things people say about us, things we even say to ourselves, aren't true. Even though they are. We self-medicate to avoid dealing with it. Hard as we try, shame lingers.

This muck makes it difficult to connect with those underlying emotions. It takes courage to dig up the things you have done and go to the place where you have shame. Yet it is essential if we are going to connect with others who are feeling shame. It gives us understanding. The exact reason may be different, but the underlying emotion is the same. We know how it feels. And that's where connection happens. We must be willing to enter our own place of shame, conjure up those emotions, and sit with the person in their despair.

The good news is we all can develop that skill.

Our young team knows all about shame, grief, fear, and loneliness. They know the feeling of being unwanted and unworthy just like me. But they didn't know their shame was a magical blessing in loving the least of these. God would use those feelings to help put a salve on their neighbors' wounds.

I remember how humiliated I was when my best friend and business partner arranged with our boss to take the business from me. Just writing these words makes my pulse quicken and my heart ache. I was unaware then that God would use this experience to help me relate to a struggling community in Africa. Even though I left working on Wall Street eighteen years ago, over half my disturbing nightly dreams revolve around the end of my career. Many of the others are night terrors. Rarely do I have a night full of joyful dreams.

For years, I believed that these were attacks from the devil to discourage and torment me. When I am awake, I am conscious of God, His promises, His protection, and His victory. I feel strong. But at night, while sleeping, I am vulnerable and ripe for an enemy attack. The more time I have spent with my friends in Hilton, the more my thoughts about my shame-filled dreams have evolved. It is my shame that connects me with the community. We share this emotion. I now believe it is God who uses the shame I felt from being betrayed by my business partner as a benefit. It is a constant reminder to understand and have compassion for my neighbor. God truly is good, even when my dreams are not filled with children's laughter as they are being chased by puppies running through fields of spring flowers.

The team and I both needed to realize and embrace this gift of shame and develop a few phrases to help relate to those around us.

Brené Brown's *Dare to Lead* once more provided helpful insight. I opened the text and read a few examples. "When someone shares something difficult with you, you can respond with, 'I don't even know what to say right now, I'm just glad you told me.'

"See? We don't need to fix it. We need to connect."

The GLT and I talked about being aware of the other person's perspective. Maybe we could build connections by understanding how they saw the world.

"Let's be aware of all the signals we send. Should we make eye contact? Look away? Reach out and hug? Give space? Respond quickly or stay quiet for a while? This really applies to me because I have the added cultural challenge of considering what my actions mean to Kenyans, not Americans.

"When someone is sharing their struggle, it's powerful to say, 'Me too.' This communicates 'I may not have had the exact thing happen as you, but I know the struggle and you're not alone.'"

We explored the differences between sympathy and empathy. Sympathy is feeling *for* the person. Empathy is feeling *with* the person. This is an important distinction. One makes the other person feel less than, while the other lifts them up.

I gave some examples of how we could completely mess this up by sharing a few clunkers.

"When someone shares something difficult, try not to gasp." The entire team laughed.

"Resist the temptation to compare and say, 'If you think that's bad, wait until I tell you this.' It's not about you; it's about them." A few eyebrows went up conveying that I've done that a few times.

"We will not do this perfectly. You guys have been around me long enough to know I make lots of mistakes, but I keep trying. As you bravely step into other people's lives in the middle of their darkest moments, you're gonna mess up too. I want to end the session with this piece of advice. When you blow it, and you will, simply be honest and say, 'You shared something difficult with me. I wish I'd responded differently. I care about you and what you shared. Can I try again?'"

"Can you repeat that?" Maggie asked.

She and each team member, including Joe, wrote it down word for word. Joe read it back to me. "Is that right? Did I get it all?" It was a tender moment.

We broke for ten minutes to grab some tea. I remained in the hall and let the excitement build in my heart to share what was next.

At 9:30 a.m., I couldn't help but smile, really big.

"Guys, are you ready for this?"

I was bouncing in my seat.

"I went to sleep last night without a plan for today's council meeting. When I woke up this morning, God laid out exactly what He wants us to do. It's crystal clear, and I feel a little foolish being so excited about it because it's too obvious."

They scooched closer and exchanged glances with one another.

Just over a year ago, when we began our leadership training sessions, Kim and I realized the GLT was inexperienced and wanted to please "the boss." They would look at me like, "I know I should know about this, but I have no idea what you are talking about." So, we tried to lighten things up. We purchased some candy-filled Wacky Monkey Clappers for that first week of training. Any time anyone agreed strongly with what was said, they would pull the lever with their thumb making the toy monkey clap symbols over its head. It may seem juvenile to you, and that's because it is! Plus, Dan loves sugar, so anything candy suits him just fine. We still use these toys to celebrate good ideas at our meetings, whether in person or virtual.

"Where's my monkey clapper?" I looked right and left and then clicked the end of my thumb like I was lighting a cigarette lighter.

Everyone laughed.

"Are you ready? God wants us to run the council the same way we run Maisha Mapya!"

Not a single clap. Just inquisitive looks.

"What do you mean?" Joel asked. As head of community care and responsible for the council, he wanted to know the plan.

"The format of our meetings will be identical to our GLT

meetings. We will set goals for the term, review our to-do lists, and build our issues list between meetings. He wants us to create a set of core values everyone agrees on. Then, draft mission and vision statements. How awesome is that? It's not something new for us. God has been preparing us for a year and a half to lead our community in this manner. We'll use the Traction system for our structure. The best thing is you know how to do it. You don't even need me around."

That last line struck a little fear in them.

"Oh, I'll be here. But you already know how to do this. God has prepared us. Isn't He good?"

Nia asked, "If you allow, may I straighten up the hall for our guests?"

It was a polite request to take a break, clean up our tea, and sit and wait for whoever shows up.

I posed a question to the team before any community members arrived. "Where is the seat of least honor at this table?"

I knew the answer. I wanted to teach them the principle in Philippians 2:3 and how "in humility we consider others better than ourselves." It's highly counter cultural. Kenyans place those in the highest position at the head of the table. That's what happened to me and Joe at the International Day of the Girl Child event. And I squirmed out of it as fast as I could, even though I was a guest there. Today, I was in charge, and we were going to honor those who society says are the least of these.

Four large tables were arranged to form a square with seats for six people along each outer edge. One table had a different colored cloth over it, signifying it was the head table. I told the team we would not be sitting there. We would be off to the side, and I explained we would give the seats of most honor to those who traditionally have received the seats of lowest position, meaning, our friends from the dumpsite neighborhood.

The first person to arrive was an older man dressed in his Sunday best—an oversized sport coat and slacks. He smiled at Maggie and Nia and sat himself at the head table. Nia politely escorted him to a less prominent seat and offered to bring him some tea.

Others wandered into the hall with their mouths open, craning their necks, looking up at the grand ceilings, admiring the bright, airy building. Some looked as though they had just been transported into Buckingham Palace—intimidated but wanting to explore.

Nia and Maggie greeted each person, "Karibu Maisha Mapya. Welcome. We are delighted you are here," while extending their hands. They alternated taking people to the buffet table for tea and small bites (sausage and muffins) and showing them to their seats.

Others entered. They were probably dressed in their Sunday best too. But for them it meant well-worn denim pants, a heavy sweatshirt, knit stocking cap, and tennis shoes that revealed a few toes. Of course, I was dressed in jeans and a Hilton's Heroes T-shirt.

Soon all the seats around the table were full. Dembe was among them. We had invited each of our six neighborhoods to self-select an older man, older woman, younger man, and younger woman to be their representatives, so I was expecting twenty-four people. Twenty-six people came! They must've thought we were giving something away. Or maybe they had never been asked to participate in any decision-making process before. We got them extra chairs and figured we'd have them sort it out themselves as to who was their proper council person. I was happy anyone had shown up at all.

Joel leaned to me and whispered, "It's appropriate for the eldest gentlemen to open us in prayer." I thought he meant me. He turned to the older man in the sport coat, named Benjamin, and asked him to open us in prayer. He graciously accepted the honor.

I welcomed everyone to the council. "Thank you for being the courageous people who have the heart to serve our community. We are humbled you agreed to meet with us today, join forces, and see what we can do to make for a better community. I am honored you are here today."

It was the first time for some of them to sit and talk with a white man. I think the complimentary opening surprised them.

"You're probably wondering what we are going to do and how we are going to do it. You've all seen what God has done here at Maisha Mapya. This was a rocky hillside a few years ago. Look at what God has done. He transformed the lone wooden structure with Judy's Academy painted on the rusted iron sheet roof into Maisha Mapya Learning Center. God told me He wants us to lead the council the same way we led Maisha. We will use all the same ideas and methods. We pray He brings the same transformation to our entire community."

I don't think any of them had any idea how we run things, but as the beacon of hope for the community, they were interested. A few may have been thinking the council members would receive special handouts despite what we said when we met them in their neighborhoods.

"What should we call ourselves? What do you think of Maisha Mapya Community Council for our name?"

They all nodded with looks of approval.

I explained we wanted to extend the Maisha Mapya family beyond the school walls to include the entire community. I told them we would base this council on Christian principles, but individual members did not have to be Christian to take part. Again they heard the words, but I'm not sure they understood the meaning. Nakuru is a predominantly Christian city, although there is a growing Muslim influence. Regardless of what they proclaim, tribal religions and traditional healers (witch doctors) are where many residents go when the chips are down.

A few heads nodded for that too. One young lady with heavy makeup and a provocative dress looked at me like, "Do you really mean that?"

"Values such as loving your neighbor as yourself will be a cornerstone for us."

Historically, when outside agencies come into our community, the process is for them to distribute goods to their neighbors. That's what brought Mama Amon to power in the dumpsite. The closer she could position herself to the rich entity, the more she took for herself. The more she got, the more temptation fed her greed. More power, more greed. The cycle created an ever-tighter grip on her reign.

I knew everyone was expecting to get some special treatment, reward, or money out of being on the council. I imagined they were wondering, *Am I becoming a privileged politician like the others, full of self-interest to enrich myself?*

God gave me precious words from out of nowhere:

"There is no special privilege of sitting on the council—other than the honor of representing your people. Let me say that again. There is no special privilege of sitting on the council—other than the honor of representing your people."

I asked if they would allow me to tell a story. I had run it by the staff before the meeting, though they weren't sure the community would understand the analogy. God prompted me to speak it anyway.

"It's an old story that gets shared when a problem seems too big to conquer and doing something, no matter how small, is better than doing nothing. It goes something like this. One day, after a powerful tropical storm, a man was strolling along the beach. Thousands of starfish had been washed ashore from the violent storm surge. The man noticed a boy off in the distance reaching down, picking something up, and gently throwing it into the ocean. He walked closer to the boy and asked, 'What are you doing?' The youth replied, 'Throwing starfish back into the ocean. The tide is going out. If I don't throw them back, they'll die.'"

I was happy to see the council members were tracking.

"'Son,' the man said, 'don't you realize there are miles and miles of beach and thousands of starfish? There are just too many to save. You can't make a difference!'

"After listening politely, the boy bent down, picked up another starfish, and tossed it back into the surf. Then, smiling at the man, he said, 'It made a difference for that one.'

"The boy was right. It made a difference to that *one*." I held up my index finger. "But what about all the others? There's always another starfish, and there's always another storm."

The council members had looks of deep contemplation. Then I said the words that changed everything. "Instead of helping one starfish at a time, LET'S RAISE THE TIDE and help everyone!"

Benjamin stood. "Let's raise the tide!" It set off a wave echoing around the council. "Let's raise the tide!"

I've heard nonprofits tell the starfish story to encourage people to join them in some small way, and maybe, just maybe, if enough people take part and do it for long enough, genuine change can happen. We had used this approach ourselves up to this point.

But God now had a fresh vision for us. Raising the tide meant creating a healthy environment, full of nutrients, so everyone could survive and thrive. The water of life is so low in our neighborhood. It's a desert with a few small springs, but He was creating an oasis of love, hope, and joy at Maisha Mapya. A place where His love reigned and all were welcome. Instead of trying to place the starfish back in the shallow water of Hilton, He wanted us to lift the tide for all.

There is so much I don't understand about how those in poverty feel. Mostly it's because I am unaware of the circumstances and feelings associated with them. Things that make little sense to those living in the prosperous outside world are completely reasonable to those crawling through the gauntlet of poverty. Because I've walked for a while with my friends, I've gained greater understanding. To them, maintaining dignity and a sense of pride is so important. My penniless friends will often spend their last shilling to buy things of extravagance, like fancy clothes, hats, belts, or shoes so as not to appear needy. They can't afford the threads, and the money would be much better spent on school fees, food, or essentials, but the need for the image of success is deep within them, even if it is a facade.

I've seen fathers spend wildly, using several months' pay to throw a party for their child. When asked, one man explained, "I was poor yesterday. I will be poor tomorrow. But for today, we have the memory of this great celebration."

They all know how it feels to be a starfish. Sometimes, they get thrown into the water and get nourishment. Sometimes they get left on the beach to suffer in the scorching sun often at Mama Amon's discretion.

If we were going to thrive as a single community, we needed to do more than make life more prosperous for people. We needed to address our divisions. Economic and tribal differences, and even the colors of our skins, created distance between people seated around a table. I stressed the importance of unity. We had to look out for the well-being of others. I told them that to make things better for everyone, something good might happen for someone else before it happens for them.

I said, "You have to be joyful for them because they *are us.*"

A lady from Gioto named Njeri addressed everyone in Swahili. Joel whispered the translation in my ear. She talked about how she was grateful to Maisha Mapya for feeding the community during the COVID-19 shutdowns and that it wasn't just the people at the dumpsite. It was people from Hilton, Guba, and Kenya Meat too. She addressed things that separated us, echoing a lot of what I had said earlier.

Then Njeri turned and looked directly at me. She said, "We're truly of one heart, just of different skins."

I realized that a woman in her forties who lives in a dumpsite in the middle of Africa appreciated the message of unity and could look past the color of our skin. Only two weeks ago, I was in America. No matter how much I loved my neighbor and talked about unity in my home country, our media and culture are transfixed on widening divisions between people along every line. I think Njeri could teach America something.

Things were loosening up around the table, and ideas flowed freely. Questions addressing the increase in gang activity came up.

"What are we going to do about security?" Followed by the standard method of dealing with gangs. "How are we going to call the police in to help us? Will you call the Chief in?"

I responded that violence is a symptom of an underlying issue. We would not treat symptoms. We would not first call the cops in to punish the people causing the problems. Instead, we would identify why the violence occurred in the first place.

One member shook his head and scowled.

I remembered a few years earlier when a young student came to Maisha Mapya with wounds on her face. We investigated and found out her mother was the one inflicting the scars. In my anger, I grabbed our head teacher and marched to find the mom. I wanted to remove the child from the home and report Mom to the authorities. That may have ended the abuse for a moment, the mom being sent to jail. But then our student and her four siblings would be without a guardian because the father had already abandoned them. My first reaction was to treat the symptom.

A more in-depth investigation uncovered that her mom had experienced the same thing growing up. Mom had the same scars as her daughter as the result of *her* mother (the student's grandmother) pinching pieces off her face using her fingernails. The behavior had been passed from generation to generation, and it was the only way Mom knew how to parent her kids. We realized sending the mom to the authorities would only cause a more significant issue.

Instead, we needed to help heal Mom. We wrapped our loving arms around her and helped her learn how to discipline her children properly. By healing Mom, we would help the children. We focused on the root cause, a lack of healthy parenting skills, to solve an abused child's problem and not add them to the scores of orphans.

I glanced to my right, and the youngest person at the table was a teenage lady from Gioto. Seated directly next to her was the wealthiest local in the room, a gentleman from London. She blushed in disbelief during most of the meeting that we included her in a place of such high honor. Having her involved in this conversation brought the dignity and hope needed in this community.

"How often should we meet?" I inquired.

"Once every three months" was the quickest and loudest response.

I said, "Thank you. Any other ideas?"

"Every week?" a timid voice added. This sparked murmuring as people responded they worked and wouldn't have the time to meet that often.

I told Joel before the meeting started that I would like the council to meet every two weeks. Finally, someone mentioned, "Every two weeks!" When we heard that proposal, I called for an immediate vote. It passed.

Next, we talked about how we would present issues to the council for discussion at future meetings.

Njeri said, "We should come tell Joel."

"But what if he is not around?" said a lone voice.

"We could have a suggestion box?"

"Where should we put it?"

"Just inside the gate, next to the security guard's office."

The council worked better than expected, and we agreed on a few ideas. This exchange encouraged me, and my confidence grew.

I promised each meeting would only last an hour and a half. It was 12:30 p.m. and time to leave. To balance the hierarchy of power, I asked a young man from Guba to close the session with prayer. He was honored and delivered a heartfelt sermonette of praise and thanksgiving.

We adjourned the meeting. But before everyone left, we wanted to take a photo to commemorate the day. The members gathered behind the head table. I made sure to be off to the side in the last row.

During the meeting, a few people wandered into the hall, including Luis from Hilton. This time, instead of his pink slipper

and green Croc, he had on a pair of matching tennis shoes. It
surprised me he didn't have a seat on the council because he is a
sober guy everyone looked up to. Quickly, six people from Hilton
surrounded him, and they debated who was going to sit on the
council. Luis told me later he declined an invitation to be their
leader. He wanted someone else to have the chance. He was
growing mentees of his own to strengthen and bring hope to his
neighborhood.

Another guy who wasn't on the council snuck in to be
included in the photo. It was Rasta D, the kid in the rainbow hat
who had attended all the Team Peace meetings at Balozi's bar. He
wasn't there to grab a seat of influence at the meeting. Rasta D
was there because he loved his nephew.

After the meeting, he asked me, "Daddy Dave, can you come
to my house?"

"Sure, give me a minute."

He sat down in front of the gate and waited half an hour for
me to finish. We walked to Hilton together. We stopped at the
mabati-covered bar owned by the guy who was murdered and went
through the bar to a small compound in the back.

"This is my brother's place."

I was trying to figure out why that was important.

"He was the one who was killed." *Oh, Rasta D, why didn't you tell
me earlier that your brother was the victim?*

Sitting on the edge of a chair was a little boy.

"This is his kid, John. They call him Bob, for Bob Marley. He's
five."

The back of the house had walls three iron sheets thick to
protect the widow and John from gang attacks. They feared K2
thrusting blades through the wall when they were sleeping. "I
spend the night here with them, to keep them safe. Do you think
John could come to Maisha? Let me show you my house."

We walked back through the bar and fifty yards through the
dumpsite. We passed Mama Amon's burned-out compound. She
was usually out bossing people around, but this time she was

nowhere to be seen. I wondered if we were finally rid of her and her minions. Bordering the pile of her structure's ashes was Rasta D's home. He lifted the broken gate at the entrance to his place, and we filed in. He introduced me to his wife and six-month-old baby. He was also raising four of the cutest puppies you'll ever see.

"Can the kid go to Maisha?"

I couldn't say no even if I wanted to. And I didn't want to. I also couldn't say yes because I had to respect the chain of command for admissions at the school. Dan, Mary, and Maggie were in charge of new student enrollment.

I told Rasta D I couldn't make any promises, but I'd see what I could do. What I didn't say was that if we didn't have room for him, we'd make room. Then I walked back toward Maisha Mapya trying to figure out how I could put my thumb on the scale without destroying the GLT's authority.

Hey Dan I met a kid that really needs help. His dad was the one who was killed. He lives behind the rasta bar. Can you see what we can do? ~ me

THE STUBBORN

October 20, 2020

I WAS FLYING high with the successful kickoff of the community council and the possibility of saving another child's soul. Before I reached Maisha, I got a text I'd been praying the entire trip for, but never thought I'd receive.

THE K2 GUYS WANT TO MEET YOU ~ ANONYMOUS

Woah, I didn't think any of them were around. I heard all of their members fled to cities throughout Kenya because the police were after them for the Hilton murders.

I thought they were all on the run? ~ *me*

4 REMAIN CAN YOU MEET ONE? ~ ANONYMOUS

With only two days before my flight, I was desperate to meet with them. Anonymous's text was confusing, but the risk didn't matter. The meeting could be in an isolated dark parking lot for all I cared.

Yes. Where? ~me

HE CAN'T COME TO HILTON ~ ANONYMOUS

So where? ~ me

KELSEY WILL PICK YOU ~ ANONYMOUS

Anonymous is like the Wizard of Oz, behind the curtain, knowing all the players and pulling all the strings. Kelsey and I never talked about who it might be. We didn't need to. We were getting the insider info we needed.

———

My heart was flooded with the blessings of this week. The council meeting went great. God brought John Bob to us. K2 wanted to meet. Mama Amon had been silent. The Chief and MCA let us do our thing. And Team Peace was going to ask the Shosh for forgiveness. Angel would be coming home. Birds may sing again.

My appetite was back in full force. I turned to Joe to see if he was ready for an early dinner. "Want to get some food, Joe?"

"Sure."

"How about Java?"

We laughed.

"Joe, He hasn't let me down."

"Who?"

"God! He hasn't abandoned us. The tide is turning. Maybe it will rise. And rise for everyone. Maybe I can get Angel and bring her back home. There are still two days to go, Joe. Anything can happen."

Just then, Kelsey came through the Maisha Mapya gate. I could hardly wait to tell her about the chance to meet K2.

"Kelsey, guess what!"

One look at her said she wasn't in the mood for playing. Her shoulders slumped, and she wore a half scowl on her face.

"You okay? What's wrong?"

"It's Shosh."

"Is she okay? Oh no . . . is she all right?"

"She's okay, just so stubborn."

"Tell me."

"She said she'd only meet with the Team Peace guys if they would answer all her questions."

I shrugged. "What's the big deal?"

"She wants to know why they attacked her son and what they would do when he was out of prison."

That seemed fine to me. I wasn't getting the problem.

"Dave, she said they would have to say it in front of a community elder *and* the Chief. The police would have to be there. If they want to meet her, they have to confess their crimes!"

My hands covered my mouth.

Kelsey said, "My heart stopped beating when Shosh was talking. She talks about being this woman of God. She wears their dress. She covers her head. She shows tenderness and emotion most of the time. But now, all she showed was wanting power and revenge."

Revenge? *I'm so sick of it.* Hasn't everyone had enough? What makes you want revenge rather than getting your granddaughter back? I don't remember the next words Kelsey said. My eyes lost their focus from listening to her. It was just faint mumbling. A mushroom cloud of despair hit me. The fallout meant there would be no peace. *Oh, Lord, how can this be happening? The violent gang wants peace. The victim wants revenge.*

"No! No! No!" My shouts turned to silence.

There was no way I could ask the guys in Team Peace to do what Shosh wanted. It would destroy what little trust had been built between us. I joined Kelsey in having a heart that stopped beating. Everything stopped beating.

"Shosh has to meet them," I said.

"She won't. One thing I know is that lady is stubborn."

Without this mini peace summit, revenge would return. Team Peace would go after the son when he got out. Maybe even Angel. It would never end.

"I think Mama Amon has her ear too. I'm not sure Shosh wants peace, Dave."

"Mama Amon is in this?" I felt like saying I hated the lady but held my tongue. I wanted to cover my ears, bury my head, and build a skyscraper on top of it. I'd had enough. I was so close. How could God whip me around like this? How could He let this fall apart now? Maybe they all were right. Maybe things would never change.

"I can't stay," Kelsey said as she walked out the gate.

"You can go to dinner without me, Joe. I'm going to bed."

"I'll come with you."

Joe always knew the right thing to say. We got in the Wasili with Wally, and Joe asked one more time if I wanted some food.

"Okay, Joe, if you think it's best."

"I do."

I went to Java and pushed food around my plate. The single act of a headstrong person prevented peace.

The grains of rice on my plate reminded me of the thousands of little people in Hilton. Some clumped together. A few stragglers off to the side. Some waiting to be thrown in the trash pile.

Enough! I wouldn't have been able to sleep for a second. I had to know if the dream was dead.

"Joe find Wally and tell him we're going back."

I texted Balozi to assemble the team even though they would be sleeping or drunk. I didn't care.

I walked into the club, skipped the formalities, and got right down to it.

"Guys, I'm so sorry."

I don't know if they had ever heard an apology from someone like me before.

"I heard back from Shosh. She said she'd only meet with you if the Chief and the police were there."

"The Chief! The police!" They yelled lots of comments I won't repeat. I shushed them before things could build.

"I appreciate your hearts to meet with her. Especially you, Isaac."

Humbly, he lowered his shaking head.

"I know you want peace, but I can't advise you to meet with her. It's not in your best interest. It's not what forgiveness is all about. I'm sorry I've failed you."

"You haven't failed, Daddy Dave. It's okay. God will make a way."

THE RENDEZVOUS

October 21, 2020

GROUNDHOG DAY with a twist. 5:30 am alarm. Smiling Barnabus Joe Jesus. Tea. Twende kazi, greetings.

The twist? It was my thirty-first wedding anniversary, and in so many ways, I was a million miles away from my wife. Physically, Kim was 9,428 miles away. In terms of time, she was ten hours behind. And emotionally, well, I was about to step into something where I would cherish her tender, confident, prayerful, loving support. Plus, I had done a lousy job connecting with her this week. She hadn't. She snuck an anniversary card and picture inside my suitcase.

The other twist: all of the uncertainty of encountering K2.

When we pulled up to the school, I asked Wally to keep the car running.

"Sure, Wafula. I'd wait anywhere all day for you. Let me know what you need." *I'm gonna miss Wally.*

Kelsey and Kat were already at Maisha. Nia was waiting at the entrance to the hall for another GLT session to begin.

"Joe, I have a meeting."

He took the cue and said, "Hey, Kat, will you stay and play

some catch with me today?" Besides being the perfect Barnabus for me, Joe was the ideal grandpa for Kat. Together, they skipped off to the playing field, Joe tossing the ball up and down, likely daydreaming of the days he wore a Little League uniform.

I handed Nia my wallet and passport. I looked at the wedding ring on my finger, spun it around a few times, reminiscing about the day Kim placed it there.

"I miss her so much."

"I know, Daddy. Everyone misses Mommie Kim."

I took off the gold band and gave it to Nia.

"Take good care of this. I'll be back before you know it."

I kept my phone in case I needed to make an SOS call. I knew nothing about where we were going or who we would meet with, and for the first time, my palms were sweating about what I might walk into. *Maybe it would be a deadly version of Triangle Island?*

I slid in the car with Kelsey eager and apprehensive to meet someone from K2. "Where are we headed?" I asked.

"Across town to a parking garage."

"You're kidding."

"Nope. Bottom floor."

I looked up to the heavens, but only saw the black interior of the car's roof. I remembered my cheeky thought in my desperation to meet with whoever this is. I'd said to myself I'd meet them anywhere. Either God has a sense of humor, or He was signaling He knew all about this meeting and I had nothing to worry about. I opted to think it was both.

Kelsey told Wally the directions to the rendezvous spot on the other side of town. I knew the location. It was secluded. No place to run. Nowhere to hide.

I still had no idea *who* we would be meeting.

The rest of the ride was silent. I battled my racing mind and filed thoughts of anything outside of communing with God to the side. I could deal with those things later. I wanted to go into this meeting with a clean slate, free of judgment and preconceived notions, ready to love and be loved in return.

Wally turned off the road. Before he could enter the parking lot, I asked him to pull over and let us out.

"Stay close by, Wally. I'll pay you to wait."

"Sure thing, Wafula."

Kelsey and I walked out of the bright sunlight into the darkness of the covered structure. We went down a few floors. The lower we went, the colder it got. I made some small talk with Kelsey to ease the tension. I make dumb jokes when I'm nervous. When "Even though it's dark, my hair still glows" came out of my mouth, I knew I was more uneasy than I thought.

The basement floor was empty except for two cars and five plastic chairs from the diner on the top floor. I wondered if anyone would show. We pulled three chairs to the far corner. I was thinking about where to get some tea to welcome our guest, but the shop was closed and there was no way to get anything.

As soon as we sat down, the dumb jokes ended, and peace washed over me, chasing away the butterflies in my stomach.

Out of the shadows, a guy walked across the garage floor. He was thin and muscular, like Damu, clothed in tattered blue jeans, a well-worn T-shirt, and tennis shoes that barely had enough fabric to stay on his feet. I didn't recognize him. He didn't smile. He didn't say a word. He looked afraid and frightening, a strange but menacing combination.

We sat. I wanted to extend my hand, but it was as still as a corpse. I thought, *Okay, this guy probably doesn't know me.*

"I'm Dave, and you're probably wondering why I want to meet with you. I want to bring peace to our community. I know there have been so many troubles."

I used the most general terms possible because I knew either this guy or his close friends just murdered two guys. I didn't want to incite him. I assumed he had the same concerns as Team Peace on the first day I met them in Hilton, so I started the conversation the same way.

"You might be wondering about my intentions. My intention is to love you and have you love me back."

All he did was stare and shift nervously in his seat.

"Do you know me?" I said.

He nodded. "Yes, you're Daddy Dave, and you're a man of peace."

How in the world does he know that? These guys' knowledge of their neighborhoods is all-inclusive.

His phone rang. He said something I didn't understand. I think it was in his mother tongue. He nodded again and handed me the phone.

What am I supposed to do with this? "Hello," I said.

Between the tinny, blown-out speaker of a twenty-dollar flip phone, the sounds of the garage, and my aging American ears, I could barely understand the English spoken on the other side. But I know rage when I hear it.

It was one of the other gang members, and there were other voices in the background too. It sounded like a barroom brawl. I imagined a room full of gangsters crowding around the phone, drinking, smoking pot, yelling insults, spewing their venom at the captive, stupid white guy on the other end of the line.

Obviously, more wanted to meet me. They just didn't know if it would be safe or a trap. Instead, they sent this poor kid to meet the man from Maisha. No wonder he looked so scared. He was torn between two parties who would never come together.

They did not give me a chance to introduce myself. Not a moment of silence to say, "I'm Dave. I'm here to love you and have you love me back." It was just an onslaught of profanity.

The guy on the phone ranted about the police and how they were holding innocent K2 members because the Team Peace guys paid a bribe for the cops to lock up their guys.

"If you want peace, go tell the cops to get our guys out," the voice demanded.

Like I could do anything about the police or that I was the only one wanting peace. I was on my heels. "I have no sway over the police."

I asked some questions to see if there were any other issues and how we might get to peace. Like a madman on a tirade, he repeated the same obsession six times, increasing the insults and tempo each time. For twenty-five minutes, I tried everything I could to move the conversation past this issue. I wanted him to feel heard but also wanted to see if there was any chance, any possibility, to end the hate.

"If we solved the issue about the guys being held by the police, is there anything else preventing peace? Are there any other issues?"

Like a two-year-old who only hears what he wants, he started in again with "The cops . . . my guys are innocent . . . there will be no peace."

Thirty years ago, I had a tape stuck in my car's cassette deck. For a year, it played Bruce Springteen's *Tunnel of Love* over and over and over again. There was a comforting ritual about hearing a tune I liked on a loop. But this repeatedly vile rant just made me sick.

It was futile. I was stuck. If I challenged him further, it could backfire, and if I ever got the chance to ask, "Do you have anything against me personally?" he might have something to respond with, and it wouldn't be good. So I stopped.

I handed the phone back to the young man standing next to me while the verbal rampage was still coming through the speaker. I shrugged my shoulders and made a face like, "I can't do anything with this."

He spoke a few words and hung up the phone like he was in trouble.

I switched my focus to establishing a relationship with the one who was tasked with meeting me. He was a lowly pawn placed in the middle of a violent chess match.

"What's your name?"

"Radhi."

Kelsey whispered something to me about Mama Amon, but I was locked in on Radhi.

"Do you want peace, Radhi?"

A hardened, distant stare communicated, "I don't even know what peace is."

"I want peace. I don't want any of your friends to go to jail. I don't want any of them to get killed or wounded. I've had enough of it, haven't you?"

I thought that with the scars on his hands, arms, and face, he would jump at the chance. There was no response. It didn't budge him at all.

I wanted to offer him something, anything, that would show I cared and that God cared too. I guessed, with all the brutality, some of his friends may have serious injuries and need medical treatment.

"I know sometimes when conflicts like this happen, people get hurt. Maybe they're sick. Maybe they got slashed. But they can't go to the hospital because the doctors will want to know what happened and you're afraid of being jailed. I don't have a doctor, but I know my God works miracles. So, if anyone in your group is sick or hurt and needs to see a doctor, I'll do everything I can to bring one to a safe place. Not in a hospital. Not a place with police."

No response.

I'm usually pretty good at getting someone to say something in the general direction I want a conversation to go, but nothing was working. I couldn't see any way forward. This wasn't a conversation. It wasn't even a monolog. This was an attempt to connect with a struggling young man. It was just me talking.

For Radhi and me, it was a dead end. It was time to say goodbye.

I pushed my chair back to stand up. The legs rubbed against the cement and made a scraping sound. Then the most unexpected thing happened.

Radhi lifted his head, turned to me, looked me squarely in the eye, and reached out. He placed his right hand softly on my shoulder. He gently pushed me back into my seat.

"Will you pray for me?"

I looked deeply into his eyes. *Where did that come from?*

He repeated, "Will you pray for me? Will you pray for forgiveness and peace—for me?"

It was the last thing I expected to hear from this man.

We bowed our heads. I prayed for forgiveness, peace, unity, and for God's kingdom to come to this earth, and to do it through Radhi.

And with the amen, the man with a heart of stone next to me had tears streaming down his expressionless face. We stood. I hugged him. Without saying another word, we walked out of the garage together. When we got to the top floor, the sunlight peeked through. Radhi made a left. I walked straight. Everything in my being was feeling the pull inside of Radhi. He desperately wanted to come with me and explore a new life.

I got in the car feeling like I abandoned Radhi.

"Wafula? You okay?" Wally asked.

"Let's just drive."

Kelsey leaned forward in the back seat and whispered in my ear, "Dave, Radhi is Mama Amon's son."

I wanted to hop out of the car and run back to him. I had no idea the poor guy suffered under her wrath. No wonder he couldn't come with me. She'd never release her talon's hold on his life. Maybe that's why he sat in silence. Maybe he was contemplating if I'd hate him the same way everyone else did because of who his mom was. He had been trapped between me, the guy on the other end of the phone, and his identity. All I wanted to do was listen and love and see what God would do.

At least I found out where we stood with the K2 guys. Nowhere. God obviously wanted us to connect. But also, quite obviously, He didn't want a similar relationship as with Team Peace. At least not now.

THE ANSWER

October 21, 2020, 4:00 p.m.

THE MEETING with Radhi had run overtime. By the time we made the long return drive to school, I'd missed lunch, which was fine by me. But I'd also lost out on saying goodbye to the grade-four students, which wasn't fine. Who knows when I'd get the chance to see them again given the state of the pandemic?

God reminded me that my visit's primary purpose wasn't to see the children; it was to stop the gangs from killing each other and leave our kids alone. Maybe next time it would be to better connect with the students. Maybe next time we'd bring peace. At least we'd made inroads with Team Peace.

Before I left, I wanted to have one last chance to look into the eyes of each teacher and have them feel the love I have for them. We assembled everyone in the hall so the teachers could share what they'd created for the compassion curriculum.

Teacher Collins stood and gave an outline of the prior week, which included how honored they were to be asked to design something like this. "All the days went well, except for the first day." Tee-hees went around the room.

My curiosity increased. I wanted to hear how they sorted out the assignment I'd dropped in their laps with so few instructions. The lesson was as much about team building as it was about creating a teaching tool for school. It turns out they spent the entire first day talking about what they were going to do and how they would do it.

As if it had been choreographed, each teacher gave a six minute presentation on a specific aspect of the curriculum. They shared the illustrations for making the Scriptures come to life, and as I heard them, they were straight from our neighborhood.

Tying their presentation in a nice bow, Collins said, "I never thought I'd be involved in creating something like this. I never thought I'd help write a book, but now we have." Like the evening they were on the video call with the American teachers, they felt pride in how far God had taken them.

We had a brief celebration with tea and cake. Barnabas Joe Jesus had the honor of cutting the first piece. They all said how quickly the time had flown.

The moment of the dreaded goodbyes was upon us. We exchanged hugs and smiles, which led to lots of swollen eyes, sniffles, and "see you soons" and "say hi to Mommie Kim." *Oh, I was looking forward to that!*

The teachers were right. Although every day overflowed with activity and emotion, the time had gone quickly. I was leaving for the airport not in weeks or days, but in hours and minutes.

———

I couldn't leave Nakuru without seeing my Team Peace brothers one more time. Plus, I owed Damu an answer to his question: What would I do if someone wanted to shoot, stab, or slice me?

Kelsey came along. Grandpa Joe stayed at Maisha with Kat. The ten-minute walk to their place was getting easier. Maybe I was adjusting to the altitude, or perhaps I wasn't spending so much energy squashing my fears with each step? I was missing Team Peace already.

I knocked on the door to Balozi's. Six kids, waist high, surrounded me. They squeezed through the door before me, giggling like they were entering the Mickey Mouse Club. I sat on a couch, and they snuggled next to me. Three of the kids were students at Maisha Mapya. One was Gakere who God rescued two years ago when Dan, Maggie, Kim, and I were in the dumpsite.

Now I was sitting next to this seven-year-old in a gang bar in the middle of the afternoon. I pulled out my cell phone to take a selfie with them all. It was so dark the only thing showing was— no joke—my brilliant crown of white hair. I got up, the kids followed, and we went into the alley outside the club and got our prized picture. The kids love to see themselves in photos. Most don't have a mirror in their home and for many, the first time they see themselves is in a photo on my iPhone. We went back inside, sat on the sofa, and they huddled even closer.

To watch Team Peace file in and gather around the pool table warmed my heart. My previous fear was nowhere to be found. "Fellas, I'm leaving tomorrow. I just wanted to come by and say, *tuonane.* This isn't goodbye. It's just 'see you later.'"

One guy started playing with his dreadlocks, another said, "Will you remember us?"

"How could I ever forget? God has bound us together forever."

I looked down to my right at Gakere and the other kids sitting with me on the couch. I hated to leave them knowing K2 was still hunting them and Angel hadn't been heard from. Although I'd made progress with Team Peace, who knew what they were really up to when I wasn't around?

I pointed to the young ones seated on the couch with me and asked. "Do you love these kids?"

"Yes. We do. We do. They are family. "

"I love them too. You know, three of them are in our school. Do you love all the neighborhood kids?"

"We do. We do."

Even the guys who had no idea what I was talking about nodded to save face.

My tone firmed and I picked up my pace. "Then you can't threaten them. Each one is just like these kids." I motioned to the little ones sitting next to me. I sat up straighter.

"They need you to protect them. You need to nurture them. You need to be their big brothers like you are for Mikey. You can't threaten them."

Most of the members nodded their heads in agreement. A few wore questions on their faces.

Again, I thought about Angel. I had to leave them with the impression that they had to change their ways. "If you don't stop saying you'll kill them, revenging one of their relatives, you're going to have to change your name from Team Peace to Team I Cut Little Kids' Heads Off!"

I don't know where those words came from. Maybe they came from a place of learning not to trust people at their word. Maybe the betrayal of my former business partner and the Kenyan family who stole the school ran deep within me. Maybe the fear of peace only being temporary was talking. Maybe I was afraid of more small caskets. But once those words were out of my mouth, I wish I could have swallowed them.

"We are Team Peace. We want peace. The kids are okay."

"Really? You all say you want peace. But there are dark violent forces all around us, and one of its biggest allies has been you."

"We want peace, Daudi. We want the darkness to leave. We want peace." Damu didn't say a word.

"Tomorrow, I'm leaving for the airport, and I have to know the kids are okay. I have to know you are Team Peace during the day, during the night, when I'm here, and when I'm gone. You have to be Team Peace in your hearts all the time."

"We are Team Peace, Daddy."

Damu circled around the pool table moving in like a lion one more time, slow, quiet, and determined.

"Well, pastor . . ."

Are we really going to do this again?

With his head tilted back and forefinger across his Adam's apple, he continued. "What do I do if someone comes at me with a panga and puts it on my throat?"

The way he said it made me think of poor Angel being grabbed by the hair and her neck laid bare to the rusty cold steel of a machete. *Was Damu signaling he was the guy?* I knew this was the gang who'd threatened her. *Was he the beast?* The way he said it made me wonder if he heard one word about what I had just spoken about Gakere and his friends.

"I don't know."

He backed off, smirked, and shook his head.

"I don't know what *you* should do, Damu. But I can tell you what *I* would do."

He put his right elbow on the pool table, index finger across his upper lip, and glared at me.

"I can't tell you not to defend yourself."

Others in the room sat up. Some leaned closer.

"What you do is between you and God. But for me, I will NEVER defend myself. You know me. I will never be armed in this community. I will never walk around with armed guards like that lady."

They all knew I was talking about Mama Amon. I thought about Radhi and the prison she kept him in his entire life.

"I walk the streets freely and without fear. And I'm a white guy. Everyone knows I have a phone and a few shillings in my pocket. And I'm old. I'm the easiest target out here."

I let my vulnerability sink in for a minute.

"You know my deal with the community. I'm going to love you and you're going to love me back. And even if you don't love me back, I'm going to love you anyway. If I'm armed, what trust does that show?"

They could tell I was serious.

"If I defend myself, I might be robbing God of the opportunity to change the attacker's heart at the last second."

Dembe, Samson, and Isaac were locked on me.

"If I defend myself, I might be taking away the chance for someone in the community to stick up for me. Who knows, maybe it's one of you guys, even you, Damu. Who knows? But I can't tell *you* what to do. For me, no, I won't defend myself. I am a man of peace. My best defense is to love you."

I could see now the others were thinking, *Would I step in to help Daddy Dave?*

I'm not sure I made any progress with Damu. He recoiled to his position, like a snake ready to strike. Was this guy so steeped in hatred that he couldn't shake off the need to retaliate? Did he have to solve his problems in the only language he understood —violence?

The silence among the other members contemplating the notion of not inflicting pain on their enemies spoke volumes. How could I get any one of them to truly understand peace?

"Pray for us, pastor. Pray for peace and forgiveness," said a voice in the background. It was Isaac. He'd asked for the identical prayer as Radhi.

I prayed and said *tuonane* one last time. On the way out the door, I gave Balozi a high five. "Make sure Mikey's at Maisha at 8:30 tomorrow morning, maybe earlier."

And with the sun low on the horizon, I made my way, unarmed, back to Maisha Mapya.

———

It was time for Joe and me to head to the last scheduled event of the trip—the GLT's final exam.

Throughout the week, I had teased the GLT by sending text messages that on Wednesday night from 4:30 p.m. to 6:30 p.m., there would be a final exam based on the fortnight's training.

Being a new member of the team, Joel replied to one text, "What do I need to do to prepare?"

I had sympathy for him, and I knew I'd give away the secret if I answered. But kindness overcame me.

Appetite. ~ me

He responded with a questioning emoji.

Dinner with some sugar. ~ me

Naturally, Dan jumped in the thread.

Did you mention optional sugar? ~ Dan

Mandatory. Some dinner, mostly sugar. ~ me

Maggie did not want to be left in the cold.

Will there be ice cream? ~ Maggie

Dan sent a final text.

I've slept with my notes beside me all week. *fork emoji* ~ Dan

Thank you, Jesus. That's our team. We met at Java and nearly emptied the dessert case while filling the air with laughter.

Before falling asleep, I received the last text of the night from a familiar source.

THANKS FOR COMING ~ ANONYMOUS

THE JOY

October 22, 2020

FIVE A.M. ALARM. My clothes were everywhere. I took four minutes to shove them in a suitcase. I felt like I'd done that with myself all this week. Shower. A final morning smile exchange with Joe. *I'm gonna miss that guy.*

We were six hours away from the big twende to Nairobi for the flight home. The two things remaining on my to-do list were to sit with Mikey for his 8:30 a.m. interview for entry to school and remember my passport.

By 7:00 a.m., I'd successfully fueled myself on caffeine, sugar, and an intense calling from God. For sure I needed a takeaway today, and asked if they had a larger cup. Joe and I had an extra moment of prayer.

Right on time, Wally was waiting for the last morning's drive to school. I'd kidded with him a lot, starting from the first second God connected us outside of Java. It had been fun; we had lots of laughs in the brief spurts of our five-minute car rides. Wally also had sat quietly and eavesdropped on some serious conversations. But now, after building a relationship for two weeks, it was time to say goodbye and share some lasting encouragement.

"Hey, Wally, I want to thank you for taking such great care of Joe and me. God gave us a busy schedule these past few weeks, and it's been great to be able to count on you to make sure we got where we needed to go when we needed to get there."

"Thank you, sir. It's my pleasure. I hope to do it again."

He turned his attention from the road for our eyes to connect. I reached over and patted his hand on the steering wheel to seal the deal. He glanced at my beaded wristband. It shouts loud the green, red, white, and black colors of Kenya.

"Tell me about your bracelet. It is nice."

"It was a gift from one of our teachers. She made it special for me. It says *Kristo Milele* (Christ Forever). I put it on five years ago and haven't taken it off since."

"Amen. I like it. It looks good on you," he said.

During our rides, Wally had shared the challenges of being young and having a girlfriend and child during the economic troubles of COVID-19.

"I want to come to the US, Wafula."

"Why?"

He hesitated.

I knew the answer to the question before I asked it. I just wanted him to hear himself speak the words because it doesn't sound great to say, "I want to go to the land of comfort and easy living."

"Do you think you will grow closer to God by coming to the US, Wally?"

He wasn't expecting that.

"Do you know the closest big city to where I live is San Francisco and only four percent of people go to church?"

"Really?"

"They also don't teach the Bible in our schools."

"I would not like that."

"In that city, it costs over three thousand US dollars to rent a one-bedroom apartment every month."

"Three thousand USD a month? That is too high."

"Do you know there's a fifty percent divorce rate in the US, even among church members?"

"I did not know."

"You'd be leaving your friends and family behind. And your culture. And your favorite foods. The sound of the music you love. Everything would be different."

He kept driving.

"Don't be so tempted to leave behind what you have to chase some shiny object. You've got a wonderful country with loving friends. You have a pastor who cares about you and teaches you God's ways. You have a beautiful girlfriend and a baby boy. You have an amazing life full of potential. I have a feeling God will keep calling you to Himself and transforming you into the image of His Son. That's the best place to live."

We pulled into the school driveway. For the first time at the end of a ride, Wallace pushed the emergency brake and exited the car. He wrapped his arms around me. "God bless you, Wafula. Thank you for what you are doing for Kenya, especially these kids. Karibu Kenya, you are always welcome here."

We shared a prayer, and he drove off. I watched his compact car disappear into the sea of vehicles.

At 8:00 a.m., the director for Nakuru Children's Trust was already sitting in the hall. He's a good friend, and we caught up on how our families were doing before we got down to helping Mikey turn his life around.

"I think we can really help this boy if he's given a chance. I know he's outside the children's age group in your program. But if there is any way to take him in, it would mean so much to him and the guys in his gang. We can set conditions that if he has a disciplinary problem or doesn't hold to the bargain, he's out."

Sounding skeptical he said, "Dave, let us see."

I check my phone. 8:30 a.m. No Mikey.

8:40 a.m. No Mikey.

8:45 a.m. No Mikey.

I started to get nervous. Why would I think the devil wouldn't put up a fight to keep this kid? He had him firmly in his clutches. Maybe Mikey got too high and forgot we had an 8:30 meeting? My heart pounded more than at any time during the trip.

I texted Balozi.

where is Mikey? I'm really pulling for this kid ~ me

I will try and find him. ~ Balozi

8:55 a.m. Still, no Mikey.

The director from NCT left to go upstairs to the admin office to chat with our staff. He had been down this road before with street boys.

The pounding in my chest was now racing through my veins. We were so close to saving him. Why was the pull of drugs and street life stronger than being on the path to education and a better life? Why couldn't Mikey swim against that current?

I paced outside the gate, going one hundred yards in each direction, hoping to see him. The street was busy, but as far as I was concerned, it was desolate because there was no sign of Mikey.

9:00 a.m. NO. MIKEY.

I slunk back inside the gates thinking of how I could persuade the NCT director to stay a bit longer. One minute later, in bounced a bright-eyed, smiling Mikey with a pregnant woman and a small child escorting him.

"Here I am, Daddy Dave! Right on time! Haha!" Mikey exclaimed.

Once again, the prodigal father opened his arms and hugged his kid. I rushed him inside. I didn't even have time to greet the lady, but she and the child came in and sat next to me, silent. I didn't know who they were or why they were there. I was just thrilled to see Mikey.

A counselor by training, the NCT director was the perfect guy to conduct the interview. He's a soft, gentle yet direct man. He was in charge of a rescue center when we met thirteen years ago and spent an immense amount of time trying to rehabilitate street kids during his tenure.

Contradicting his earlier story, Mikey said he, in fact, had a mom. I glanced at the lady sitting next to me.

"Not her," he said.

Mikey's mom had kicked him out for scavenging and hanging out with the guys at the dumpsite against her will. It was where he began doing drugs. His mom even turned him in to the authorities, and he spent six months in juvenile hall. Now he is a regular in Hilton because it is easy for him to get drugs. I'd never heard someone speak so freely about things that might cause them shame. There was no remorse in his drug habit. He said it matter-of-factly.

"Last week me and the guys hunted Mama Amon with pangas," he said. "We almost got her."

I thought that would kill his chances to get into school. But, the director recommended we rescue this boy before his drug use became uncontrollable. He suggested we take him to a boarding school to change the influences around him. Mikey needed healthy, new surroundings.

My soul rejoiced that this boy, who only a week earlier was lost, stoned, and without hope, had experienced God's touch. God used Balozi, the other guys in the gang, a quick email to the NCT board, and the director to give Mikey a chance. It was a moment worth celebrating.

I almost forgot there was a woman and a young boy seated next to me. They looked familiar, but I was so focused on Mikey I couldn't recall meeting them.

"This is John. You know my boy, Bob?" she said. "You know my husband. He was the one who owned the bar."

I was still struggling to put the pieces together.

Mikey spoke up. "Mr. Daddy Dave, she is the one whose husband was killed. She is my aunt. Bob is her son, remember?"

"Yes. Yes. Oh, how could I forget little John Bob Marley?"

But I had forgotten. The pace and intensity of the events of the past two weeks had run me over, and I'd never followed up with my team. I had texted Dan but forgot to follow through. I escorted John Bob and his mom up to the admin office to meet Mary, Maggie, and Joel, and to remind them of the story.

I pulled my team aside. "I know I don't get involved with the intake in our school. But this young boy *must* come to Maisha. He needs us. The community needs this healing too. Let's go to his house now and do an assessment."

At this point, it was 10:00 a.m., and Joe and I had to leave to make our flight in sixty minutes. There wasn't sufficient time, but I urged the team to go to Gioto with me anyway.

We walked through the streets, and formerly nameless faces lurking around corners were now my friends—Dembe, Samson, Isaac, Balozi, Biggie, and so many others. We enjoyed glances even though we didn't stop to say hi.

We got to John Bob's home, which was ten feet behind the bar where his dad had been torn apart by the ruthless K2 gang.

I introduced Dan, Maggie, Joel, and Mary to John Bob's mom, then watched them go into action. They were in their element, doing what they did best, loving the people.

"Are you guys okay from here?"

"Yes, Daudi."

I smiled, turned around, and walked out. I wasn't sure when I'd see them again. The sigh of satisfaction said it would be okay. I hurried back toward Maisha Mapya.

On my way, Samson stopped me, grabbed both my shoulders and looked deeply into my eyes. His strong, massive hands could have snapped me like a twig. "Thanks for chancing Mikey for school."

Nothing more needed to be said.

Vic's driver (yes, that Vic who helped rescue Angel) was right on time at 11:00 a.m., and I hopped in with Joe. Safe in the car, I shut my eyes for a moment to reflect on the endless miracles God had done. I exhaled. Soothing euphoria soon replaced the adrenaline I had become so used to running on.

"Well, Joe, what did you think of all that?"

"Just amazing, Dave. It was the experience of a lifetime."

I lowered the bill of my cap and rested, privately praying and thanking God for everything—for the International Day of the Girl Child; the special treat of having the fourth graders in class; the healing among our GLT; the staff writing a book on compassion; launching the community council; for everything about Anonymous, John Bob, Mikey, Balozi, Dembe, Isaac, Samson, Radhi, Kelsey, Wally, Steve, Terri, Joe; and, of course, for Kim, who was wearing out her prayer muscles. I couldn't wait to see her. The only uncertainties left were Angel's homecoming and Shosh's stubbornness.

And despite it all, I still hadn't gotten COVID-19 or been stabbed in the face.

I drifted off to sleep before we left Nakuru County. Then the buzz in my pocket woke me. *Why didn't I put that thing on silent?*

Just seen Mikey totally sober and the biggest smile on his face ~ *Kelsey*

You can't do that to me [crying emoji] ~ *me*

She sent a photo of nine random guys just sitting somewhere in Hilton. I didn't recognize any of them.

Damu wanted me to send this to you. ~ *Kelsey*

I wondered why.

He says most of his friends in this photo have died. Even he has killed a lot of people. He wants to carry this with him to remember how far he has come because HE CAN'T KILL ANYMORE. ~ Kelsey

I knew Damu had vengeance. But a killer? I'd never sat that close to a murderer before. I had looked for God to do a miracle, but I was amazed that God was able to change a heart that quickly.

Wow. Is this a new revelation from our talks? ~ me

Yes. And get this. He says he can't kill even if someone comes at him. ~ Kelsey

After stalking me around the pool table for over a week, God looked into the bottom of what was left of Damu's heart and made it new. Damu couldn't kill anymore. Not even if someone came at him with a gun or knife, or put a machete to his throat.

How is it that God, who is love, can send a messenger across the world to be present, to listen and encourage a dark heart, and as a result, turn a killer into a man of peace in a week?

I tried to read the text to Joe but couldn't speak. I simply gave him the phone with my trembling hands. He almost got through reading the thread before the phone buzzed again.

Two of the other members asked if you had flown yet. One asked about Kim. Your team is missing you too ~ Kelsey

Before I could respond, I received a picture of a smiling Damu, holding an empty Johnny Walker Gold Label Reserve whisky bottle with plastic red roses sticking out the top.

This guy says he is praying for your wife. ~ Kelsey

Are you ready? ~ Kelsey

Probably not. ~ me

Shosh's big son was at Balozi's telling stories. He hasn't been at any of the meetings. They were talking about the issues in the community and pastors and wazungu stealing. Then he says, "do you know the one who will really help his community? It's the Man from Maisha." ~ Kelsey

Balozi's face lit up. He loves us. ~ Kelsey

THE BREAKDOWN

October 22, 2020

THE TEXTS on my screen were prayers come true.

HE CAN'T KILL ANYMORE. Even if someone comes at him.

Balozi's face lit up. He loves us.

With a smile in my heart, I slept most of the way to the airport. I was so out of it, I thought the images of having a murderer unable to kill anymore and a gang leader feeling loved were a beautiful dream. The heartbreaking vision of Radhi walking in the opposite direction out of the parking garage was a nightmare.

Joe was silent on the ride. I wondered what he was thinking. Maybe his brain was trying to sort everything out. He was quiet on the flight too.

We said our goodbyes in the Frankfurt airport, and he ambled off. Usually, as people walk away, they get smaller in the distance. Joe seemed to get bigger. I stood a moment and watched this gift of a man who was gentle, kind, peaceful, and loving stroll down the terminal rolling his carry-on behind him before he disappeared. I never did learn what he meant when he said he and Sandy were married by faith. I just remember the smile on his face when he said it.

Some use the expression, "He was an angel." To me, Joe was more than an angel. He is a man who's spent his life loving God, learning from God, and being obedient to the will of God. When asked to step into an unknown situation, one that was potentially deadly, he trusted and obeyed his God. He was everything I needed.

He was Barnabus Joe Jesus.

October 23, 2020

The plane took off at midnight, and I slept more on the flight home than I had any single night in Nakuru. When we landed at San Francisco International Airport, I wanted to abandon my luggage and run straight to Kim. Once, I made it through customs and saw my bride, we embraced like newlyweds.

I realized I hadn't spoken with her much while I was in Kenya. My days had been so full, and I was so exhausted, that I didn't have the time during the day or the energy at night to update her.

"How was it, sweetheart?" she asked.

"Just amazing."

Then I rambled at the pace of an auctioneer:

God was so good . . .

How about the guy texting the pic of flowers for you . . .

What about getting Mikey into school . . .

And little John Bob . . .

Angel's still hiding . . .

I never got a fever . . .

And oh, seeing Lucy and Martin . . .

And the stupid GLT meltdown . . .

I was so happy watching them call you . . .

Mama Amon is a nightmare . . .

And the council meeting was so successful . . .

What about not getting stabbed in the face . . .

How about Damu not being able to kill anymore . . .

And Balozi feels loved . . .

Oh, and poor Radhi walking out of the garage in tears back to Mama Amon's . . .

I was having this conversation as much with myself as with my wife. Merely stringing disjointed fragments together, my attempt to explain everything that had happened made little sense. But she was patient with me, and I soon got back into the familiar rhythms of life. I slept in my own bed, ate my favorite foods, visited with my biological kids, had video calls with the GLT, and got back into the gym.

Day after day, snippets of what was happening in our neighborhood streamed in via text.

October 26, 2020

I just saw Dembe. He said we are in peace. Peace. Just like daddy dave told us ~ Kelsey

October 27, 2020

and just like that the atmosphere changes when Samson spots a spy near Balozis ~ Kelsey

October 28, 2020

K2 were seen yesterday in town. They had dispersed far but are obviously returning. ~ Anonymous

The yo-yo of texts added to the unrest in my soul. Joy. Fear. Never knowing what to expect. Pure uncertainty. Up and down. Day after day after day.

November 3, 2020

Last night Mama Amon's second son [Radhi's brother] came at 1am to burn Rasta Ds house. He didn't manage ~ Anonymous

More fear. The image of Rasta in flames a few hundred yards from where his brother was killed flashed through me. A text from Kelsey confirmed the threat.

Rasta D's fence got burnt. He realized it before it spread. The guys are so fearing. They were all so sad today. ~ Kelsey

November 4, 2020

Rasta D cut his dreads ~ Kelsey

Did Rasta cry out, "God make it stop! I'll change. I'll leave the gang. Make it stop!" and cut his dreads as an offering? Did the threat on his life force a desperate cry to God to make the terror stop? Or was it a symbol of a changed heart? Maybe he shaved his head to disguise his appearance from the police for what he might do in revenge.

November 8, 2020

Dembe says hi. He is good, that guy, his face is so bright, he is thinking he is trying to mentor the younger ones ~ Kelsey

Joy. Pure joy! I imagined Dembe's super expressive face bursting with hope. Would he be the one to help raise the tide?

November 9, 2020

The police shows up just before we started the hanging contest. They walked through the bar. Kat and I were sat outside and as they walked through. the first one didn't react, the second one started and then greeted me, the third one his jaw just hit the floor. Not everyday you find a white female with 20 gang members, definitely not everyday you find her with her young daughter too! In the end the second one thanked me for loving the guys. The third one is probably still in shock!! It was fun, the guys felt loved, we talked, we laughed and they can't wait for next time. ~ Kelsey

More joy! But it was short-lived.

November 19, 2020

THEY'VE ARRESTED SIX K2 GUYS FOR THE MURDER OF THE 2 GUYS. MAMA AMONS GRANDSON IS ONE. ~ ANONYMOUS

I was numb except for my aching heart—even her grandson was involved. Generation after generation trapped and enslaved in the devil's chamber. *Will this curse ever be broken?*

November 21, 2020

MAMA AMON HAD A STROKE. ~ ANONYMOUS

Maybe a grandma like her *had* emotions—mine were getting pounded too. Day after day, the texts poured in, adding to the strain. They were relentless. Bipolar messages of terror and joy. I never knew what was about to come.

November 22, 2020

You won't recognize the guys when you come back. Isaac is the next to remove his dreads...change is happening. ~ Kelsey

Then on December 2, six weeks after returning to California, I received the most crushing text of all.

7 WERE KILLED LAST NIGHT ~ ANONYMOUS

The phone slipped from my fingertips back to the table, back to where it was when this all began. I refused to look at it. Had they gotten Angel, Shosh, Dembe, Samson, Balozi, and Isaac? Did they get Dan? Ohhh, did Damu not defend himself and the gang? Is Team Peace dead?

The next time I picked up my phone.

10 MORE MURDERED ~ ANONYMOUS

I thought I knew what it felt like to be numb, but I was wrong. How could God allow this? Did it even matter that I risked my life on that trip? Seventeen lives had been taken in a two-day rampage a few miles from Hilton. *Will this ever stop?*

I scrolled through the texts on my phone. Kim looked at me like I had received a cancer diagnosis. I looked at her like the prognosis was terminal. *Are more murders coming to my community?* I was hyperventilating.

"Kim, I need to go back. They need me."

Despite my downward spiral, I wished I was in Nakuru with Team Peace, Kelsey, and the GLT. My systems were on overload. My stamina spent. I was lost at sea without a compass and no stars in the sky to guide me. I wasn't sure what was happening. *Lord, help me. Where are You? What should I do?*

Then I got a message from the Lord Himself. "Wait."

So I waited. And prayed.

———

As hard as I tried to share with Kim what had happened during the trip, I couldn't organize my thoughts. I saw images in my head, but the phrases to describe them escaped me. I thought it was jetlag, but physically, I had made the adjustment in record time. I woke up at sunrise and went to bed at sundown. But the words just wouldn't come out. Inside, I was a twisted mess.

Another week went by. Then two. I tried to write the events down. All I could do was stare at my pen. *Maybe if I tried typing, the words would flow?* I just looked at my fingers on the home row and a blank Google doc. I feared something was wrong with me. I didn't know what.

Instead of typing what happened on my trip, I Googled "unable to put your thoughts in order." The first result to pop up read, "simply write a stream of consciousness letter." That only added to my frustration because nothing was simple. Nothing was flowing. Another result that popped up was an article on symptoms of a nervous breakdown.

It turned out, I didn't have writer's block. I was experiencing a nervous breakdown. God's wisdom to wait was more brilliant than my response to jump back into the fire. *How would I have helped anyone while I was in that condition? I couldn't even think.*

I decided the best way to deal with mental exhaustion was to try once again to get my thoughts down on paper. Any thought would be good. Whether they made sense or not didn't matter. Even if it was only one word, I just had to break the logjam in my head. Like pieces of a puzzle, I figured I could assemble them later. I asked our youngest son, Scott, a philosophy graduate, to drive from LA to Northern California and spend a weekend with me. We had been all over the world serving together. Maybe he could coax what was in my head out and on paper.

Scott drove up, and over two days, we sat in the local Starbucks and things spilled out of my brain. He made some order of them and typed out eighteen thousand words, about forty pages. I could only imagine what people were thinking as two men sat in the corner booth, laptops plugged in, talking intensely and occasionally sobbing. The blockage in my mind was breaking, and God was building a story of love and forgiveness being more powerful than hate. He wanted the world to hear it.

I actively waited. I prayed. I wrote. And God healed me.

God continued to move in our community. They never rest, and neither does He.

The additional seventeen murders threw gasoline on the pace of the investigations to hunt down the killers. The Chief and special task force arrested nine guys on nine counts of murder. They were put in prison and hadn't been able to bribe their way out—yet. There were no arrests of Team Peace members. Not one.

Gang violence was at a stalemate in Hilton, at least for the moment. One side was wounded with their leaders in jail. The other side felt tranquility because they were living in their homes and sleeping again at night. It didn't mean, however, there was peace.

Three more guys from Team Peace cut off their dreadlocks as an outward symbol of a desire to leave gang life. They wanted peace. I agreed, but I think what they really wanted was Jesus.

Mama Amon remained in exile from the dump recovering from her stroke. Would she rise out of the ashes of her compound like a phoenix and rule again? Or would the wind blow away the charred remains? For now, it seemed the people of the dumpsite were free from her tyranny. Her pastor friend continued to exploit the residents and share the profits with her. And, Radhi, her son, the one who might be connected with the guys who chopped up seventeen people in December, kept pleading to meet me again.

January 4, 2021

One hundred eighty-one children, who had been in COVID-19 lockdown, returned to Maisha Mapya and became students again. Nineteen little lambs were unaccounted for. Maggie searched for the lost ones every day hoping they would join their classmates.

One of the sweetest to return was Angel. She had been tucked away so tight in hiding I never did get the straight story of where she was or how she came back. But none of those details mattered. She was home safe with her shosho, had her Maisha Mapya uniform on, and was ready for class. I was thrilled beyond belief to know she was alive and back in the place she belonged. I praised God for sparing her life. I wonder what marvelous things He has in store for her.

I was getting better every day. My nerves were healing. My thoughts were clear and focused on the King. Finally, God let me know it was time to return to Nakuru. The "Kim, I need to go back," declaration I spoke in November was ready for action. Individually, I invited seven people to accompany me on the trip. But unfortunately, not one could make it, not even Barnabus Joe Jesus. He was busy establishing a food bank in his hometown.

Kim and I agreed that I would travel by myself because I wouldn't be alone. I'd have dozens of people praying for me. And the God who answers prayers living inside me.

THE REMODEL

March 1, 2021

BAGS PACKED. Negative COVID-19 test result in hand. The test was much friendlier this time. A self-administered sample using a Q-Tip, not an emergency room nurse with a coat hanger pleading with me not to punch her.

I didn't have Joe to keep me company in the airport, so for the first time in thirteen years of flying to Africa, I checked into the Paris YotelAir during the layover. I had great Wi-Fi and texted with Kim for over an hour. Then I laid down in a comfortable bed and slept for four hours. It was the best $68 I'd spent in a while.

March 3, 2021

I landed in Nairobi at 6:30 a.m., breezed through customs, and got a ride directly to Maisha. The warm sun on my skin was comforting, much different from the thirty-five-degree mornings I left behind in Northern California. Nakuru, which means "City of Dust" lives up to its name during the dry season of January and February—the toxic dust and fumes from the dump torture my eyes, nose, and throat. But now that the calendar had turned to March, it's my favorite time of year. The weather is perfect, fifty-five degrees in the morning and seventy-five, maybe eighty, in the heat of the day. Afternoon rains wash away the cares of the day and provide much-needed water for my friends in the community.

The beauty of the facility at Maisha Mapya hit me as soon as I walked through the gates. The piles of stones, sand, and other building materials from seven years of constant development had vanished. The main wall to the second floor, where the classrooms are, no longer looked like you were standing outside the Vatican. Instead, bright murals with the "Fruit of the Spirit" and a train with each car having the grade level above and the class photo in the window decorated the twenty-five-foot-tall structure. The color palette was straight out of Disney's *The Lion King*.

Dan was first to run and greet me. "Daudi! Karibu!" Maggie, Mary, and Nia trotted close behind.

I hugged them all.

"Wow, you guys, I love what you've done. It's pure joy!"

"Wait till you see the Amani office," Dan said.

We turned and walked up the driveway. I peeked into the hall on the way. Three adults from Hilton were huddled around a table learning to read.

There's an eight-foot gap between the hall and the ramp to the second floor where a thirty-foot high scaffold supports our ten-thousand-liter water tank. We built a storage area under the stairs when we erected the ramp. When I left in October, it was a mess, filled with lots of construction leftovers.

I had to do a double-take. In place of rebar, crooked two-by-fours, and paint buckets was a lovely atrium with a bright blue roof matching the halls. It fit in so well, as if it was part of an architect's master plan. Large double glass doors invited me to step inside. On the right was a planter with a luscious garden of succulents. Above it were two colorful ten-foot-high murals. One depicted Noah's ark with a rainbow above it. The other showed

Jesus sitting in a garden with children of all colors surrounding Him. On the left, there were couches with comfortable cushions. If they had filled the Amani with water, you'd feel like you were on the Jungle Cruise ride at Disneyland.

At the far end of the room, a door invites you into a secret space that offers something unique for schools in Kenya—a library with open access for students to choose a book of their own to read. We encourage the children to explore and identify their interests. It provides a beautiful opportunity for our teachers to see what excites each child.

It's a spectacular space.

Outside the Amani is the assembly area for the students. When I left in October, it was a dirt patch with a flagpole. Today it was paved with a colorful, round Maisha Mapya logo fifteen feet in diameter.

Nia laughed at the look on my face over its size. "We call it the helipad," she crowed. It's certainly aptly named.

Each Monday and Friday, the entire student body gathers here to raise and lower the Kenyan flag. The children and staff pray, sing worship and the National Anthem, and pray some more.

We walked upstairs to the admin office. It looked straight out of the movie set of *The Devil Wears Prada*, with a brilliant blue and white "Karibu Maisha Mapya" displayed on the reception desk. Our school motto, core values, and logo were professionally printed on the windows of Maggie's office. The floor inside was carpeted. The walls were bright. There were new light fixtures and mirrors bouncing light around. Tastefully arranged sunflowers sat cheerfully in glazed pots. Tall, wispy arrangements were in the corner. I imagined this is what fancy offices at nonprofits in New York or Nairobi looked like.

I thought I was in the wrong place. My eyes enjoyed it, but my spirit held me in check. Were we losing our simple charm? Were we focusing on the spoils of the world? I kept these thoughts to myself. If I had said anything to the team, my disappointment would heap shame on them and crush their enthusiasm. But what

I saw fine-tuned my radar to check if pride had crept into Maisha.

Yes, the facility at Maisha Mapya looked flawless. Everything in its place. Very orderly. Very polished. Very corporate. Very quiet.

I didn't like it one bit.

THE RETURN

March 6, 2021

GROUNDHOG DAY WAS BACK—ONLY different. A single bed in the
hotel room. 5:30 a.m. alarm. No smile from Joe. Shower. Silence.
Head to the Sapphire Restaurant for breakfast.

I looked at the spectacular Rose Diamond buffet and giggled,
remembering Joe's breakfast charades, before I ordered four hard-
boiled eggs and a few breakfast potatoes. Thankfully, one pot of
mixed tea did the trick. But the silence of not having someone
across the table from me made the morning lonely. I cracked the
eggs, peeled the shells, and discarded the yolks. I heard the salt
granules hit my china plate.

It was Saturday morning, and the GLT arrived at the hotel
right at 11:00 a.m. for fellowship and leadership mentoring. It was
our first chance to get together without the distractions of a busy
school day. I wanted to observe how they related to one another in
a relaxed setting with their guards down. Was the unity problem
we had back in October active, napping, or gone forever?

I discussed writing this book and that a few chapters addressed
the conflict and beautiful healing we experienced in the fall. I
wanted to get their approval to share this intimate part of our

history publicly. The conversation also created the perfect opportunity to address the joyless feeling I was experiencing at Maisha, especially in the admin office, and how all their whispering was giving me a headache. Their laughter was gone. The spontaneity was dead. The atmosphere in the admin was the proper decorum if the Queen of England was coming for tea, but not for a young, energetic team trying to change the world.

I read chapter thirteen of this book out loud. I was concerned it might pick at the scab of our divisiveness.

"Are you okay with this being in the book?"

Each one approved.

"It will be a good reminder for us," Nia said.

I tore a sheet from my small yellow Steno pad and ripped it into twelve pieces.

I've learned all of our staff have opinions, but social protocols limit them from feeling safe to share them. We've talked about this openly, and we can now voice our opinions by secret ballot when discussing sensitive issues. I passed each person two scraps of paper.

"Please answer either yes or no. Do you like the way the admin office feels?"

I wrote my answer, then instructed, "Next, please write why you answered yes or no."

I collected their responses without reading them and set them aside.

"I'm going to share my answers. Mine is a definite no. I feel uncomfortable in the office. It's so quiet. We're very professional, but where has our joy gone? Is it on vacation in Mombasa?" Only Dan laughed.

I knew I stepped on one of Nia's toes. She has a forceful personality and loves efficiency. Her high standards and Rose Diamond training had come with her to Maisha, where they are valued and rewarded, but the hotel prided itself on catering to the elite. The clientele of the Rose Diamond would love this space, but was it right for who we are and whom we serve?

"How are we doing with our unity? Are we getting along? Are we okay?"

Lord, please don't let this be a full-on meltdown like last time. I don't think we will be able to put the pieces together again if we do.

Maggie spoke up. "I am learning that we all have different ways of doing things. I am learning if I am working and someone insists I stop doing my activity to do the thing they want, when this happens time and time again, my heart hardens, and I just won't help. I get angry because they think my work is not important. And if I ask the same person for help and they never do, I will not ask them anymore. I will just bury the anger."

The team chewed on that for a while.

She continued. "Why don't we interview ourselves and ask, 'What is it we are doing to others? What is it about me I need to work on?'"

"I love that, Maggie. Can we agree to do that, team?"

They all agreed, and we avoided the opportunity to keep biting each other.

"How about some lunch?" I said with a smile.

THE CHALLENGE

March 6, 2021, 3 p.m.

IN THE FIVE months since I had left the inaugural meeting of the Maisha Mapya Community Council, I intentionally left them alone. I repeatedly turned down the opportunity to observe the sessions via video call. To succeed, this movement must come from the people in the community. They were going to have to figure it out. They are the experts on their area, not me. I want them to discover that God's given them more resources than they realized and that they can look within the community for help instead of relying on me or Maisha Mapya to solve all their problems.

I was curious to see if the council had matured, fallen apart, or morphed into something else entirely. Within the hall the table was set for twenty-four. As the meeting started, I counted nine empty chairs, which spoke volumes. I grew concerned that "fallen apart" was the answer.

Seventy-four-year-old Benjamin, donning his trademark sport coat, opened the meeting in prayer. After the amen, he wasted no time. "All of these chairs used to be full." His finger wagged around at the vacant seats. Maybe he sensed my disappointment?

"When you didn't come for a few meetings, some dropped. Then, more and more left."

I wondered if, in a couple of months, it would just be me, Joel, and Dan staring at each other in the echoes of the hall.

"But don't worry, Daddy. They were only here for handouts."

He pointed around the table with a fatherly look of approval. "The ones who remain here are the ones to make a difference."

The resolve in their eyes said Benjamin knew what he was talking about.

Kevin from Guba said, "Welcome, Daddy Dave, we will make the difference."

"Abigail from Kenya Meat, *karibu nyumbani* (Welcome home)." "We will make the difference."

"Daddy, daddy, daddy. It's me, Dembe, from Team Peace. Welcome, welcome back. We missed you."

"Zawadi Gioto, karibu sana, we make difference."

"Makena, London, welcome, Daddy Dave. We are glad you are here. We will make the difference."

Round and round they went until each person on the council had introduced themselves. Members of the council from different areas were sprinkled in among each other. I marveled at the beautiful collage God created. *Tuko pamoja*, we are one.

Now I was the one with the fatherly look of approval on my face. "It's wonderful to see you all. I am Dave from Maisha. Together, with God's help, we will make the difference."

Leah lowered her mask, revealing her concerned face. "How's Mommie Kim?" She has a handsome son in grade five at Maisha and has been friends with Kim for nearly a decade.

"She's doing a bit better and ever so wishes she was here with you. She's heard all about the council and is so proud of each and every one of you. She sends her greetings and love. We pray for God to heal her, and maybe next time she can be with us."

"Please tell her we love her. And Joe, where's Joe?"

"You know how much Joe cares about feeding hungry people. He's with his wife in Connecticut setting up a food bank in his hometown. He wishes he could be here too. He sends his greetings."

I opened my Bible. "Please, let me share a story with you from God's Word."

My pages in Numbers 13:26–33 were still crisp as I had only recently written notes on them. I'd read the story once or twice of how God had empowered Moses to lead the Israelites out of bondage in Egypt and then stood on the cusp of entering the promised land. I knew the ancient story, but I hadn't thought of its contemporary application until now. As I looked at the council, I wondered if, like Moses, we were on the verge of something big too.

"The Lord told Moses to select twelve people to explore the land of milk and honey, 'The land I am *giving* Israel.' God made a promise. 'This territory is yours. I want to give this to you.'"

"Why would they have to explore it if God was giving it to them?" one council member asked.

"That's a great question. Let's see how God answers it." I turned my focus to the Bible in front of me. "The twelve people were not ordinary community members. Some Bible translations say twelve 'spies,' but that isn't the most accurate term. God said, 'Send one *leader* from each tribe.'"

"Would it even be someone like me, a council leader?" another asked.

"Exactly. These are people like you. They are the leaders of their neighborhoods. This was written for you. And Moses gave them specific instructions for what to look for in this new land. What were the people like? Strong or weak? What was the land like? Was it good or bad? Was the soil fertile or poor? Were there many trees?"

"Our land is bad. Nothing good is here. There are no trees, only rubbish," one of the members added.

"Moses said, 'Enter the land boldly! Bring back some samples of the crops so we can all see.'"

I think Moses knew about the crops. He knew they were

fantastic. God promised him the land was fertile and the place was good. But sometimes, people who aren't as trusting or close to God need proof.

"They did as Moses told them. They went and explored the land for forty days. Imagine. That's quite a thorough investigation. When the leaders returned with a report, they even brought back some of the fruit."

"Oh, I want to hear this!" Dembe said.

"They reported that the land was indeed magnificent country, a land flowing with milk and honey and spectacular things the leaders had never seen." I wanted the council members to comprehend how much greater God's gifts are than anything they could imagine. "Have you seen the Rose Diamond?"

Almost all shook their heads no. "I see the plastics. I pick them," Zawadi said. "Nice. Get twice for them."

I could barely hear her, but she was referring to the discarded single-use shampoo and lotion bottles she'd find while scavenging. Zawadi and her friends get five or six cents a pound for the "virgin" plastic bottles from the Rose Diamond, compared to two and a half cents for ordinary plastic water bottles. In the course of a month, she might find eighty or ninety pounds of them worth four dollars.

Benjamin informed everyone at the table. "It is the top hotel in the land."

I held up a bunch of grapes between my thumb and index finger. "I got these from the Rose Diamond today. Aren't they beautiful?"

Dembe's mouth was watering. His hand extended. "Grapes are my favorite. May I take?"

Everyone laughed.

"Sure. Pass these around, and everyone can inspect. First with your eyes, then with your mouth."

Each person took a single purple grape.

"Those are good. So big and full of juice!" Dembe exclaimed. "May I finish them?"

Everyone busted up.

"In a moment. In a moment. Let me tell you about the grapes in the land God promised Israel. Would you like to hear?"

"Yes. Tell us," Dembe said.

"Verse twenty-three says, 'They cut down a cluster of grapes so large it took two strong men to carry it on a pole between them.'"

I held up what was left of our puny cluster. "These are Rose Diamond grapes from the finest hotel in the land. God's grapes take two men with a pole to carry them. God's grapes are the size of watermelons!"

"Never mind, Daddy. I want those!" Dembe now had the council howling, including me.

"But listen to this. Pay attention. All twelve leaders saw the same land. They all saw how majestic it was. But ten of them, ten of twelve, said the people there were too powerful and the cities too fortified. 'Some of the people were huge!' they cried."

"One of the leaders, Caleb, could sense where this report was going. He tried to get them to listen to God's way. He interrupted before it could get out of hand. 'Let us go at once to take the land.' Why would he say this?"

"It was the land God promised them. God is trustworthy," Dembe said with such confidence it was as if he were Caleb.

"Yes. Caleb went on to say, 'We can certainly take it!'"

"Joshua and Caleb saw the same things as the other ten leaders, the same giant grapes and the same giant men; however, they interpreted them differently from those who were listening to their own voices. They were aware of the same dangers, but instead of being paralyzed by fear, Joshua and Caleb were inspired by God. Their confidence in God was the source of their courage. They said, 'The land we explored is a wonderful land! Don't be afraid of the people or the land. The land is ours. It's a gift from God. Do not be afraid to go to the new place God wants you to be!'"

I pointed to my Bible. "An argument broke out. The ten said,

'No, we can't go against them. They are stronger than we are.' God was ready to move them into the promised land, but they were afraid, rebelled, and spread negative reports all over Israel."

"Why do people do that, Daddy?"

"Don't we do it too, Dembe? Our world in 2021 is really good at being negative with each other. We grumble. We point fingers. We're good at reporting the awful stuff. Everything is doom and gloom. Everything is falling apart. It's the terrible and tragic stuff that gets all the headlines."

Dembe's face recoiled, and he pouted.

"The ten went on to say, 'The land we explored will swallow up any who live there.'"

"Like it swallow us," Zawadi added.

She and her friends in Gioto knew all too well what that's like. Because when it rains, sinkholes are formed, and the dumpsite can literally swallow you whole. You don't dare step foot into it.

"It eat my cousin," she said.

"Oh, I'm so sorry, Zawadi," I said. "That's terrible. And it's the same fear these leaders had, and they continued to spread the destructiveness of fear. 'All the people were huge. They were giants. They were nine feet tall! We felt like grasshoppers next to them. That's what we looked like to them. GRASSHOPPERS!'

"Moses's leaders were overwhelmed by focusing on the threats. They only talked about the obstacles and never about God's promise. They made every difficulty bigger than life. They made every challenge impossible. Their fears influenced those who hadn't been there.

"Because the leaders panicked, the people panicked too. They all wept and cried out, 'We wish we had died in Egypt! Why is the Lord taking us to this new place only to have us die in battle? Our wives will be slaves. Let's run and return to Egypt. Let's choose a new leader who will take us to Egypt.' The leaders spread their foolish fears rather than having faith in God's truth."

I figured I'd made my point and didn't have to include that Numbers 14:36 says the ten leaders who rebelled by spreading fearful reports were struck dead with a plague. Only Joshua and Caleb entered the land of milk and honey.

"God wants us, this council, to move forward into 2021. He has new things He is about to do this year, but if all these fears hold our hearts prisoner in everything that goes before us and behind us, we will stand at the brink of this new way and pull back. We will say, 'This isn't what I expected. I quit.'"

Looking around the room and seeing the empty seats, I thought maybe that's what our absent brothers and sisters were stuck in.

"But the Lord is calling us to move forward. Joshua and Caleb had ears to hear. Do you? Let's look at the end of the chapter together."

Benjamin turned the pages of his Bible along with me.

"The ten leaders were saying they saw themselves as grasshoppers. They, the leaders of God's chosen nation, Israel, didn't see themselves as God saw them. They didn't see they were awesome, powerful, and made in His image, ready to step into the land He promised them. They didn't view themselves as more than conquerors, as it says in Romans. Instead, they saw themselves as grasshoppers. Mere insects!

"It is a confession that, in their sight, they think they are inept. They think they are incompetent. They think they are powerless. They think they are small. They think they are incapable. They think they aren't enough. Truly, they think they're still slaves."

"How could they not believe God?" Dembe said.

"Oh, I think we do that more than we would like to admit," I replied.

"The text says, 'We are grasshoppers in our own sight, and so they will see us this way as well.' If we, as a council, have a similar mindset and see ourselves as grasshoppers in the community, what difference can we make? You saw a locust swarm yesterday. Do we see ourselves like them?"

Benjamin interjected. "If you allow, may I clarify? Locusts are tough. Grasshoppers are weak."

These people are the experts here. In so many ways, I know so little.

I went on with my pregame locker room rally speech. "If we get stuck in that dead mindset of, 'We can't change this area. We have nothing to offer. We're going to get squashed if we try. We'd better play it safe,' then that's exactly how the community and the rest of Nakuru are going to view this council. If we view ourselves this way, why should we be upset when others say, 'You have nothing to offer.' If we don't believe God can deliver a miracle here, then everyone will say, 'You don't matter.' But God has been doing miracle after miracle since the beginning of time.

"If we don't believe it, then the rest of the community will go somewhere else for answers. They will find some other group to belong to. They will go and drink more. They will join gangs. The violence will never end.

"I want it to end forever, Daddy." Maybe Dembe was thinking of all his fallen friends.

"Me too. And our God lets us choose. We can listen to Him, move forward, and enter the land of milk and honey, or we can listen to our leaders who believe they are right in their own sight but are fools. They thought of themselves as mere grasshoppers. They felt they had nothing to offer. As a result, if you keep reading in Numbers 14, God says, 'Therefore you will not enter the new. You will not enter. You will wander in the wilderness, going in circles for forty years until your entire generation dies out.' The entire mindset had to die away before His people could enter the land promised to them."

"They did wander," Benjamin declared.

"And that's exactly what happened. For forty years, they roamed in the wilderness. Then, finally, a whole way of thinking died, and a new group of people said, 'We're tired of going in circles and not doing much. We want to enter the promised land. We want to go where God promised a land flowing with milk and honey, tea, and chapati. We want to be a part of that. We want to help create that.' And when that new generation arose, God said, 'Come, I've been waiting forty years for you.'

"May it never be said of us that an entire generation had to die off for us to step into the new that God wants," I exclaimed. "Aren't you tired of this?"

I had to take a moment to catch my breath.

"So, what does this look like? What does it mean to move into the new?"

Dembe shrugged. Benjamin contemplated. Several other council members had blank stares on their faces.

"It means we come together and share ideas. It means we have the courage to seek God. Then follow and obey what He says. As we do, the entire community will become more peaceful, more loving, more patient. The fruit of God's Spirit will be our bounty. We will leave the violence behind. It means beginning to understand that not everyone gets the same thing. It means being joyful for your neighbor who is lacking and may receive something to ease their suffering while you receive nothing. It means if you have a talent or skill, you would freely share it with others for the greater good. It means if you are frustrated you will not take it out on the vulnerable.

"For me, I need to let go of some of the stuff the world has told me is so important. The world has divided us in so many ways, even in our neighborhoods, language, tribes, and politics. But God calls us to be one in Christ Jesus.

"Let us dare to be new. Let us not wander in the wilderness any longer. Let us dare to trust God, move forward together, and see what happens. Can we agree on that?

"It will start with the proper mindset. It will start with faith. It won't start with harvesting ripe fruit and giant grapes. It will start with tilling the field, planting, watering seeds, and pulling weeds."

"I like that. How do we do that?" Benjamin asked.

"Here's what I ask you to do this week. I want each one of you to be like the twelve leaders Moses sent out to investigate the promised land. I want you to take a fresh set of eyes back to your neighborhoods and find one person who is succeeding. Next Saturday, come back with the good things that are happening in your community and give a report to the council. What are the success stories in the area you represent? Next week, we will all share. We will all learn something and be encouraged."

I looked around the room.

"Please know sometimes I am not like Joshua or Caleb. I am like those fearful, doubting leaders. My eyes focus not on God's promises but on my own worries. I get depressed. I complain. I don't see any way out of the pit. I can be quick to forget how God has sustained me through previous challenges. But if I come back to His word, He teaches truth, He lifts my head, He shows me beauty." I smiled at them. "Beautiful things like everyone sitting around this table.

"Now, will someone pray for us to end the meeting? I notice we always respect the older men by giving them the honor, however, I'd like us to take a fresh mindset and have a young lady close us in prayer. Let us dare to be new."

One lady looked at the others. The other women avoided eye contact with anyone, especially me. Finally, a quiet lady in her twenties cleared her throat and began.

"Lord, thank You for the gift of this day. Thank You for loving us and protecting us. I never thought a day like this would happen, Lord. I never thought I could make a difference. Please change my eyes from being a grasshopper. Never let it be said we are nothing. And when I feel like I am nothing, tell me, 'no.' Remind me I am your child. Give us courage, Lord, to be like Joshua and Caleb, and follow You to the promised land. Thank You, Father, for this council and each of its members. Give us courage. Amen."

THE HOMECOMING

March 7, 2021

I'D PLANNED on Sunday worship at Pastor Edgar's church, Trinity Vineyard, but when the alarm sounded, my heavy body said to roll over and rest. After the stress breakdown I had from the last trip, I promised myself I wouldn't push to the brink every day. I called Edgar, apologized, said I wouldn't be making it, and asked him to dinner on Monday. Most of the day was spent editing chapters of this book. I talked with Kim on the phone for over an hour, which soothed my soul.

March 8, 2021

Monday morning. Time to see Team Peace. The main contact I'd had with them in five months was exchanging texts with Balozi —where he couldn't help but make the occasional request. Some things he asked for were on behalf of the children in the community. Others he asked for things for himself. Would I pay for a rasta band to make an album? Would I buy him a printer? This was followed by a photo of a machine suitable to print *Time Magazine*'s latest edition.

Much like the council, I wanted to know if Team Peace and I would be starting all over again. Or, would we still be brothers? Would they look at me like a dad? Would the devil have wedged divisions between us? How was Damu? Had he lived up to his promise not to kill again?

The iron door outside the bar was unlocked, and I strolled in with Kelsey to find ten guys lounging on the couches. Balozi was asleep, barefoot, wearing jeans and a Bob Marley One Love T-shirt. His dreads wound up on top of his head like a pineapple.

All but Balozi jumped up. "Daddy Dave, karibu nyumbani!" It was a homecoming.

A dozen more young men filed in. I overheard two of them whispering, "He said God would make peace, and now there is peace. I am sure Daddy is Moses."

It was a far cry from the first time I entered this place with Kelsey. Back then, fearful, sleepless skeletons of men filled the place, questioning whether they should kill their neighbors before their neighbors killed them or just give up. But today, every face smiled at me. Laughter filled the air as much as the conversation.

Even Samson smiled. He released me from a bear hug, his massive hands shaking my shoulders. "I never thought. I never thought Mikey would see inside a school."

Damu entered, still wearing the sleeveless T-shirt. Would he start up with his "Well, pastor, what if a guy wants to kill me" routine again?

"DAVID!" A grin replaced Damu's scowl. His full-faced smile revealed beaming white teeth. "HOW'S MAMA?"

"She is okay. Better, but just okay. She wants to thank you all for your prayers."

Dembe, with wide eyes and an even wider smile, chimed in. "Daddy, tell them about the story. Tell them. Tell them."

"What story?"

"The story Daddy, the story, the one about the grapes and grasshoppers."

"*Dakika moja* (one minute)," I answered.

I sat at the head of the pool table with Balozi, and the guys settled into their spots. Kelsey, with a look of great satisfaction, grabbed a chair at the opposite end.

"It's been long since we were together. I've been praying to see your faces again, and here we are. Who wants to pray and give thanks?"

From his perch in the corner, dreadlockless Isaac volunteered. He looked like a new man with his head nearly shaved. As soon as he was finished, Dembe shrugged his shoulders and turned his palms up. "The story, Daddy. It's time."

I repeated the story I shared with the council of Moses being on the edge of entering the promised land. When I got to the part about him selecting leaders to investigate the territory, questions arose.

"Are we leaders?" Rasta D asked.

I answered the question with a question. "Do you have influence? Do people around here care about what you do and what you have to say?"

"Some do."

"Okay then. You are leaders of those who follow."

Dembe said, "Don't forget the grapes. I love the grapes. Did you bring?"

I shared that part of the story, continuing, "God is ready to give something new to Hilton. He is ready to give peace. Are we ready to embrace it? Are we ready to step into the new land of peace, forgiveness, and love He has for us?"

"I like peace," Samson said.

Balozi, clearing the sleep from his eyes, added, "We are Team Peace. We are ready."

I knew the desire for peace ran deep within Balozi. It's a primary tenant of his rasta religion. I'm learning more about it in hopes of bringing him and his friends to the complete truth of the Bible. There are so many things I didn't know. Rastafarians believe the Old Testament, but like many offshoots of Christianity, they miss the deity of Christ and His work on the cross.

The meeting ended with a challenge. "How do we see ourselves? Are we helpless? Incapable? Inept? Are we mere grasshoppers?"

———

Dinner time couldn't come fast enough. Not that I needed food. I was hungry to see Edgar. We'd texted a few times since we were together in October, but there's nothing like sitting down face to face and breaking bread. Being able to see and hear the emotion behind the words creates better understanding and builds stronger bonds. Plus, I laugh a lot more when I'm with someone in person.

I'd been twisting Edgar's arm to get him to start a Trinity Vineyard branch at Maisha Mapya. Our community, including the staff, desperately needed a shepherd. He always responded politely without committing. From the day I met him in 2018, the look in his eyes had always communicated a desire to help the Hilton community. He has a heart for the least of these. I don't know what his hesitation was, but he's curious.

Kelsey's a better arm twister than I am. The main reason for our dinner was for her to convince Edgar to come to Hilton, meet Team Peace, and have a small Bible study at Bob's gang bar. She succeeded.

"When would you like to do this, Kelsey?" Edgar asked.

"Tomorrow."

His nervous laugh was followed by "Really?"

"Yes, Edgar. Tomorrow. Come. Come."

He surrendered. "Okay then. It's settled. I will see you tomorrow at ten o'clock."

I sat quietly wondering if he would really show up.

THE STUDY

March 9, 2021

KELSEY ARRIVED at Maisha at precisely 10:00 a.m. Alone.

"Where's Edgar? Is he coming?" I asked. She shrugged with an impish grin.

I peeked out the front gate and saw Edgar hustling up the street—a droopy, white plastic bag hanging from his right hand.

"You made it!"

Edgar laughed.

The five-minute walk to Bob's Bar was enough time to flush that initial adrenaline from my system. On the way, Edgar handed me the warm, squishy bag. It weighed ten pounds. And there was a bone sticking out of it.

My nose couldn't detect what was inside because COVID-19 had hijacked my olfactory system in December. It's the strangest thing. Some days my sense of smell is spot on and I can enjoy all the beauty a rose has to offer. Other days, everything smells like a cigarette butt. And sometimes I wonder why I even have a nose in the first place other than to hold up my glasses. Today, if my nose were eyes, I'd be blind. But I guessed the bag was filled with something to eat.

Just like I had set out our best dishes, tea, and snacks for the six people from Team Peace on the first day they came to Maisha, Edgar wanted to honor those he would meet today. It was his version of, "I'm going to love you. Maybe you'll love me back?" Team Peace, like everyone in Hilton, eats meat about as often as Halley's Comet shoots across the sky. Anything more than tea was a special treat.

I was imagining what Edgar must be thinking. He was headed into a gang bar. That thought alone should be enough to raise the hair on his neck. And this establishment was owned by a man savagely murdered by another gang. Imagine stepping inside that dark room about to meet the rivals of the killers—to hold a Bible study. For the first time ever. Some will be in mourning, numb with grief. Others will be outright enraged, wanting to spill blood.

The payoff for his obedient steps could be gigantic. What if God's light pierces through the darkness? What if peace and forgiveness replace hate and vengeance? Is this what God was about to do through Edgar? I was proud of him for even making an attempt.

We walked through the gauntlet of Hilton, past the tall, haunted building with two wild dogs in close pursuit. I bet they knew what was in the bag. I stood taller, puffed out my chest, and made certain not to make eye contact with them.

Bob's Bar was on the border of Hilton and Gioto. I used to avoid it since it was rumored gang guys hung out there. Now, because of how God can bring the most unlikely people together, it's my club too. Kelsey led the way through the entrance, and we emerged on the sunny side. The place was perched on a hillside. In the foreground was the vandalized social hall. In the distance, there's a panoramic view of Lake Nakuru National Park. The sky was clear and the view breathtaking. It's hard to believe that only a stone's throw away, cheetahs, rhinos, and lions flourish. There are even Rothschild giraffes standing nearly twenty feet tall.

It fascinated me to learn there are nine subspecies of giraffes, each with a unique pattern depending on the geographical region.

I'd never noticed. I just knew giraffes were tall and liked to eat the leaves of the acacia trees prevalent in the game park. I guess humans aren't the only things God made with different outward skins. At first glance, I doubt many people notice the difference between the giraffes. They just see something tall. And beautiful. And graceful. With spots. Giraffes fill us with wonder and make us smile. But for some reason, sometimes the beauty in humans is overlooked. Our grace goes undetected. Why is it that often only the difference in our spots is acknowledged, magnified, and used to divide us?

Between the bar and the deceased owner's shack, there was a gathering place. We sat on rickety wooden planks under worn sisal bags that shaded the dirt patio. A dozen guys loitered about, not sure whether to sit with us. Then they saw the bag with the bone sticking out, and, like the dogs, stayed close in case there might be something for them to eat.

Biggie leaned against the back railing, taking in the conversation. I'd never heard him that quiet. My ears were grateful. Isaac sat to my left, and Dembe sat to my right. Edgar and Kelsey squeezed next to Isaac.

Before Edgar could start, Dembe tugged on my T-shirt. "I've already got a great story for the council." He smiled like he knew the mystery behind Cinderella's glass slipper.

Edgar locked in on fifteen people who were brave enough to explore what God might have for them. After a brief prayer, he began teaching. "One day an expert in religious law stood up to test Jesus by asking him this question: 'Teacher, what should I do to inherit eternal life?'"

Most of the boys were listening and watching Edgar's every move. Two new ones eyeballed me trying to figure out who I was. A couple more insisted they were sober, but their breaths betrayed their secret.

I warmly smiled at them all as Edgar continued.

"Jesus replied, 'What does the law of Moses say? How do you read it?' The man answered, 'You must love the Lord your God with all your heart, all your soul, all your strength, and all your mind. And love your neighbor as yourself.'

"'Right!' Jesus told him. 'Do this and you will live!'"

"I want to live!" exclaimed Dembe. Edgar continued his teaching. "The man wanted to justify his actions, so he asked Jesus, 'And who is my neighbor?'"

I was paying more attention to the reaction from the guys than the words Edgar spoke. I know the story. I've preached it. But I turned to Luke's gospel in my Bible, chapter ten, to follow along.

Jesus replied with a story about a Jewish traveler who was stripped of his clothes, beaten, and left for dead. A Jewish priest walks by, sees the victim, and crosses the road to avoid him. A Jewish temple assistant sees the man, comes close to get a better look, and walks on. Then a traveler from Samaria, a sworn enemy of the Jews, sees the man and stops. He bandages the man, puts him on his own donkey, and takes him to a hotel to heal. The Samaritan had to be on his way, but before leaving, he paid the innkeeper for another night's rent and told him if the injured traveler needed to stay longer, to let him, and he would pay the entire bill.

My preschool level of understanding Swahili could only interpret so much, but I knew as Edgar went on he was talking about our actions, not only our words, reflecting our heart.

Jesus then asks the question that had me sitting in Africa, 9,500 miles away from my wife, making new friends. It's the question that also challenges me on who I cross the road to avoid.

Edgar related the question to the group, continuing with the parable. "Jesus asked, 'Now which of these three would you say was a neighbor to the man who was attacked by bandits?'

"The man replied, 'The one who showed him mercy,' to which Jesus said, 'Yes, now go and do the same.'"

Listening to Edgar's words and seeing the reaction on the guys' faces, my heart told me my neighbor is everyone.

Everyone sitting around me knew what it was like to beat someone. They also knew what it was like to be lying on the side of the road, bloodied and beaten. They all knew what it was like to have people pass them by.

Edgar switched to English and said, "If you see something, someone who is hurting or needs help, you can't just walk by. So, the lesson is to not be like that priest who saw the man lying on the road and looked at him as a problem. This may mean not being like your pastor, even though your pastor may be a good person. Instead, be like Jesus who is goodness itself. Love your neighbor. Even love people others may think are your enemies."

Many of the boys shifted in their seats. Dembe looked at me like, "Do you agree with that, Daddy?"

Isaac said, "Amen."

Would this story be enough for Team Peace to consider helping their enemies? Would it be the start for them to not look at others as enemies but rather as neighbors? Would it be the catalyst for them to stop beating people in the first place? Would it be enough for them to forgive the guys who were in prison for killing Rasta D's brother?

At the end of the study session, Isaac prayed. "Show us who our neighbors are, Lord. Help us not beat our friends. Bring true peace to our land. Amen."

Kelsey then excused herself and returned a few minutes later with a massive pot of ugali, a favorite Kenyan staple. It looks similar to, but tastes nothing like, cold mashed potatoes. It's a mixture of white maize flour and water. Some say it tastes like popcorn. It always looks like homemade white Play-Doh to me. One lady in Hilton had been so excited to have Jesus brought to her troublesome neighbors that she insisted on making it.

"Daudi, how do you take your ugali?" Balozi asked.

"I don't take."

We shared a good chuckle. Not indulging in the meal made the difference between us apparent, but our friendship and laughter more than overcame it. But like the giraffes, it's only a spot. I'm discovering that in Jesus's kingdom, it's okay for you to be you and for me to be me. We celebrate and learn from our cultural differences, wrapping them in Jesus's love.

Today's Bible study and meal weren't like the day I first met that gang on Triangle Island in 2007 when things felt so distant. Today, we connected. Today, we had a local pastor who spoke the local language and told jokes and stories the locals understood. Today, we brought local food, not white bread and milk.

The secret contents of the warm, white plastic bag were finally revealed. It was full of *nyama choma* (roasted meat). Edgar handed the bag to Rasta D so he could have the honor of serving it to his family. After all, this picnic was in his brother's backyard. Kelsey set out the rest of the food, and fourteen men and one woman completed the morning feast of roasted meat, ugali, and the Word of God.

This wasn't about showcasing me, the foreigner with access to money. It was about them, and their access to God's bountiful treasures of forgiveness and love. It said to the gang, "You are not forgotten. You are not alone. Let me introduce you to someone who will never leave you, or me—His name is Jesus."

I lingered, enjoying watching my friends consume an enormous amount of food in record time. With his stomach full, Isaac took three steps to the back entrance of the bar. "Okay, it is time."

I thought he was telling the boys it was time to leave. Instead, he stretched his long, thin arms to the top of the doorjamb, grabbed on, and hung. Young men like to prove their strength to each other and establish a pecking order. These guys are no exception. It's a custom they have when Kelsey visits. They hold contests to see who can hang the longest. Kelsey is good for one minute and twenty-seven seconds. Kat's record is one minute, twenty-eight. *Sorry, mom.* Isaac holds the title of king at four minutes and twenty seconds. I made it sixteen seconds and quit before I needed ice and a physical therapist.

While they continued to impress each other, I walked out of the front entrance. I often like to leave them to themselves, diminishing my influence. Sitting in the shade of the blue, peeling *mabati* wall was a small boy. Alone.

"Whose child is this?" I did not direct those words to anyone, but a young man fifteen yards away heard the cry of my heart.

"How old is this boy? Why isn't he in school?" I asked.

"You know his brother, Thomas. He goes to Maisha."

"Thomas, whose dad passed last year?"

"Yes. Want me to get the mom?"

He took off before getting an answer. I sat on the ground next to the boy as his bare feet stroked the dirt. He tilted his head to look at me. Didn't smile. Didn't say anything. Then looked back down. His yellow-tinted, mini-dreadlocks were filled with debris picked up from somewhere.

The mom came. "Hi, Daddy Dave."

"This is your son? How old is he?"

"Four."

"Why isn't he in school?"

"He starts PP1 at Maisha in July."

"Oh, he should come before then. Allow me to speak with my staff. Someone will be in contact." They walked away together. I could feel myself about to nudge the intake team again.

———

Kelsey exited the bar rubbing her arms, confirming I made the right decision not to show off. She flashed me her phone. The text message read:

I want to come.

"Who's that from?" I asked.

"Remember the guy from the parking garage?"

"How could I forget."

"I invited him to Maisha tomorrow."

I glanced at Edgar in the doorway. He turned and took one

last look before leaving Bob's, and we walked back toward Maisha. Edgar's smile was gone. His words were missing too.

After a few minutes, I broke the silence. "What's going on, Edgar? Shilling for your thoughts?"

He stopped and looked at me with the softest eyes imaginable and said words I'll always remember: "I saw Jesus today." We walked another hundred yards before Edgar continued. "I have never said these words out loud, but they have been in my heart. What would it look like if we wanted Trinity to reach this group?"

"I don't know, Edgar. But let me know what God puts on your heart and we'll help find the resources." I wondered if he was thinking he didn't want to be like the priest or temple assistant he just taught about in Luke 10. Would Edgar just pass by, or would he stop, have mercy, and help these hurting neighbors? Maybe he was questioning why we go to such an effort to avoid the people Jesus hung out with.

Back at Maisha, I rushed to track down Mary, Maggie, and Dan to see if we could change Thomas's little brother's life. They circled around me, and I made my pitch to enroll him early.

"Let us step into the new and do this," Mary said. "Shall I call the mom?"

THE CRY

March 10, 2021

5:30 A.M. ALARM. Shower. Silence. Four egg whites, potatoes, and tea. Wasili to school. No Wally to liven things up.

I arrived at Maisha at eight o'clock. Close behind, Thomas, his mom, and pint-sized brother ran to catch up with me at the gate. Mom had shaved the little one's dreads and given him a bath. The boy had found his smile too. I didn't think it could grow any bigger until Mary handed him his uniform. Julia Roberts could take lessons from him.

Mary trotted him to the PP1 classroom and introduced him to Teacher Faith, who tenderly picked him up. "What is your name?"

"Devin."

"Can we welcome Devin to our class?"

Thirty-one children, sitting eight to a table, stood in unison. Devin's gaze left Teacher Faith's. He turned to see kids just his size. He clenched his fists and pressed them into his cheeks, making his smushed little grin that much cuter. In a sing-song voice, they greeted him. "Welcome. Welcome. Welcome, Devin, to our class."

"We're so glad you are here, Devin." Faith walked to the only empty seat. "Here are your new friends. Karibu, you are most welcome."

With the same gentleness she had lifted him, Teacher Faith placed him on the floor. The sound of his new Bata shoes squeaked. As he sat, the children, still standing, clapped and sat themselves. I'm sure the angels in heaven rejoiced too, God having rescued another soul from the pit.

———

Kelsey was still glowing from Edgar's Bible study with Team Peace. "That was so awesome. I never thought something like that would happen."

"God's moving. Maybe He's got more in store?"

"Yeah, maybe. Let me wait at the gate for Radhi."

I entered the Amani office and asked God to bless and fill the space. Since walking out of the parking garage in October, Radhi had been on my mind. I still felt the pull in his heart for leaving his mom's tyranny and breaking free, but at that time, he couldn't muster the strength to step into an unknown world that offered peace, forgiveness, and love. And now he was standing at the entrance of the Amani with Kelsey.

Radhi was smaller than I remembered. Fighting the urge to smile and reveal his brown teeth was of no use. He rocked back and forth, rubbing his hands together, waiting to hear whatever came out of my mouth.

"Thanks for coming, Radhi. Good to see you, Kelsey. Karibu Maisha Mapya. Welcome, please have some tea."

Only Radhi's eyes moved. His hands remained folded in his lap. Kelsey looked at him. "It's okay. *Ni sawa.* You can take." She poured him a cup of mixed tea and offered bread and butter.

"How are you? I heard you wanted to meet," I asked.

"Yes."

"Do you remember our meeting last time?"

326 • DAVE HATFIELD

"Yes. Yes, I do. I want peace." It was more of a response from him than I expected.

"I know you do. I want peace too."

"I want peace more."

I can only imagine.

"Radhi, when we left the parking lot together last time, I could feel the pull in your spirit to come with me. I know you wanted to, but you just couldn't. I know you wanted to follow me in another direction."

He froze. "How can you know my mind so well?"

"That feeling was God's Spirit tugging at your heart. He wants in. He loves you and wants you to be His child. He wants peace on earth. Do you know peace begins with forgiveness?"

Radhi nodded.

"It means that when someone hurts you, you don't revenge."

His gaze intensified. "I won't. I won't." He lowered his head. "I won't anymore. I will NEVER." I wondered if he thought I was accusing him of something.

I'd thought about this day and how I'd make an eloquent, persuasive pitch to get one rival from each gang to meet peacefully. I would be like a prosecutor, laying out the case. Now, there was no need. I could sense it. God had already moved in Radhi's heart.

"Are you willing to meet with someone from the other side and ask for forgiveness?"

"I want it. Peace and forgiveness."

"I know you do. But would you be willing? You wouldn't be talking for everyone in K2. It would be just between you and one guy. If I can find one to meet with us with the same understanding—would you do it?"

"Yes."

I glanced at Kelsey. *Can you believe what you are seeing?*

Radhi added, "I will. I understand."

God gave me the answer I dreamed of so fast I didn't know what to do next.

"All right, let me see what I can do. Please stay. Enjoy some tea. You and Kelsey can leave whenever you want."

With the promise of a meeting secured, I prayed as I walked out the door. *God, please make a miracle happen.* By the time I got twenty steps away, standing on the helipad, the doors of the Amani office flew open. They rebounded so fast I thought they might come off the hinges. Radhi sprinted out with a wild look in his eyes.

Before I could take a step toward the Amani, Radhi was on me. *Oh no! He's freaking out. Is Kelsey okay?* He jumped and stopped eighteen inches from my face. His eyes spellbound.

Arms spread wide, he shouted, "I want to get born again!"

It was the clearest thing I'd ever heard him say. A look of wonder washed across his face and he looked skyward.

I. Was. Stunned.

I wanted to bring him into God's magnificent kingdom right then before the devil could snatch him back. But wisdom flashed in my mind that I shouldn't be the one to do it. Too many people in the neighborhood thought God only worked through me, the guy from the West. I'd heard them debate among themselves if I was Moses, or Elijah, or the Apostle Paul. I wanted them to know that it is God alone, not Daddy Dave, who is the Savior. I wanted them to know God works through everyone He calls His own, not just me.

"That's so awesome! Will you come to church with Kelsey and me on Sunday?"

"Yes! Yes. I want to come."

"We'll make it happen."

With that, Radhi floated out the gates of Maisha Mapya. I wondered how long that joy would last when he got home to Mama Amon's place. Would she cast a spell on him? Would she tell others in the gang to persuade him against going to church? Would she sacrifice her own kid if she found out?

I dialed the phone to share this amazing news with Pastor Edgar.

"You'll never guess what just happened."

Still reflecting on his experience leading Bible study in a gang bar the day before, Edgar didn't even venture a guess. I told him the news and asked if he would bring another lost soul into the family of God on Sunday.

"I would be so honored, Dave. Jesus is so, so good."

———

I stood with Kelsey staring at the gate for a good five minutes. "Do you think Radhi will come on Sunday?"

"He's been through so much, Dave. He wants to. I just don't know if he's in charge of his own life."

I was full of nervous energy and couldn't sit for meetings in the admin office. I turned to Kelsey. "Let's go."

She followed without even a reply. We headed straight for Balozi's. The atmosphere in the neighborhood had come off the boil from October. People were doing some business. Others were just *mrandoo*. The regulars were well into their drinks already.

We swung the bar's door open, and I plopped on the couch. A couple of young guys grabbed chairs like I was about to hold a meeting.

"Hey, guys. Relax. I'm just here to greet you."

Balozi came out from the back room. "Hey, Dave, how's you?" Samson followed him. "Dad! Let me buy you a soda."

Ever since Mikey got into school, Samson has offered to buy me a soda. I never accept because I know he doesn't have a spare nickel, let alone money to buy me a sugary drink. "Come on, Dad. Come on, you never take," he said.

"Okay, my friend."

"Fanta?" he asked.

"How about a Coke."

"Coke?"

"Yes, Coke."

He lowered his voice, looked me square in the eye with raised eyebrows and confirmed again. "Coke."

"Yes, Coke."

"Haha, Dad wants a Coke." When he approached the door, he stopped, turned around, and lifted his index finger in the air. "One, Coke?" I couldn't tell if he was happy because I had finally accepted his gift or if he and Balozi had been in the back enjoying a few too many beverages of their own before I arrived.

"Yes, just one." I wanted to ask for one for Kelsey but figured that might be pushing it.

He giggled, shook his head, and shuffled out. *"Baba anataka kokakola.* Dad wants a Coke." I could feel his smile even though he was walking away from me. Three minutes later, he was back with a bottle of "the real thing" in hand. He smashed the top on the corner pocket of the pool table and the cap came spinning off. He smiled, handed the recycled glass bottle to me, and then grabbed the straw from his shirt pocket. "Here you, Dad. One Coke."

He went to sit next to me on the couch and almost squashed Kelsey. The entire scene had her quite entertained.

"You know, Daudi," Samson said like he was holding court. Immediately, I thought he was buttering me up for a big ask. *Did he have another kid who needed schooling? Maybe a relative this time? Did he want a car?*

I interrupted and looked around the bar. "Is Dembe around?"

"Dauuudi." Samson giggled and wrapped his massive arm around my shoulder. He pulled me close. "You know . . ." *I was preparing to get out my checkbook wondering how much this bottle of Coke would actually cost me.*

Samson continued. "You know we love Angel and even Shosh." I glanced at Kelsey. *Where is this going? Is the next phrase going to be "but we need to get her uncle . . ." or "but someone must pay . . ."?*

Balozi chimed in sounding like a proud uncle. "We love all the kids."

"We talked after you left last time. The day Isaac cut his dreads, we all agreed to go and talk to Shosh. Me, Balozi, and

Isaac. Even if she still had issues with us. We were going," Samson said.

Balozi grabbed a chair and squeezed between the couch and the pool table. "Dave, we went and talked with her. She was toiling (scavenging in the dumpsite). When she saw us, she picked up her rod and made a face. I raised my palms, showing I had nothing. 'We're cool. We're cool,' I told her. She lowered the rod. We asked if she would forgive us for raiding her place. Man, the look on her face was wow—amazing. We said we were sorry for scaring Angel. We promised she had nothing to fear from us ever again."

My eyes watered and I settled into Samson's embrace. For a moment, I was completely relaxed and silently in prayer thanking God for the miracle of forming peace in their hearts.

Samson added, "Shosh even told us the hiding place and Rasta picked the girls one by one and brought them home. Now we guard her."

"Wow. Thank you. Thanks for looking after all the kids, especially the girls, around here. You guys really are Team Peace." Now I sounded like the proud one. "Doesn't it feel good?"

Samson smiled. "How's the Coke?"

THE APPEAL

March 11, 2021

My time at breakfast became shorter and shorter. Living in the silence of my head was wearing on me. I couldn't wait to get to school and be with people.

Dan was in a conversation with the security guard at the gate when I arrived. "Danny! Good morning!"

"Haha, Daudi. How are you always so happy this early?"

A dark sedan stopped in front of us. The blacked-out passenger window rolled down. A man wearing a blue disposable paper mask said, "Get in."

I looked at Dan.

"Daudi, it's the Chief."

Dan and I got in the back seat.

"You haven't come to see me," the Chief said. I worried for a moment before he continued. "But I knew you were coming. How have you been? How is your wife?"

The car drove five hundred yards from Maisha and stopped at a postage-stamp-size empty lot. Somehow, the Chief had heard we were looking for property to expand our school. "I want to make sure there are no land disputes. I will show you some few plots," he said.

The parcel was nice. It was flat. It was close.

"How much is it, Chief?"

"Five million. Do you want?"

A quick calculation pegged it at $45,000 US dollars.

"How big is it?"

"One-eighth plot."

I covered my mouth and whispered, "Dan, that's $360,000 an acre."

Seven years earlier, we had paid $49,000 USD for a plot six times the size. Even then, I thought it was ridiculous. Our back fence borders a slum a stone's throw from a smoldering dump. Now prices had skyrocketed. How was that even possible?

"Thank you for the tour, Chief. It was very kind of you."

"Do you want?"

"No, thank you."

"We have others. Same size. Same price."

"Thank you again, Chief. I didn't know small plots were this expensive. We can't afford anything close to that."

"How much can you afford?"

"We might be gifted five acres from another ministry. We'll just hope that happens."

"Where is it? In Nakuru? I can confirm if it is legitimate."

I couldn't tell if he genuinely wanted to help or if there was some way for him to profit by getting in the middle of the transaction. The car drove around the block one more time and stopped in the same spot in front of the plot. After three minutes, I had to end the silence.

"Thanks again, Chief. Dan and I can walk from here. I've been sitting too much, so I can use the exercise. Thank you again, sir. I'll make sure to see you before I leave."

The Chief made a prophetic statement of his own as his car pulled away: "Keep doing what you are doing, and this place won't be a slum in five or ten years."

I'd managed to escape again without insulting him and without committing to having money change hands.

————

My mind was fixed on which Team Peace member would want to reconcile with Radhi. The first to come to mind was the father–son pair, Dembe and Isaac.

Dembe's engagement with the Maisha Mapya Community Council, positive influence during meetings at Balozi's, and sparkling eyes during our private conversations led me to believe he may be the person from Team Peace to patch up relations with the K2 gang. And if not, at least maybe he wouldn't shout obscenities, make accusations or threats and reignite the war.

And the more time I spent with Isaac, the more my curiosity was piqued. He was thoughtful, contemplative, and had a soft spirit. Isaac also looked at me like a dad. *Maybe he would be the one?*

Kelsey and I invited them both to Maisha at noon for tea. They entered the Amani. Dembe immediately said, "I have a good story for the council, Daddy," and sat on the couch next to me, glowing. Kelsey found a chair, and Isaac reclined on a cushy inflatable sofa.

"What did you think of Edgar's message at Bob's the other day?"

The two men sat quietly, wondering what the correct answer was.

"It's okay, just share what you thought." I was looking for the one who was brave enough to speak first. Isaac smiled and deferred to his dad.

Dembe grinned and rubbed his hands together. "Okay." Then he rubbed his face. I sensed he was looking to give the answer he thought I wanted to hear. "The pastor is okay. Edgar is good." He set his hands on his lap only for a moment before he rubbed his face some more. He looked at Kelsey, then me.

That's it? He's good.

Now Isaac had permission to talk. "It made me think I've heard that story."

I waited. He wrestled with the recliner trying to sit up.

"It made me think Jesus is telling me not to have enemies. Why am I fighting my neighbors? Why do I want to take revenge on my friends?"

Dembe fired his index finger at Isaac. "Because of what they've done!" His crazed eyes widened, then narrowed repeatedly. I was taken aback because he had been so reasonable during all our meetings. He had been a ray of hope. But once things moved from God interacting with others, like the counsel, to a specific situation in his life he didn't like, it all changed.

I didn't want this to slide downhill to the place of listing all of K2's offenses. "Do you guys really want peace?"

"Yes! I want them to stop!" Dembe said.

"What about Rasta D?" Isaac sat back, folding his arms across his chest. "Who is going to defend his brother?"

I wanted to shout, "You can't defend a dead guy!" But maybe he meant who was going to defend Rasta's brother's honor?

"I know you are angry. I know you are hurt. I know every time you see sorrow on Rasta's face, it brings you pain."

Since the morning Rasta D woke up to discover his brother outside his home torn apart by K2, he has been tormented. When he rolled him over, his brother's insides had spilled out. He won't ever unsee that, no matter how much he drowns himself in alcohol or numbs himself with drugs. We all felt it, but none more than Isaac, who had been friends with Rasta D since the day they were born.

"God knows all about this, Isaac."

Dembe's eyes were still gyrating. "What's He going to do about it, Daddy?"

"God has been dealing with conflicts since the fall. Just think. There first was Adam, then Eve. Who came next?"

"Cain and Abel," Isaac said.

"Right. What happened between them?"

Again, Isaac knew the story. "Cain killed Abel."

"So, God has been dealing with clashes between people forever. He knows how you feel. The Bible says, 'Dear friends, *never* take revenge. Leave that to the righteous anger of God. For the Scriptures say, "I will take revenge; I will pay them back," says the Lord.'"

"He knows if you revenge, you may feel good for a moment, but you will have remorse forever. You will also trigger the full wrath of your enemies. The circle never ends. Everyone loses. Everyone suffers. Everyone cries. We should leave the judgment and punishment to God. It's our job to . . ."

Before I could finish, Isaac said, "Love our neighbor."

"That's right. Do you understand peace begins with forgiveness in your heart? It means that even though someone did something to hurt you, you won't revenge. You will forgive."

Dembe said, "Yes! They need to say they are sorry and make and oath they will never do anything ever again!"

Isaac listened.

"If I can get one guy from the other side to meet with you, would you be willing to ask for forgiveness and seek peace? No matter what they have done?"

They both stared into the emptiness.

"He would come with the same understanding. To ask you for forgiveness and seek peace. Would you be willing to do that?"

Without moving his head, Dembe eyed Isaac. Isaac dead-eyed him right back.

My trip was half over. *When would I have a chance like this again?* I pressed. "You might be wondering who."

Dembe glared, huffed, and folded his arms. Isaac tilted his head, his eyes losing focus as he lifted his index finger to his lip in contemplation.

"It's Radhi."

Dembe muttered something. Isaac's eyebrows shot up. Asking them to meet with one of Mama Amon's sons was a stretch, but he was the only guy from K2 who had been willing to meet with me. And he'd just cried out to be born again. He wants forgiveness from God and the people he's hurt.

"He has been your neighbor for a long time. Would you be willing to make peace with Radhi? Not for the entire group, just between you and him. Would you be willing to do that?" My eyes ping-ponged between the two men.

Come on, Lord, move their hearts.

Again, neither man moved. "Ask yourself, which of you will be the Caleb of Hilton and step into a new way? Are you willing to be the first to bring peace to your people?"

At that, Isaac said, "Yes. I will do it." Dembe shot a look at his son.

"I'm proud of you, Isaac," I said. "Let me see what I can do. Thank you for coming, Dembe. Thanks for coming, Isaac."

I stood. They followed and walked out the same gate Radhi had the day before. But Dembe was blasting outrage in Isaac's ear the entire way. I wondered if Isaac was about to lead the cloud of grasshoppers into the new land God had prepared for them or if the devil would use Dembe to stir up hatred in Isaac.

"Well, Kelsey, this should be interesting. I think Isaac really wants to patch things up. Do you think Dembe will let him?"

"I never know about those two. Sometimes Dembe gets in Isaacs's face so much that Isaac complies just to shut his dad up," she replied. "Maybe he will come, maybe not."

THE REPORT

March 13, 2021

I'D BEEN THINKING all week about the success stories the neighborhood leaders would harvest to share with the council. I expected to hear tales of small shopkeepers making a living during COVID-19 because of their cunning and hustle.

Dembe strutted into the hall like he owned the place. He lifted his eyebrows and smiled as he went by me. I wondered if he'd completely forgotten how he stormed out of the meeting about forgiving Radhi. Before he sat, he waved a peace sign in the air and burst out, "I've got two great stories to tell!"

I was as excited to hear as he was to share. *This is gonna be good!*

After an opening prayer and introduction of the twelve members at the table, I set the scene to share the successes in our neighborhoods. I dreamt of hidden gems mined through careful investigation by my leaders. I was going to use them as a template and then replicate the achievements throughout the community. It would spur a tsunami of economic activity. The tide for all the starfish would rise.

"I know you've been good spies this week and have uncovered

some great stories. We aren't helpless grasshoppers. We are the mighty people of God."

I turned to Dembe. "Okay, my friend. Let us have it."

He clapped his hands together, beaming. "Okay. A thief got caught, and . . . they beat him!"

I blinked twice. Hard. I flashed back to the empathy training with the GLT and strained to manage my face. *Don't say, "What?!" Don't say, "Are you nuts?"*

"Thank you for that, Dembe. You mentioned you had two."

He slapped the table, stood, and yelled, "And a lady got an inheritance. She got a goat!" His right arm extended and his index finger surveyed the crowd. His hands found his hips. He nodded. "How about that!"

My blinking continued like I had sand in my eyes.

"That's good. Thank you." I scanned the room, looking for someone to rescue me. "Any others?"

The next man exclaimed, "I am the success story in my neighborhood!" He didn't give any details about why.

I was still stuck digesting Dembe's words. All week he had been bursting at the seams to tell me these stories. To him, they were important. To him, God showered blessings. To him, a thief getting caught and beaten and a lady getting a goat was success.

To me, it revealed that my assumptions about my community were miles off base. My planned strategy of analyzing the stories, identifying common themes, and giving a rousing talk of how we could learn from these people and multiply their success went down in flames. I did not understand how my community thinks or what they valued. Their choices weren't wrong but rather illustrated that I was unaware of their thought process and expectations. The thief getting caught and punished spoke to a desire for justice. The lady getting an inheritance displayed the mindset that we cannot solve our problems ourselves; we need an outside force to give us things. The exercise screamed the starting point for repairing the community was miles behind my elementary understanding.

Finally, sport-coat clad seventy-four-year-old Benjamin put his elbows on the table and pointed to a woman on the other side of the room. She was lean, muscular, maybe in her forties, and wearing a peach-colored cotton bonnet pulled down to her eyebrows.

"This lady is doing something. She pays her bills."

I snapped out of my funk. "May I know your name, ma'am?"

"They call me Wawira. I come from Guba."

"Tell me more."

"I have a shop, and I work casual jobs. Sometimes I load rocks, sometimes I nail. I do wash, too. I do anything."

Benjamin was still wagging his fingers toward her. "You see, she, she is doing something."

"I have to," she said.

"Why do you have to?" I asked.

"I have kids."

"How much do you make a day, Wawira?"

"Two hundred, three, four hundred" (about two to four dollars a day).

Benjamin said, "The young men make more than her, sometimes six or seven hundred. But they spend it on alcohol and drugs. They do not have any left to eat, so they rob."

"Why do you think she can make it on less than them? Why can't they make it?"

"I have to," she said. "I have kids."

It opened a discussion between the members about the importance of motivation. Wawira owned the responsibility of providing for her children. The young people were without hope and only lived for today. They partied their lives away.

"Is this something we all agree on?" I asked. "Is this the difference?" Two young men hung their heads. The rest of the group enthusiastically approved.

"How can we help motivate the youth toward positive activities? How can we change their mindset so they are not helpless grasshoppers? Can we agree this is the next task for our leaders? Find out how we can motivate the youth. What can we do to help them not be idle?"

The council had their next assignment, and I had mine—would Radhi show up for church and join the kingdom of God tomorrow?

THE KINGDOM

March 14, 2021

KELSEY ARRANGED to pick up Radhi outside the gate at his mom's house for a ride to Trinity Vineyard Church at 9:30 a.m. Mama Amon's large new home was twenty-five minutes from her profit center at the dumpsite where she'd been burned out of her compound and banned by the Chief from ever returning.

Kelsey texted me at 9:34 a.m.

can't find radhi and his phone is off. ~ Kelsey

noooooo ~me

going past the gate to mama amons home now ~ Kelsey

Radhi wasn't a lost lamb who'd wandered off. He'd been chained to Mama Amon's wolfpack his entire life. And now he was the lone son still living with her. Kelsey gathered her courage and didn't back off.

Five minutes later, she sent another one.

at her house now ~ Kelsey

Kelsey sent the driver, a man who knew Radhi and his mom well, to investigate. Six minutes later, I read on my phone:

how long do I give it before I go and rescue the driver from inside! ~ Kelsey

I know him. He can handle himself. Come on, Jesus. Do Your thing. ~ me

Amen ~ Kelsey

I think she was sending me updates knowing I would pray for her, rather than wanting to give me a play-by-play. Kelsey could only wait two minutes. Her love for Jesus and Radhi compelled her to open the car door. She prayed and took five steps toward Mama Amon's lair as Radhi and the driver emerged from the house. Standing on his tiptoes, Radhi waved.

He was just getting dressed! Wahooooo! ~ Kelsey

Lol. Fear not. ~me

He had taken extra time bathing and putting on his Sunday best for the big occasion. It turned out his best was the same uniform he'd worn each time we've been together—black jeans, a black T-shirt with CHS in cardinal red letters, and a bright blue pair of New Balance knockoffs with teal shoestrings.

Radhi and the driver strolled closer to the car. Kelsey heard their laughter and put her freak-out back in its box. Mama Amon then darted out of her haunt. With her hands on her hips, she scowled as her son got in the Wasili and drove off. The more I prayed for her, the more I was reminded of Frankenstein's monster's admission: "I am malicious because I am miserable." And I held out hope that if Radhi could turn his life around, perhaps Mama Amon could too.

today is going to be amazing. the enemy is trying hard to disrupt it ~ Kelsey

Too many tears for me already today. ~ me

Jesus has the victory ~ Kelsey

Kelsey sent me a photo with her in the front seat of the car and Kat and Radhi in the back.

Got room for me? ~ me

———

They were sanitizing their hands and getting temperature checked when I arrived at Trinity.

"I'm so excited about this day. How about you, Radhi?"

He looked down as he scribbled patterns in the dirt with his tennis shoe. It reminded me of how Christians long ago would draw an ichthus fish in the ground, secretly revealing their faith to others in the brotherhood.

We walked to the open-air church and sat in socially distanced, gray plastic chairs. The space between us had Radhi on his own island. I would have loved to know his thoughts. Was he scared? Was he expecting a supernatural zap from heaven to make all his troubles disappear? Would he wake up from the nightmare of his life? No more pain. No more tears. A clean slate without secrets. A loving mom. Would he be able to experience joy?

Edgar's sermon was in English, and I couldn't tell how much of it Radhi understood. But he sat there patiently, mostly attentive, until the final amen. I heard the pastor's message, but my heart was already standing at the gates of heaven, ready to welcome Radhi, praying he would have the courage to go through with it.

Pastor Edgar greeted us at the back of the church with an

engaging smile peeking out from behind his mask. He may have been the most excited of all.

"Well, Radhi. Are you ready?"

"Yes. Yes, I am. Will you call me Joshua, pastor? Please. From today, I want to be known as Joshua."

With a gentle bow and pleasant grin, Edgar replied, "Of course, Joshua."

We formed a circle. I put my right arm around Radhi and my left on Kat's shoulder as Edgar invited him to make a decision that would forever change his destiny.

"Radhi, if you would like to be forgiven of your sins, enter the kingdom of heaven, and become one of God's children, who will forever be known as Joshua, please, with your whole heart, repeat this after me."

Dear Lord Jesus, I know I am a sinner. I ask for Your forgiveness. I believe You died for my sins and rose from the dead. I turn from my sins and invite You to come into my heart and life. I want to trust and follow You as my Lord and Savior.

The young man humbly declared every word. At that moment, Radhi became the true Joshua.

Joshua raised his head with tears streaming as Edgar handed him a small, red, Swahili Bible. I looked at my right arm still on Joshua's shoulder and saw the green, red, white, and black beaded wristband with the words *Kristo Milele* (Christ Forever). One of our teachers made it for me five years ago, and I'd been wearing it ever since. I struggled to take it off, but with God's grace, I was able to remove it. I placed it in the palm of Joshua's hand and gently wrapped his fingers around it.

"Welcome to a new kingdom. God will never leave you or forsake you. I want you to keep this as a reminder." Joshua slipped the wristband on, looked directly into my eyes, and embraced me. The young man who indecisively walked away from me in the parking lot a few months earlier had experienced the forgiveness and love we prayed for. His demons were on the run.

"Are you ready for tomorrow, Joshua? Are you ready for a new start with Isaac?"

"I am."

When I got back to the hotel to shower, I looked at the tan lines on my bare wrist. They were some of the most beautiful things I'd seen in a long time.

THE SUMMIT

March 15, 2021

ANOTHER BREAKFAST alone gave me plenty of time to think about what could happen today.

Peace treaties usually aren't about peace.

Geronimo, the last Native American leader to formally surrender to the US military, spent the last twenty years of his life as a prisoner of war. "Germany surrenders! The War is Over!" were the newspaper headlines at the end of World War II.

Peace treaties are about a superior opponent having their boot on their enemy's neck, forcing them to sign a formal agreement. They will quit. They will fight no more. All the world must see who is the winner and who is the loser.

The hearts of the vanquished may be full of bitterness. But because they want the suffering to end, their brothers to have all of their limbs, and their children to not grow up orphans, they capitulate. They say, "We've had enough! We've reached our pain threshold and beyond. We surrender. We will live our lives in humiliation." Many times, the losers become slaves to the victors.

Peace treaties are about one side winning and the other surrendering.

Today, there wouldn't be any headlines. No pens. No paper. No treaty. No media snapping photos. Not even an amateur video on Facebook. There would just be a simple, life-changing meeting between two former friends still in their twenties who were now mortal enemies. They would lay down their bloody knives and machetes. Their violent actions and hatred for one another would be the thing surrendered today. Their hearts' plea for forgiveness, and genuine forgiveness granted, would be the signature on this treaty.

That was my hope.

On my way to our mini-summit, I had to make a quick trip to the West Side Mall to get a COVID-19 test to allow me to fly to California. I feared the coat-hanger test that might await me. It took four days to recover from that experience with Nurse Suzanna back in October.

I arrived at the lab at 8:00 a.m. I was the only patient. Thankfully, it was a simple swab; however, it was administered by a lab technician. It's one thing to stick something up your own nose and wiggle it around. It's another thing entirely to have someone else do it. The damage was minimal, although I'd feel it for a couple of days. I was in and out of there in thirty minutes.

On the drive to Maisha, I received a text from Kelsey.

I got Isaac :) ~ Kelsey

I rocked back and forth in the passenger seat like a little kid trying to speed the car up. I got dropped at the gate and dashed up the hill to the kitchen to double-check with Florence that the team had set up tea in the Amani office.

Florence smiled. "It's already there, Papa." She, as much as anyone, wanted peace among her neighbors. She wanted the streets to be safe for her seven-year-old Rooney and all the kids.

On my way to the Amani office, Kelsey and Isaac entered the gate. Isaac was dressed in a white and gray tank top, black jeans, black Adidas knockoffs, and a black visor. Kelsey wore blue jeans and a plain, black V-neck T-shirt. Her signature sunglasses rested on the top of her head, and an optimistic smile lit up her face.

I interrupted their conversation, motioning for them to join me in the Amani. "Karibu, welcome. Come have a seat." I opened the doors and loved what I saw—a small table draped in white cloth with two thermoses, one with hot milk, one with hot water, some tea bags, a bowl of sugar, bread, butter, and jam. Very welcoming.

Isaac entered as I held the door open. We exchanged glances. I was glad to see he brought his soft eyes, with lashes Kim Kardashian would envy.

"Thanks for coming today, Isaac. It's a big day."

He just smiled and looked down.

"Are you ready for this?"

He gently clasped his hands together. "I think so. I want peace."

"It's within our grasp. Do you have any questions?"

"No. Not for you."

I stepped out to greet Joshua, who was waiting in front of the hall. As soon as he saw me, he waved. He was clad in his favorite, or only, black T-shirt with the letters CHS on the chest, black jeans, and bright blue tennies with the teal shoestrings. He'd topped the look with a black TREND baseball cap. Naturally, I was in my standard black Hilton's Heroes T-shirt and jeans. Joshua and I are easy to dress.

We sat and enjoyed the beverages. Joshua's smile said he was beginning to like coming to Maisha Mapya, or that he couldn't wait to be friends with Isaac again. I couldn't tell.

"Thank you for coming today, Isaac. Thank you for coming, Joshua."

"Joshua?" Isaac said. "Who's Joshua? That guy is Radhi and has been his whole life."

Joshua looked down embarrassed by how his new identity was received.

I said, "Radhi got born again yesterday."

Isaac's eyebrows shot over the top of his head.

"He's a new creation. And he's got a new name—it's Joshua."

Isaac squinted one eye while the other was wide open and tense. Joshua squirmed.

I reclaimed their attention from each other and began. "It takes a lot of courage to do this and I'm proud of you. I've told you both the story of Moses sending the twelve leaders to explore the land God had promised His people with the instruction to report back what they found. Even though they saw the amazing blessings of the land, with grapes as big as watermelons, and God Himself had promised this land was especially for them, ten out of twelve men came back and reported fearful things. They only saw troubles, the things they thought were standing in their way. They saw the people living there as giants. They saw themselves as weak and powerless. They couldn't make a difference. 'We are like grasshoppers,' they said. But God hoped they would see themselves as He sees them, as conquerors."

Both men were riveted, hanging on my every word.

"They were afraid to step into the new. Yet there were two leaders, two men just like you, named Joshua and Caleb."

The former Radhi grinned.

I continued. "They said, 'Let's change the way things have been. Let's go with God and dare to enter the new way.' The two groups argued, and the side of the ten who saw themselves as helpless grasshoppers won.

"God said, 'Okay, I'll wait for those who are ready.' And then He had the Israelites wander in the desert for forty years until that generation and their mindset died off." Watching them while I spoke, I prayed they understood the message.

"Today, I am asking you to be like Joshua and Caleb. Be the generation to step into the new. Be the generation to bring peace to Hilton. You two can be the ones who make a difference. You may only be two people, but this is how things change. It can start with you two. And it can start right now."

I was so fired up, I could have forged into the promised land alone and defeated those giants. You could have tossed Goliath in the mix too.

"Isaac, even though your dad battles with Joshua's mom, and Joshua, even though your mom battles with Isaac's dad, you two can be the ones to break the curse. You don't have to continue the war. You can have a new mindset. I'm asking you to be like Jonathan and David, whose parents were enemies but who themselves were best friends."

No one knew trouble from being born into the wrong family more than Joshua. I couldn't fathom life with Mama Amon as my mother.

"I'm not asking you to make peace between your groups." I made sure not to use the word gangs. "I'm asking for this to be just between the two of you. We will start there. Will you lay down your weapons? Will you abandon your hate?"

Their eyes were fixed on me.

"So, here's how this is going to go. I'm going to ask each of you to apologize for the things you have done, to say 'I'm sorry' out loud, and ask the other for forgiveness. You will say to each other, 'I'm sorry. Will you forgive me?'"

Joshua's eager heart jumped in almost before I finished. "I'm ready."

"I know. You've been waiting for this from before we met in the garage in October. Go ahead. Ask Isaac."

Without the usual clearing of his throat or shifting in his chair, he started. "Isaac, I am sorry for what I have done. Will you forgive me? I want to be friends again."

Isaac stared at Joshua. And then stared some more. He took a visual polygraph. I glanced at Kelsey. As much as I wanted to say something to relieve the tension, I knew this was between them.

Finally, Isaac responded. "Yes. I forgive you."

"Okay, Isaac. Your turn."

The silence returned to the room. The top of my head started to itch, but I didn't dare move. I wanted Isaac to search his heart and make this decision without my nudging.

His head tilted sideways, his eyes looked down, his mouth turned down too. "Joshua, will you forgive me for the things I've done? I am sorry."

"Yes. I want to be friends again."

If it had been a peace treaty ceremony, they would have set their pens down. But this wasn't a document to be signed. It was genuine repentance to be honored. They just looked at each other, not knowing what to do next.

"All right, guys, shake hands."

Both men stood, slapped hands, and pulled each other closer. They bumped right shoulders, and it grew into a full embrace. Joshua was fighting back tears of joy. The sight of these two brave, humble, courageous warriors putting their armor down, being vulnerable, and hugging each other, melted me.

Two Christians, one brand new, forgave each other for the most violent and heinous deeds. And division dissolved. I wondered what the world would be like if Christ's entire body did the same. Would our churches be full if everyone felt welcome and unjudged by the people surrounding them?

Forgiveness is an invitation to friendship and unity.

We all sat down. I reached for the pot to pour more tea.

"Radhi, Joshua, I have to know," Isaac said in a stern tone.

Joshua searched for Isaac's eyes, then looked down.

"I have to know what happened that night. Many say you had a bloody panga in your hand. I have to know."

This may be the shortest truce ever.

I grew concerned and jumped in. "Isaac, Isaac, hey, before he answers, please allow me to say this. I want to clarify some things. Forgiveness means that even if someone does something to harm you, you will not hold a grudge. You make a conscious, deliberate decision to let go of the vengeance toward him even if he has hurt you or your friends. Even if he did it. Forgiveness is about you releasing your anger and letting God deal with it. It means you forgive Joshua, even when he doesn't deserve it. Do you understand?"

Isaac simply sat. I couldn't tell if he was contemplating my definition or whether he was ready to forgive, even if Joshua had blood on his hands.

"I will tell him," Joshua said staring at me.

"Were you there that night?" Isaac demanded.

Joshua turned his gaze to Isaac. "Yes. Yes, I was there."

"Did you have a panga?"

"Yes. Yes, I did."

"I knew it!"

Oh, man. Where is this headed? I don't have time to patch this back together. My bags are packed, and my plane leaves in a day and a half.

"I was traveling from my place up there," Joshua said. He pointed off in the distance. "I needed it to get through the brush."

He wasn't very convincing, even to me. I feared what was next.

Unshaken, Joshua continued. "But it did not have blood on it. I was not there for that. Some of the guys went and attacked. I went to Kiprop's house and hid until it all stopped. You can ask him. I did not do it."

Isaac stood, looked down on Joshua, and puffed out his chest. "Are you sure?"

"Yes, Isaac, I swear."

Isaac's eyes intensified into lie detector mode. He read each one of Joshua's cells. One thing I have learned is that what these guys lack in formal education, they make up for in their ability to read people. It's what keeps them alive.

"Okay." Isaac sat for a moment, his eyes darting around the room. He filled his lungs and exhaled.

My heart started beating again. Without further prompting, the two men stood and shook hands. This time I think it was for real. Two minutes later, they were outside the Amani office, taking selfies together and laughing like the old days. The reunion was beautiful. The peace I was experiencing gave me a vision of these two friends rising out of the water with their bitterness, hatred, and darkness washed away. They would be true brothers in the Lord.

The Lord gave me words. "Hey, do you guys want to get baptized?"

Joshua, who had accepted Jesus as his Savior the day before, answered before my last syllable was spoken.

"Yes!"

"How about you, Isaac?"

"Yes, maybe, but I have some questions."

I'm learning Isaac is one who listens well, asks his questions, and mulls over his responses. It makes for decisions that stick.

"Fire away."

"Well, in my church . . ." *What church? Really? Church?* ". . . you have to go through classes before you can get baptized. Do I have to do classes first?"

Oh, man and his religion.

"That's a great question. I've read this book." I held my Bible in the air. "There was this guy, John the Baptist, who baptized people in the Jordan River."

Isaac nodded.

"They didn't have to take any classes first. And he dunked Jesus. So, I'm gonna go with that. No, Isaac, you don't have to take any classes first."

"Okay, but I smoke."

I'd never seen Isaac with a cigarette, so based on him recently cutting off his dreads, I knew he meant weed.

"I smoke. I'm addicted. Can I smoke and get baptized?"

Now that was a good question!

"Well, Isaac, if you're asking me if you have to have your entire life cleaned up before you can be baptized, I'd say absolutely no. You can come as you are. Let's commit our lives to Jesus and see what He will do with them."

I was thinking of my constant battle with sin. It's relentless. I stumble all the time, and Jesus loves me anyway. He picks me up, dusts me off, encourages me, and says, "Keep going." He promises He will always be with me.

"Okay then. I am in."

The sight of these two men asking for forgiveness, shaking hands, and hugging a few moments ago was powerful. The image of them being baptized together would be too much to take in.

I phoned Pastor Edgar. The same Edgar who said he experienced Jesus by giving a Bible study in a gang bar six days earlier. The same Edgar who brought a rival gang member to the Lord yesterday. The same Edgar who was learning to see the poor as Jesus sees them and was beginning to understand why Jesus loves them so much. I may have been giggling as I initiated the call. I would have loved to see his face when he heard my news.

Unfortunately, I got his voice mail, so I left a message for him to call when he was free. But I was bursting with happiness, and I couldn't wait even a minute for his return call, so I sent a text too. (I've always been the type who wants to open all the presents on Christmas Eve.)

How would you like to do a double baptism of 2 rival gang members? ~ me

Hey Dave, this would be awesome! We can do it this weekend. ~ Edgar

Can we do it before? I leave day after tomorrow. ~ me

Oh wow I didn't know it was so soon. Let's do tomorrow. ~ Edgar

My phone rang, and the joy in Edgar's voice lifted my spirits even higher. "We're Kenyans, you know, so we must plan a breakfast," he said.

I'm an American and just wanted to get the business done. Isaac and Joshua have to get together and publicly declare their new Lord, their new kingdom, and their new family—right now! Who needs breakfast?

But I deferred to Edgar. This was his turf.

"I'm thinking we do a simple tea and eggs and bread for the meal. Have a talk, some worship, and baptism. Are they inviting their friends and family?" he said.

Nice sentiment, but NO WAY. I was not risking this entire thing blowing up. How could Mama Amon, Dembe, some still-vengeful Team Peace guys, and Joshua get together? No way! At least not yet.

"I'm not so sure. Let's keep it simple. How about if I bring Dan, Maggie, Nia, and Joel?"

"Awesome. I will bring the worship team. We will take care of everything. See you tomorrow at nine."

Nine o'clock in the morning couldn't come fast enough.

THE AWESOME POWER OF GOD

March 16, 2021

SOMETIMES MY STOMACH gets ambushed by the local pathogens lying in wait in the food. I didn't know whether to have breakfast at the hotel or be brave and eat what Edgar would offer. I didn't want to offend him by declining the meal. Instead, I played it safe and had my standard four hard-boiled egg whites, breakfast potatoes, and a cup of mixed tea in solitude at the Rose Diamond. I wished Joe was here to witness the victory that was coming for the kingdom of God. Even more, I longed for Kim. I'd never be able to adequately express what was about to happen. Why would God not want her to see this with her own eyes and have the memory etched into her heart?

I consumed the last drop of tea, and it was time to leave. I knew I'd experience Kenyan worship in a few minutes, but I wanted to connect my heart with songs my soul survived on through thick and thin over these years. There's something about worshiping in my native language that resonates with me.

I ran back to my room to listen to "Isaiah 6" by Todd Agnew one more time. The song is about Isaiah entering the presence of God. Todd's husky, emotional rendition always touches something deep in my spirit. Isaiah sees God exalted on His throne, surrounded by angels. Witnessing the majesty, glory, and holiness of God, Isaiah realizes he is unworthy. He is unclean. But he's seen God. Once you've seen Him, you are consumed with His beauty, His forgiveness, His compassion, and with His love. Isaiah now knows God is real. But he could not approach Him because he wasn't worthy.

The more I encounter God, the more I realize I'm not worthy either, and I am amazed that He considers me at all. Let alone be the apple of His eye for whom Christ died.

God cleansed Isaiah and took away his sin. God spoke that into Isaiah twenty-seven hundred years ago. He spoke it into me thirteen years ago. And He was about to further speak it into Joshua and Isaac today.

———

I headed to Maisha to get Dan, Maggie, Nia, and Joel and drive to Trinity. This team of beautiful people, each coming in their own brokenness, each who realized God cleansed their lips as well, squeezed into the Wasili, and off we went. Together, we had cried tears of sorrow, tears of shame, and I hoped we would soon be fighting back tears of joy. There wasn't much talk, only the anticipation of a miracle.

I couldn't help but wonder if Joshua would make it. Would Mama Amon make one last attempt to imprison his soul in darkness? Oh, how I pray she is next to cry out to the one true God for salvation and be free from her misery.

Kelsey picked Isaac at 8:30 a.m. to head to the church. She texted me on the way.

he didn't bring anyone ~ Kelsey

> *It will be supportive to have Maisha and Trinity teams there. No loose cannons. Well, except maybe me. ~ me*

Haha! ~ Kelsey

I sensed her joy. I imagined Isaac talking softly, smiling, and laughing with her. God had me appreciating Kelsey's sacrifice in serving Him and the encouragement she was to me.

Thanks so much for spending so much time helping these past two weeks. I'm sure it disrupted your schedule. I really appreciate it. ~ me

You are welcome. I love it. We make a good team. The driver dropped Joshua at church today. They kept time! ~ Kelsey

Edgar greeted us the moment we stepped foot on the church property. He was dressed in salmon-colored shorts, Sperry topsiders, and a brown hoodie with a cute teddy bear stitched on the front.

I looked at Isaac and motioned to the pastor's attire. "See, no classes or discipleship certificates are needed."

He laughed, relieved. Edgar lowered his mask. His grin added to the joy.

"Come, come, let's get together." Edgar waved us in, and we strolled to the tent where the worship team meets to pray before the Sunday service. Worship Leader George and a lady from his team stood to greet us. We filed in and sat on rustic couches with simple, comfortable cushions. Directly in front of me was a table made from a varnished wooden top placed above painted used tires. It was cute, clever, and functional.

"Well, guys." Edgar clapped his hands. "Today is a great day. We're going to have a talk about what baptism is really about, have a bit of worship, and then go into the water together." His eloquent accent sounded especially sweet. The men standing before us, Angel's attacker and Mama Amon's son, already forgiven by God but about to formally recognize it, radiated God's goodness.

Edgar opened his Bible, and for the next fifteen minutes, the rest of the conversation was in Swahili. I understood every fifth word or so. Where my lack of understanding was a benefit when Mama Amon was cursing me, it was breaking my heart not knowing every syllable he spoke. I was in an invisible isolation chamber, only being able to study Edgar's tone and the body language of those sitting in the room. I sure could have used Isaac's observation skills.

I heard a lot of *uhurus*, which means freedom. *Oh, yes, Lord, set these young men free from the captivity of the enemy. Set them free from the old generation of hate, revenge, and unforgiveness. Usher in peace, freedom, and love. Bring in the new.*

Everyone listened attentively to Edgar. No one more so than Isaac.

Looking straight at Edgar, Isaac replied emotionally in Swahili. Again, I didn't understand a word. My phone pinged. I looked down and received a Slack message from Nia who was sitting two feet away from me with her thumbs frantically typing. Then another ping, and another one.

I silenced my phone and kept trying to understand Edgar's and Isaac's Swahili. But it was too rapid. I set my phone on my thigh, trying not to appear like I was looking at it. It didn't matter because the two men were riveted by one another. With my head steady, my eyes flashed up and down.

Here's Nia's text of what Isaac was saying:

I've known Christ for long. But I've had questions.

Isaac's face softened more.

And I've seen I'm not worthy.
So I asked Dave questions.
Whether I can smoke and get baptized.
All I'm requesting is for understanding.
And for you to hold my hand. I'm not perfect, but don't leave me.

After a moment of silence to process what Isaac had shared, Edgar turned to Joshua. Joshua composed himself and replied with confidence.

Nia continued to text me what he said.

As you all know I'm a seed from a bad tree.

Oh, Joshua. *I know you never stood a chance.* I could see the shame on his face as he clearly communicated the curse he was born with.

I've been through so much challenge in the family, friends, and community.
I'm happy to be born again.
When Dave prayed and asked whether I wanna be born again I was scared.
I told him I need to think, but I went home and made a decision.
And I have fully confirmed that I wanna be born again.

I didn't need a translator to understand the conviction in his voice.

Please pray for me.

It was the same plea as when we met in the parking garage. Joshua understood the challenges ahead and knew only God could help him. Experiencing the pandemic had put an exclamation point on God's words in Proverbs 16:9—man makes his plan, but God determines his steps. The cries of all of our hearts should be, "please pray for me."

My team sat in silence, contemplating the humble words of these two warriors. They'd battled with Joshua's mom from the day each one joined Maisha Mapya. For Dan, it's been nonstop. For a few years, it was just the two of us encountering the ruthless, corrupt structure she created at the dump as its self-appointed dictator. I'm sure Maggie still has nightmares from Mama Amon's tirades. Nia appears tough on the outside, but the suffering caused by Mama Amon's greed breaks her each time. Joel deals daily with the aftermath of her reign as he leads the Community Council and the fifteen thousand they represent.

I saw them all standing together and marveled at the way God reconciled the differences between the leaders on my team a few months earlier. God forgives and reconciles us to Himself so we can forgive and reconcile with others. During our training sessions, He convicted each one. They humbled themselves, asked each other for forgiveness, and then reached out for a meeting with me. They had a mechanism for conflict resolution that, while painful, was free from physical violence—something that my gang friends had never been taught. Now we stood together, bound by God's love, supporting Isaac and Joshua. I wondered if they saw themselves like these men, reconciled with God and then with each other.

"Let's head over," Edgar said. We entered the tent. The chairs were gone. A six-foot-tall wooden cross and a giant tub filled with water were all that remained, and a crowd of witnesses to stand with the new family members. Everything necessary for a proper baptism.

George strapped on his guitar, and the rest of us formed a loose circle, clapped our hands to the beat, and worshiped. I struggled to know the words, but my heart knew the melody: love and forgiveness. And Christ's sacrifice on the cross for us. My spirit entered the temple, the one described in Isaiah 6, and my heart joined the angels singing, "Holy, holy, holy is the Lord Almighty. The whole earth is filled with His glory."

Edgar was the first to climb the stairs and wade into the water. Now I understood why he wore shorts. He let out a small yelp. I couldn't tell if he was cold or kidding. Kelsey wasted no time as she stepped in front of Isaac. She wanted to welcome Isaac in before she baptized him. He must have gotten the memo because he was in shorts too. He smiled big before hitting the first rung, and it only grew from there as he ascended the stairs.

Edgar read from his tablet. "Isaac, do you believe in God the

Father, the maker of heaven and earth? And in Jesus Christ, His only Son? And in the Holy Spirit as the giver of all life and grace?"

Immediately he responded, "I do."

"Do you renounce all spiritual influences known and unknown which aren't from God?"

"I do."

"Do you confess your need for forgiveness of sins and, with a humble heart, put your hope in God's mercy and your whole trust in Christ as your Lord and Savior?"

Shaking his head in affirmation, he said, "Yes, I do."

"And with His help, do you seek to follow Him, becoming more like Him until you see Him face to face?"

"Yes, I do."

Edgar gently lifted Isaac's hand. Isaac plugged his nose. Kelsey, adding tears to the water, stood ready, as Edgar adjusted Isaac's arm to cross his body. Kelsey placed her hand on his back.

Edgar spoke. "Isaac, I baptize you in the name of the Father, the Son, and the Holy Spirit."

And they lowered him into the water.

His smile was the biggest yet when he came back up. He was overcome, turning his back toward us, choking back the emotion. George had been strumming heavenly melodies the whole time.

Kelsey exited the tank, followed by Isaac. Edgar remained, ready for the next miracle. I labored to climb the stairs in my jeans. Joshua was fidgeting and grinning, waiting his turn. He kicked off his teal blue tennies and climbed the stairs, skipping a rung with each step.

Edgar's dialect switched instantly to Swahili as he read the same words of invitation. I had a tingle crawling through my body, and it was everything I could do not to wail. The victory for God's kingdom for Mama Amon's son to be standing in the water with me about to be baptized was just too much.

Joshua replied to Edgar's questions of faith in English. "Yes, I do."

My head bobbed. I believed the words, but I struggled to trust this moment was happening.

Again, Joshua replied, "Yes."

As Edgar began the phrase, "*Nakubatiza kwa jina la baba na mwana na roho takatifu* . . ." (I baptize you in the name of . . .), Joshua mouthed the words to finish the sentence. In the name of the Father, the Son, and the Holy Spirit. Then came his "I do."

Edgar crossed Joshua's arms across his chest. Joshua closed his eyes. There was serenity on his face. We lowered him into the water and then lifted him.

Joshua came up out of the water, glory shining from his face. Trembling, he brought his hands up to cover his expression. The shaking in his shoulders spread to the rest of his body. All Edgar and I could do was hold him. And wait.

I didn't want to let go. I knew fresh challenges lay in front of him, as the enemy would intensify the fight to torment Joshua's soul. My grip, even combined with Edgar's, would never be strong enough. The only hands powerful enough would be those of God Himself.

We released our hold.

Joshua faced me.

Through the tears, he declared, "I am not a grasshopper, Daddy Dave." His gaze turned upward to heaven, and his arms spread wide. "I am a child of God."

For the first time in his life, Joshua was truly free of his mom's clutches. He still lived under her roof, but his heart was free. Completely free. Free of guilt and bitterness. Free of revenge. God gave him the desire of his heart—forgiveness and peace—along with a bonus. Joshua's soul had a new home.

THE HOPE

March 17, 2021

ALONE ON THE FLIGHT HOME, the joy on Joshua's face consumed my mind. He was living in the bliss of asking for and being granted forgiveness from his Heavenly Father and his enemies. His rivals a few days earlier were now friends. I saw Joshua's unbound radiance, and Jesus lit a fire in my soul. And the Holy Spirit went to work on my heart.

Even though I thought I had forgiven those in my past who had wronged me, the Holy Spirit convicted me of harboring hidden bitterness. I had crawled into my own poisonous prison of judgment. I was the jailor.

But I also held the keys. I thought I had forgiven the pastor who kicked me out of church and the Kenyans who stole my school. I thought I'd made peace with my former business partner and all the others on Wall Street. But based on the freedom I saw in Joshua, I realized I had to forgive at a deeper level. I wish I could look into my mom's eyes and speak words of forgiveness for telling me I was a mistake through her cursing shrieks. But it was too late—she's gone from this earth. I'll have to live with that.

Feeling the same assurance that I had when God told me He

would be with me and to go to Kenya and make peace with the gangs, He told me to make peace with my own sources of pain.

I took out the phone where the initial text of Angel's horrors began. I searched with tears for any means to contact my old pastor, my former best friend, and finally the Kenyan family who proclaimed Christ but worshiped mammon. To contact them would take humility, courage, and obedience. And for God to once again deliver on a promise.

I couldn't wait to land and continue paving the forgiving path Joshua had forged. I prayed for reconciliation, but even if my offer was met with a cold shoulder, I committed to making the effort. What else could I do to defeat my bitterness?

How would they respond? Would they think I was self-righteous? Would they understand that I feel no one was more guilty of offenses than me?

Joshua was right. We are not feckless grasshoppers. We *are* children of God. Hearing that truth ignited a passion inside me to be part of the generation to bring God's love and forgiveness back to hurting people. And everyone is hurting. I had watched religion fearfully sit on the sidelines parsing unknowable things about an infinite God or arguing about whether to open church doors or wear masks or whatever our petty disagreements were. I had also witnessed Love humbly lower itself and reach out to the lost living in a dumpsite and give them maisha mapya—new life.

God wants His kingdom to come on earth as it is in heaven. He wants us, His body, His church to be so loving, forgiving, and beautiful that we are irresistible to a broken, divided world. He wants to begin with me. And with you too. We are not grasshoppers.

There's nothing worse than a small casket. I still see way too many. Thank God there's not another one with the name Angel on it. Praise Jesus there's not a big one with the name Radhi on it. But instead there's another crown at the foot of the throne in heaven with the name Joshua.

There's nothing better than Maisha Mapya—a new life

founded on the forgiveness and love of Christ. Let us be the generation to see many more.

THANKS FOR READING MY BOOK

Writing the story was super impactful for me. Did this book help you in some way? If so, I'd love to hear from you. Kindly email me at davehwrites@gmail.com.

Maybe you feel like you need to talk about what you have read? We've created a *discussion guide* to help you. It's perfect for churches, small groups, friends, and families to explore the concepts presented in the book. A free download is available at dave-hatfield.com/discussion.

Please consider leaving a review on Amazon, Goodreads, or wherever you hang out online. Reviews are essential to help readers select books that fit their interests. They also help authors have their stories heard.

Is your heart moved to help the community you learned about? Then join the Living Stone Global family at livingstoneglobal.org. You might even find a precious child there who needs a sponsor like you!

Thanks for reading and sharing this story with your friends!

AUTHOR'S NOTE

This is a true story. For much of this book, I have relied on photos, shared stories from others who were present, and my memory. The dialogue is an approximation of what was actually said. Most of the texts are actual messages, but I adapted some to protect the sender's identity. Any typos or grammatical errors were present in the original texts. Some events have been condensed. For their privacy, I have changed many characters' names and physical characteristics. Of course, if you are in law enforcement, any resemblance to particular individuals is coincidental.

Dave invites your feedback on *I Am Not A Grasshopper* via email at davehwrites@gmail.com. He is available for speaking engagements in person or online. You can find out more about Dave, his mission, and his speaking schedule at www.dave-hatfield.com. Or find him online on FB, IG, and Twitter at @davehwrites.

GLOSSARY - FAHARASA

Amani: [Swahili] Peace and tranquility
Asante: [Swahili] Thank you
Baba anataka kokakola: [Swahili] "Dad wants a Coke"
Burudika: [Swahili] Enjoy
Chakula: [Swahili] Food
Chakula na maji: [Swahili] Food and water
Chang'aa: [Swahili] Homebrewed alcohol, similar to moonshine.
Dakika moja: [Swahili] Literally "one minute"; I'll be with you in a moment.
Dawa: [Swahili] Literally "medicine"; a drink of hot water with lemon, fresh ginger, and honey.
Fundi: [Swahili] Literally "expert"; practically used for construction expert.
Gioto: [Kikuyu] Place of garbage; the name of the dumpsite.
Guba: A neighborhood in Nakuru just a 10-minute walk north of the school.
Gum: [English, British] Cobbler's shoe glue sold and sniffed by street boys to numb the pain of the hardships of life on the street
Habari yako: [Swahili] Hello, how are you
Hakuna gum kabisa: [Swahili] No sniffing or huffing glue

Hakuna Mungu Kama Wewe: [Swahili] The title of a worship song in Swahili meaning "There's No One Like You, Lord."

Hakuna pombe: [Swahili] No drinking alcohol

Jiko: [Swahili] Wood-fired cooker

Karibu: [Swahili] Welcome

Karibu nyumbani: [Swahili] Welcome home

Kristo milele: [Swahili] Christ forever

Mabati: [Kenya] Brand of corrugated metal sheet, primarily used for roofing and walls.

Maisha Mapya: [Swahili] Literally "new life"; the name of the school.

Makanga: [Swahili] Literally "conductor"; the caller on a matatu, similar to a ticket collector on a train

Mambo: [Swahili] Informal slang greeting similar to "what's up"

Matatu: [Swahili] A popular means of public transportation, about the size of a 8 passenger van.

Mpesa: [Swahili] Digital payment system, much like Venmo in the states.

Mrandoo: [Swahili] Hanging out

Mungiki: [Kikuyu] A notorious criminal organization, often referred to as Kenya's Cosa Nostra, Yakuza, or Kenyan Mafia.

Mzungu: [Swahili] Literally "wanderer"; is used to refer to white people.

Nakubatiza kwa jina la baba na mwana na roho takatifu: [Swahili] "I baptize you in the name of the Father and of the Son and of the Holy Spirit"

Nakuru: [Maasai] Literally "City of Dust," Nakuru is the 4th largest city in Kenya, and has an urban and rural population of nearly 1 million inhabitants. Nakuru is a city in the Rift Valley region of Kenya, resting about 6,000 ft. above sea level.

Nyama choma: [Swahili] Roasted meat, most often goat.

Panga: [Swahili] Machete

Piki or pikipiki: [Swahili] Literally "motorcycle"; is used to refer to motorcycle taxis.

Queen cakes: [English] A bakery treat similar to sponge cakes but without being overloaded with sugar.

Sawa sawa: [Swahili] Okay

Shamba: [Swahili] Farm

Shillings: [Swahili] The currency of Kenya (sign: KSH; code: KES)

Shosho: [Kikuyu] Grandmother

Sukuma wiki: [Swahili] An East African dish made with collard greens, onions and spices

Tuko pamoja: [Swahili] "We are together, we are one"

Tuonane: [Swahili] Literally "see you later"; often used as a familiar parting phrase

Twende kazi: [Swahili] Let's go to work

Ugali: [Swahili] A stiff maize flour porridge, a staple and favorite

Uhuru: [Swahili] Freedom

Uji: [Swahili] Literally "porridge"; served in a cup as breakfast for the children at Maisha Mapya

Umoja: [Swahili] Unity

Wasili: [Swahili] Literally "to arrive"; it is the company name of a mode of public transportation similar to Uber.

Wazungu: [Swahili] Plural form of mzungu, white foreigners

ACKNOWLEDGMENTS

Thank You, Jesus. I am forever grateful to You, the God who created me and reached down and saved me. You are now my Lord, Savior, and best friend. You have been at my side for every beat of my heart and every keystroke in this book. Your Bible was written to me so I would know the truth and know how much You love me. I've written *I Am Not A Grasshopper* to bring You honor and glory and to let You, and the rest of the world, know how much I love You.

Words alone (and I've written over a million this year) are inadequate to express what my wife means to me. Thank you, Kim, for over thirty-two incredible years. Can you believe we get closer to each other every day? I marvel at the way you love and support me. You've devoted your life to God, our family, and me. Along the way, you have allowed God to lead our family into places we'd never dreamed of, from palaces to slums, in nearly thirty countries. You have offered your life and health as a sacrifice to our Lord. Thank you for supporting me in every step of writing this book by drying my tears as I struggled with my past hurts. Thank you for your tender, confirming smile as God transforms my heart.

To my brave thirteen-year-old son, Andrew, who is now a grown man, husband, and father: Thank you for having the courage to go on an adventure with your dad that changed both our hearts—you invited Jesus into yours, while He filled mine with purpose. And we grew inseparable in the process. I am so grateful that you know you are not a mere grasshopper, but you are a child of God.

Hey, Scott Hatfield. Thanks for being with me since day one of putting this story on paper. You cared enough to help your dad break the logjam of trauma that had a hold on him. You also made the final keystroke on this work as the last editor. Thank you for twenty-five years of joy. And thanks to the Torrey Honors Institute at Biola University, who taught you how to think at a deeper level and communicate well.

I am blessed with friends who have encouraged me through the process of writing this book and in my walk with Christ.

A million thanks to those who read this manuscript as it was being developed and encouraged me anyway, no matter what mess was written on the page—Meg Roberts, Dixie Walker, Marti Ross, Glenda Cohen, Sam Hayashida, Ryan Reynolds, and Jill Ramseur.

How could I ever thank the grammar experts who made my clump of words readable? My editor, Carly Catt, was ever encouraging and allowed me to maintain my voice. And the world's greatest volunteer proofreader, Kathy Rider, who ~~red~~ read over 200,000 of my words and had enough ~~read~~ red ink to finish the job!

I'd never written anything longer than a one-thousand-word email before authoring this book. Thanks to all you Author Tubers who posted free content and challenged my thinking of how to tell a story. That's you, Jerry Jenkins, Abbie Emmons, Bethany Atazadeh, Shaelin Bishop, Mark Dawson, and others. But it was Lisa Cron's *Story Genius* that taught me so much about how to develop a story. It was invaluable advice for this inexperienced first-time author.

Thank you, Brené Brown, for writing *Dare to Lead*. The principles in your book have influenced the leadership style of our organization. Thank you for your research and commitment to developing capable and compassionate leaders.

Simon Sinek, your work in *Start With Why* is a foundational block in how we lead our organization. Thank you for challenging us to understand why we do what we do and for us to do something excellent, with meaning and purpose.

Deep thanks go to my friend and dear brother, Mzee Charles Mulli. You are a Kenyan national hero and a personal hero to me too. Daddy Mulli, your dedication to love the least of these is humbling. Your willingness to listen to my small but significant story and respond with, "I am fully convinced that *I Am Not A Grasshopper* will be a blessing to millions worldwide," was so uplifting.

Since the beginning, two amazing people have been with us, Steve and Brenda Madsen, who have always said they were with us every time we have said YES to God.

For all the folks at Starbucks, Gold Country Roasters, Nairobi Java House, and countless other coffee shops around the world who have allowed me to stay in their establishments entirely too long while enjoying their addictive brew and utilizing their free internet—thanks for keeping it coming! And to the Christian artists who filled my head with the sounds and messages of heaven. Especially you, Todd Agnew.

Blessings and soul-felt gratitude to the churches worldwide who have participated in this chapter of God's story. Thank you, Big Trees Community Bible Church, Cornerstone Fellowship, Grace Hills Covenant Church, Refuge Church, Mountain Christian Fellowship, Copper Canyon Baptist Church, San Andreas Community Covenant, Burson Full Gospel, First B Jackson, Trinity Vineyard, and many others. Thank you, Pastors John, Steve, Ray, Karl, Shawn, Sean, Kurt, Rob, Mark, Dave, Jeff, Bart, and all the rest.

There have been many organizations instrumental in moving forward the mission of the Living Stone Global Foundation. Thank you to everyone at Unseen for helping clarify and amplify the vision of LSGF. To Taproot for continually supplying professional volunteers. And Salesforce, Google Nonprofits, Canva, Midwest Food Bank and Kapu Africa, Gilani's, Rotary, Lion's Club, and countless others.

Asante sana marafiki in Nakuru for accepting the love I have offered you. Thank you for loving me back. I am forever grateful for all you have taught me and how we have walked together these past few years. Thank you, Chief, for being a friend and advocate for making Hilton a better place. And thank you, Anonymous, for having the courage and faith to reach out to me. I hope to meet you someday.

To every single staff member, parent, and community member who has made Maisha Mapya the beacon of hope it is today. We've been through a lot and cried tears of joy and tears of heartache. And we've done it together. As the African proverb says, we are going far—together.

Incredible champions have made the work of LSGF possible by sacrificing to help those who needed help in our community. Your generosity has eased suffering, created opportunity, and built hope. Thank you, Jeff and Danise Rapetti, Chuck and BethAnn Crary, Bob Summers, Jonathan McGowan, Kim Hankins-Kujawa, Lori Ingram, Kathy Northington, and the many others who are too numerous to mention. A big thanks to everyone who's been adventurous and traveled on a mission trip, including the Dream Team and the Nakuru Kenya Dental Team. May God grab your heart and give you passion for His purpose. All of your contributions, big or small, have combined to make a miracle happen.

Thank you, Shawn McCamey. We are grateful your printer always had enough ink to print out page after page! Lori Tribble and Sue Reeves, thanks for keeping our books straight so I could have one less worry. Dan and Salome, your banana bread, chai, laughs, presence, and prayers have kept us going. They are all appreciated and deeply needed.

There are many dear people who I may have overlooked in these acknowledgments. Please forgive me for that, too. I'm positive that I've forgotten someone, probably several precious someones, who have been a part of the Living Stone Global movement. Thank you for your forgiveness and grace!

In closing, I want to say, "I'm sorry" and ask, "Will you forgive me?" to everyone I have hurt. God continues to transform my flawed heart. Hopefully, it's more beautiful today than yesterday. Your gracious forgiveness is something I crave and will cherish.

Finally, to the children in our community who inspire us: You make life worth living! We love you all!! Thank you for being awesome. :)

ABOUT THE AUTHOR

Dave Hatfield has been telling authentic stories about life in Africa for over a decade as founder and director of encouragement of the Living Stone Global Foundation.

Dave has a passion for making everyone feel welcome into the body of Christ. No matter who you are, what you have done, where you live, or whatever else it is that makes you feel unworthy of the love of God—and others. Dave and his wife have been serving the Gioto dumpsite community in Nakuru, Kenya, for fifteen years.

His greatest joys are being a child of the one true King, a husband, a father, and a grandfather.

You can find out more about Dave, his mission, and his speaking schedule at www.dave-hatfield.com.